KILL
BIN
LADEN

KILL
BIN
LADEN

**A DELTA FORCE COMMANDER'S
ACCOUNT OF THE HUNT FOR
THE WORLD'S MOST WANTED MAN**

DALTON FURY

*The views expressed are those of the author and do not
reflect the official policy or position of the Department of
Defence or the U.S. Government.*

ST. MARTIN'S PRESS ❧ NEW YORK

www.stmartins.com

Design by William Ruoto
Title page photograph © Reuters/Corbis
Maps by Jonathan Bennett

LIBRARY OF CONGRESS CATALOGING-IN-PUBLICATION DATA

Fury, Dalton.
    Kill Bin Laden : a Delta Force Commander's account of the hunt for the
world's most wanted man / Dalton Fury.—1st ed.
        p. cm.
    ISBN-13: 978-0-312-38439-5
    ISBN-10: 0-312-38439-4
    1. Tora Bora, Battle of, Afghanistan, 2001.   2. Bin Laden, Osama, 1957-
3. United States. Army. Delta Force—History.   I. Title.
    DS371.4123.T67F87 2008
    958.104'7—dc22

2008024263

10   9   8   7   6   5   4   3

Dedication

Personally . . . to my wife and daughters who let me *live the dream* and whose undying spirit and love made it all worthwhile.

Professionally . . . to the intelligence shop, the *backroom boys*, an eclectic band of truly indefatigable and dedicated experts in rationalism and empiricism. These men are hell-bent on unwrapping the delicate secrets of international terrorism and have my utmost respect.
They include

Randy B.	Roger H.
Brian C.	Danny M.
John C.	Kelley P.
Jerry D.	Glenn P.
Jimmy D.	Jamie R.
Jody F.	John S.
Walt G.	Dennis S.
Eddie H.	Shannon T.
Tim H.	

Contents

Foreword

I t's about damn time. Finally, we can read, be inspired by, and follow the heroic actions of 1st Special Forces Operational Detachment (Delta Force) while they hunt down Usama bin Laden. Never before has the brave but ultimately doomed effort to find and kill Usama bin Laden been accurately written about. Dalton Fury is uniquely qualified to write this account because he is one of this great nation's elite soldiers, a Delta Force operator, and he was there. This is only the third time a former member of SFOD-D has written about the world's premier counterterrorism organization. However, this is the first time that actual combat operations have been detailed in such a compelling and honest manner.

To become a member of Delta Force you first and foremost have to have a great military record—a proven record of excellence. You then have to go through a "selection course" designed to test your every fiber as a soldier. First, you go running through the woods with a sixty-pound bag and weapon on your butt for up to forty miles a day, every day for a month. This course reduces most men to tears of frustration and resignation. If you make it through this course and no more than three in one hundred do, you then have a six-month training course that turns a great soldier into a super one.

Kill Bin Laden is a tribute to all soldiers and especially to the Delta Force operator. The author takes us inside Delta so that we can better appreciate and support those protecting and fighting for us in this war on terror.

The brilliance of *Kill Bin Laden* is the manner in which the author shares the complexities of combat and shares the credit for successful operations with the entire organization. It is easy to forget when confronted with these "managers of violence"—these supremely talented and staggeringly brave "operators"—that without great intelligence, staff officers, and brilliant logistic operations nothing happens. That without competent and caring leaders, without the best noncommissioned officer corps in the known universe, none of the remarkable accomplishments celebrated in this book could have come to pass. Fury gives the full measure of credit where it rightfully belongs: to his men. It is one of the traits of a great leader.

This spellbinding book is simple, and in that simplicity lies its brilliance. The author does not hide his love for his fellow soldiers, his admiration for their bravery and intellect, and his appreciation for their dedication to each other and to this great nation. It is Fury's directness, his self-deprecating look at himself while taking the blame for the inevitable mistakes and his unflinching credit to his men during their many successes that rings so true in these pages; you are reading about serious combat from a serious combat leader. Fury is a great soldier and leader. He is also a passionate and articulate writer: *Kill Bin Laden* is worthy of all three parts of him.

This book is so good, so topical, and so necessary that you need to stop reading this foreword and get to it.

—Colonel David Hunt (U.S. Army, Ret.)

Acknowledgments

I found the tattered little green notebook while cleaning out a closet, and as I slowly leafed through the pages, I seemed to no longer be sitting safe in my home, comfortable at my kitchen table. Instead, the scribbles transported me back five years, back to the dirt and rocks of the high peaks of the Spin Ghar Mountains in Afghanistan, where I served as the Delta Force troop commander and senior ranking military officer at the Battle of Tora Bora. Our orders were to kill or capture the most wanted man in the world, Usama bin Laden, and bring back proof.

For years, I had given sporadic and not-so-serious attention to piecing together a book about that important time. The story of the famous battle had been told and retold in newspapers, magazine articles, and books and broadcast on television, but most of what was revealed was in error. Some reports were little more than flights of fantasy that might as well have been about a military action on the far side of the moon. The record needed to be set straight, but for me to publish a book about the extraordinary and secret military operation would be difficult if it was based only upon the available public record.

Then I came across my notebook, and the faded pencil and pen scribble marks brought it all back to life. Lacing the little pages are my handwritten notes of actual words spoken by bin Laden, along with hundreds of numbers and letters that identify people, locations, and quantities, as well as my real-time thoughts, guidance, orders, and ideas. Without such detail, this story could never have been much more than a broad and general description of the battle. These notes provided the path to take a reader right into the dark heart of Tora Bora, that forlorn and notoriously well-known mountain range forever etched in America's psyche.

By the summer of 2006, I had completed about 90 percent of the manuscript, but was still undecided about taking it public, for the desire to maintain secrecy is monumentally strong among Delta Force alumni. Then I received a telephone call from Dr. John Partin, the top historian at the Special Operations Command (SOCOM) in Tampa, Florida, who asked if I would be interested in helping SOCOM write the classified historical narrative of what had happened at Tora Bora. History is only history if it's accurate, and is usually best told through the first-person accounts of people who were there.

As I mulled over that request, it became obvious that this story was going to be told, with or without me. The time had come. I made it clear that I would help SOCOM, but that there was a good chance I would also publish my own version some day. The historians at SOCOM had no problem with this and signed me up under their standard consulting agreement that required that I disclose no classified information, which I would never do anyway.

So, with the formalities out of the way, I headed south and met a Green Beret officer who was moonlighting inside the SOCOM history office that had been tagged to re-create the official version of what happened at Tora Bora. He is now a lieutenant colonel and holding down a different job, but at the time, he was the SOCOM deputy historian. This officer is a very detail-oriented guy and a consummate fact-checker, question asker, and professional in every way. He worked diligently for months digging for every nugget of information he could find. We spent sixty hours together working on that official history, and I'm certain there isn't another man alive who knows more details about what happened at Tora Bora than he.

Throughout the months, his consistent stance was to tell the truth by presenting facts and honoring all participating organizations—not just Delta Force. To do so, he remained absolutely objective and gave every angle an honest look. His work is complete now and is one of the latest additions to SOCOM's official, and of course secret, history.* My experience

---

* An unclassified version of the SOCOM history of Tora Bora is part of the 20th Anniversary History: 1987–2007 (U.S. Special Operations Command), pp. 93–98, which can be publicly accessed at http://www.socom.mil/Docs/Command_History_26Feb07webversion.pdf.

with this project served as the final bit of convincing I needed to bring my own unclassified story to the public.

Years before the path ever led down to Tampa, the first person I had reached out to about this project was Sir Edward Artis of Knightsbridge International, a world-class humanitarian and disaster-relief organization. I'm deeply indebted to Ed, a Vietnam veteran, for his unyielding motivation, sound guidance, and no-strings-attached support over the years.

Two true experts in the fields of terrorism and special operations forces, Peter Bergen and Hans Halberstadt, deserve credit for pushing this work from the "good idea" stage to reality. Their insight and guidance have been priceless and I am indebted to them for picking me up when I faltered along the way.

Chief Warrant Officer 3 Mike Durant, my longtime friend and also a retired special operator, deserves a great deal of thanks as well. Twice a *New York Times* bestselling author, Mike was one of the first people I contacted for moral support and expert advice. As always, he came through in spades.

My attorney, the remarkable Kevin Podlaski of Carson Boxberger LLP, a former special operations lawyer, skillfully undertook to navigate the muddy waters of the approval process with SOCOM—an approval that never came. Kevin's calm voice of reason, his attention to the finest details, and a poker-faced patience, as part of a careful process of review with other knowledgeable advisors, reassured me that this book is free of any sensitive or classified information that might help any adversary of the United States of America.

Another longtime special operations expert and successful author, Steve Hartov, also helped to guide me through the maze of telling an important story while still protecting secrets. I'm deeply indebted to Steve for his expert advice, persistent doses of motivation, and steady hand throughout the crazy business of book publishing. Without his extraordinary and delicate midwifery, this journey would have been aborted long ago.

Many others helped this work come to life, and I consider them friends for life. A great number have chosen anonymity because of continuing affiliations with the world of special operations. They know who they are, and that I am tremendously grateful that they cared enough to help. As my good friend Hans Halberstadt says, book publishing is a team sport. But, all of that having been said, as the book's author any errors or oversights, and the views and opinions expressed, are ultimately my responsibility and mine alone.

Finally, I am greatly indebted to Scott Miller, my savvy agent from Trident Media Group, and his colleagues there, who believed in this book from the beginning and never wavered or flinched in bringing it to life. The terrific folks at St. Martin's Press also earned my deepest respect, particularly my editor, Marc Resnick, and the head publicist, John Murphy, who combined to make this an enjoyable journey. Late-inning thanks also go to Jim Hornfischer and the very talented Donald A. Davis.

Key Characters

THE WARLORDS

Hazret Ali Pashai general of the Eastern Alliance Opposition Group and senior warlord employed by the CIA to hunt down Usama bin Laden. Former engineer with the Soviet-era mujahideen who helped carve the hundreds of caves in the Tora Bora Mountains.

Haji Zaman Ghamshareek Pashtun leader of the Eastern Shura and slippery subordinate warlord to General Ali. Zaman was a former mujahideen commander during the Soviet-Afghan War and posed a serious threat to Ali's power base in Nangarhar Province.

THE CIA

Gary Berntsen The chief of all Central Intelligence Agency assets inside Afghanistan. Berntsen aggressively pursued Usama bin Laden, and when the U.S. military initially refused to help confirm that bin Laden was in Tora Bora, he risked everything by sending his own team.

George Gary Berntsen's deputy chief. The leader of Team Jawbreaker Juliet, the CIA point group leading the hunt for bin Laden at Tora Bora. A champion in forcing General Ali to use American commandos in the Tora Bora Mountains.

Lieutenant Colonel Al Special Forces officer assigned to the CIA's Special Activities Division, a critical member of the CIA Jawbreaker Juliet team, and liaison to the 5th Special Forces A Team deployed to Tora Bora.

Adam Khan An Afghan national who became an American citizen and a U.S. Marine. The CIA borrowed him from another government agency to support military special operations in Afghanistan.

THE DELTA OFFICERS

Lieutenant Colonel Jake Ashley Delta Force squadron commander of the team that participated in the Battle of Tora Bora. His requests for specific authority and assets to prosecute the battle were denied. Veteran of the Battle of the Black Sea in Mogadishu, Somalia, in October 1993.

Lieutenant Colonel Gus Murdock Jake Ashley's predecessor as the Delta squadron commander. Hand-picked by Maj. Gen. Dell Dailey to head a new subordinate unit inside Joint Special Operations Command (JSOC) known as Advance Force Operations. Murdock also was a veteran of the Battle of the Black Sea in Mogadishu, Somalia, in October 1993.

Lieutenant Colonel Mark Sutter Subordinate officer to Gus Murdock and commander of the Northern Advance Force Operations. He took the enormous risk of committing three of his men to Gary Berntsen's joint CIA and JSOC team to move into the Tora Bora Mountains and confirm or deny bin Laden's presence.

Dalton Fury Code-named Redfly, the assault troop commander given command of all American and British military forces during the battle.

THE BOYS OF DELTA FORCE

Sergeant Major Bryan Code-named B-Monkey, the reconnaissance troop sergeant major who led the second Mission Support Site to enter the battlefield at Tora Bora.

Sergeant Major Ironhead Squadron sergeant major and senior Delta noncommissioned officer operator in the battle. Personally led resupply missions deep behind enemy lines.

Sergeant Major Jim Code-named Grinch, the assault troop sergeant major who led the first Mission Support Site to enter the battlefield.

Admiral U.S. Air Force combat controller habitually attached to Delta

Force. He was ordered to participate in the mujahideen's daylight assault on al Qaeda's prepared positions. Abandoned during the fighting and forced to escape and evade back to friendly forces.

Catfish Assault team leader present at the Battle of Tora Bora.

Crapshoot Assault team leader present at Tora Bora and also at the capture of al Qaeda facilitator Gul Ahmed a year later.

Dugan Muscular sniper sent to the battlefield within hours after arriving at the schoolhouse.

Hopper Recce team leader who volunteered to participate in the mujahideen daylight assault on al Qaeda's prepared positions. Abandoned during the fighting and forced to escape and evade back to friendly forces.

Jester Encyclopedic-minded sniper sent to the battlefield within hours after arriving at the schoolhouse.

Pope Recce team leader who chased retreating al Qaeda fighters straight up the middle of their prepared positions.

Scrawny Sniper and member of Jackal team during the Battle of Tora Bora. Classmate of Dalton Fury during Ranger Course 10-84. Participated in the capture of al Qaeda facilitator Gul Ahmed.

Shrek Sniper sent to conduct a "singleton" reconnaissance of Gul Ahmed's village and participant in the Battle of Tora Bora.

Ski Recce team leader present at Tora Bora and also at the Gul Ahmed capture.

Stormin' Also known as "the Bod." Delta assault team leader at Tora Bora and at the capture of Gul Ahmed a year later.

Preface

In February 2002, just six weeks after returning from a rewarding but frustrating combat tour in Afghanistan, my mates and I in Delta had refitted, reblued, and recocked and were anxiously awaiting our next mission in America's war on terror. While also juggling the responsibilities of being husbands and fathers, we anticipated the proverbial "word" and speculated about our future, whether orders might send us to Yemen, Iran, Lebanon, Somalia, or any of a dozen other countries infested with Islamic fanatics.

By then, some two months had passed since the Battle of Tora Bora in December 2001, and news stories had begun permeating the world's press claiming that America had squandered the opportunity to kill Usama bin Laden inside Afghanistan. Stories describing a failure by American special operations forces to accomplish their mission surfaced in newspapers and magazines and on Internet Web pages. Soon followed the usual flurry of books, feeding news-hungry and curious readers and intended to make a buck. It was hard to sit there and read that stuff and listen to what was spilling out of the television sets.

The mission, of course, had been to kill bin Laden, the most wanted man in the world. It was a mission so important that it couldn't be assigned to just any American military or intelligence force. No, only two months after the terrible attacks of 9/11, this truly was a mission of national, maybe even of international, significance. The best commandos America had to offer were needed.

The task ended up in the hands of about forty eager and very willing members of America's supersecret counterterrorist unit, formally known as the 1st Special Forces Operational Detachment—Delta. More informally, the elite and mysterious organization is more popularly referred to as Delta Force. Inside our building, we refer to the organization simply as "the Unit."

The American generals not only wanted bin Laden killed, but they also wanted proof. A cloudy photograph would do, or a smudged fingerprint. A clump of hair or even a drop of blood. Or perhaps a severed finger wrapped in plastic. Basically, we were told to go into harm's way and prove to the world that bin Laden had been neutralized, as in "terminated with extreme prejudice." In plain English: stone-cold dead.

In fact, the only inflexibility of the decision makers surrounded the eventual disposition of the terrorist mastermind's remains. On this they were absolutely firm. We were to leave the body with our newfound friends in Afghanistan—the mujahideen, or as we called them, the "muhj."

The Delta warriors got some help with the job, helpers who were as good as you could get. A dozen commandos from the famed British SBS and another dozen or so U.S. Army Green Berets stepped up. And, as usual, the Central Intelligence Agency was there first. Six CIA intelligence operatives and technicians provided umbrella leadership, cold hard cash, and guns and bullets for the effort. The Agency would link their intelligence collecting, interrogation, and a multitude of other skills to this clandestine military force.

A few talented U.S. Air Force special tactics commandos and several top-secret tactical signal interceptors rounded out the eclectic group of brave souls who ventured into Afghanistan as that cold winter closed in, far from home, far from help. We all would join to lay a modern siege of epic proportions. Inside one big-ass mountain range called Tora Bora we went up against bin Laden and his seemingly impenetrable cave sanctuary burrowed deep inside the Spin Ghar Mountains.

Over the years, since the battle ended, scores of news stories have surfaced offering tidbits of information about what actually happened in Tora Bora. Roughly 75 percent are complete conjecture and speculation, bar stool rumors and I-know-a-guy-who-was-there war stories. But as time passes these skewed stories of events may become historically accepted as factual information; if no one sets the record straight, such yarns may someday grace the pages of student textbooks. Unchallenged, a lie often becomes history. Fantastic and exciting stuff, but utter hogwash. Trumped-up fantasy and fiction.

I've scrutinized hundreds of stories containing even the slightest hint about bin Laden's status or the battle, and few reveal anything worthwhile. The media reports were sketchy because the media was not where the action was. But the public does not generally care if the story is accurate or not, since news has become entwined with entertainment.

The same public pushes the demand for information and seeks vicarious thrills, wanting to be thrown into a world of mystery, intrigue, action, and uncertainty. To experience a place where bravery and sacrifice carry the day, but also a sanitized place where nobody has to get hurt. No pain is felt. No blood is spilled.

The high peaks of Tora Bora provided a fantasy backdrop for dozens of reporters who camped in the foothills a few miles from the front lines, perched upon an odd place we called Press Pool Ridge. Because the time-sensitive story submitted via satellite phone secured their next paycheck, scrutiny and accuracy were sometimes sacrificed in order to soothe an excitement-starved general public. After all, who was to say what exactly happened at Tora Bora, particularly if a television camera wasn't present? Afghan warlords fed the press frequent briefings, and the very, very few people who might challenge whatever was reported would not talk to the media. Delta and the SBS avoided the press.

British newspaper writer Bruce Anderson penned my favorite story in a February 2002 edition of the London *Spectator*. His account provided significant impetus and motivation for my literary attempt to tell the true story. Although his article was full of international intrigue, shadow warrior mystery, and cries of rival elite counterterror units, it also fell far short of the truth on several counts.

Anderson claims an undisclosed member of the SAS, Britain's famed Special Air Service commandos, shared the information that the American Delta Force wanted to kill bin Laden. That Delta fought in Tora Bora. And that two squadrons of 22 SAS commandos, roughly 130 men, fought alongside them. American author Robin Moore made the same claim in *The Hunt for Bin Laden*. See how an error grows?

Well, they got it half right! Yes, Delta was there, but those large SAS squadrons were not. It was a group of twelve brave members of the British Special Boat Service, or SBS, men equal to America's most skilled Navy SEALs, who ventured into al Qaeda's formidable stronghold alongside Delta.

Each of us, to a man, American and British alike, wanted to take the final shot, to drop the most wanted man alive with a single bullet. Or at least be witness to our mate's skill of arms and accuracy.

Finally, and something I hope to sufficiently explain, America's generals were not alone in losing this one. The generals provided the game land, but it was Delta's responsibility to develop a hunting strategy that would harvest the trophy buck. Since this particular trophy buck eventually eluded his hunters and got away, the questioning about why and how quickly surfaced among scholars, military strategists, politicians, and the public. The Monday-morning quarterbacks portrayed a military blunder and cried mission failure.

If Delta couldn't deliver the goods or offer proof of having achieved the objective, then, yes, it was a failure. Even the most seasoned operator, our squadron sergeant major, said to me before we left the battlefield, in true realist fashion, "Sir, what was the mission? We failed!" A tough pill to swallow. An even tougher point to argue.

However, battles often veil the valuable lesson that failure at the strategic level by men and women in conference rooms can easily obscure an enormous tactical victory by the boys on the ground.

Pete Blaber, one of the brightest minds to ever serve in Delta, once said in reference to manhunting, while we were in another third world dump, that a hunter must venture into the woods time after time before he harvests the big one. Bin Laden got away, but not before we kicked his butt around the block.

The fact is that we went into a hellish land that was considered impregnable and controlled by al Qaeda fighters who had helped defeat the Soviet Union on that same turf. They had stalled the attempts of Afghan military forces to get rid of them. We killed them by the dozen. Many more surrendered. The vaunted complex of caves and bunkers was crushed and destroyed, one by one. And we heard the demoralized Usama bin Laden speak on the radio, pleading for women and children to fight for him. Then he abandoned them all and ran from the battle-field. Yes. He ran away.

We also eventually had to leave that game preserve without the main trophy, but we didn't turn our back to the fight and we never flinched.

I was the senior ranking American military officer at the Battle of Tora Bora. As a Delta troop commander I was given the honor of leading about ninety or so Western special operations commandos and support personnel and helped draw up, along with some of Delta's most talented sergeants, the tactical concept of the operation to hunt down and kill bin Laden. This had nothing to do with me being the best man for the job. I wasn't specially selected for the mission. Truth be told, I was simply in the right place at the right time.

Primarily, this book is to set the record straight, so to speak, as much for America as for our British friends. Much is written about the presumed failure of the general officers calling the shots at U.S. Central Command, or CENTCOM, back in Tampa, Florida. The critics argue that the generals engineered what amounted to a spectacular military blunder for three basic reasons: One, by not committing additional conventional troops to the battle; two, by opting to rely on Afghan proxies to do the dirty and dangerous groundwork while relying on American bombing from 30,000 feet; and, finally, by relying on the Pakistanis to seal off the border to prevent bin Laden's escape. The generals, however, were not operating alone. Civilian political figures were also at the control panel.

I will leave the overall strategic debate to the critics and scholars, for I was not in those air-conditioned rooms with leather chairs when they came up with some of the strangest decisions I have ever encountered. And I could care less. When it comes to tactical issues on the ground, in the dirt and rocks and snow, face-to-face with the enemy, American general officers and political decision makers typically are not involved in the tactical planning. They provide the macro task, issue vague guidance, and articulate the big-picture intent. Ultimately, they approve or disapprove the final plan. Tora Bora would be no different.

At the end of the day, the men and women farther up the ladder normally take the word and recommendations of us—the guys on the ground. At some critical times, that did not happen with the complex fight in Tora Bora. Instead, at times, we were micromanaged by higher-ups unknown, even to the point of being ordered to send the exact grid coordinates of our teams back to various folks in Washington.

Many times we had to think and act instantly, with no guidance at all, but that is why Delta picks the kind of operators that it does. They have to be able to think as well as fight. The muhj allies turned their guns on our boys to stop an advance. Rival warlords weighed their military decisions according to personal agendas. When we arrived in Afghanistan in December 2001, the United States was pulling troops out of the area in a weird ploy to trick Usama bin Laden while stripping us of a quick-reaction force. The muhj that were supposed to be doing the bulk of the fighting, and were sucking up the glory, routinely left the battlefield when it got dark, at times abandoning our small teams in the mountains. Some people within the U.S. command system were extremely reluctant to commit highly trained forces because they might get hurt. Some of the highest-ranking people in the Pentagon had no idea of what Delta was trained to do. The CIA bought loyalty out of duffel bags filled with American cash only to learn later that money does not buy everything in Afghanistan. Some of this might have been funny had it not been so serious.

When one of these problems would come up, and they frequently did, trying to figure out what to do was always a puzzle. Particularly for a tired operator standing in subfreezing temperatures on a snowy mountain without radio contact, talking to people who didn't understand him while guns blazed away nearby. But for the Delta boys, it was just another day at the office.

My intent in this book is very narrow, to provide an accurate and firsthand account of this pivotal battle. The first one ever. It is likely to be read for enjoyment, pondered by historians, and studied by leaders who will be asked to fight tomorrow's battles. Finally, it documents the valor, courage, skill, and professionalism of my Delta mates and the other commandos who fought there.

Woven throughout these pages is an inside look at the extraordinary nature of the Delta Force operator. However, it's not my intention to tell the complete story of Delta. Necessarily, that remains classified. This is simply the way I saw things.

The story is true. The people are real. It is important to understand that no part of this work is written from journalistic accounts or magazine stories about Tora Bora. My personal notes, religiously penciled in a small notebook during the battle, were the primary source. My personal recollection of events that I failed to capture in writing at the time helped fill in some details. Dozens of discussions with teammates over a beer in the squadron bar when the fighting was done added crucial operator insights to the story line. The recollections and strong memories of many former teammates complete the work.

Some of these brave men may question this writing as a breach of my personal integrity. Going into the book, I expected to be vilified and scratched from the invite list for events involving former Unit members. That happened. I have been tagged persona non grata—"PNGed" we call it—by Delta's higher headquarters, the Joint Special Operations Command. After all, standards are standards!

Some, equally professional and committed, may applaud this effort. Many have already. Regardless of the ethical line they choose, all of these men pride themselves on remaining anonymous, unsung, and quiet professionals. They are deserving of an enormous debt of gratitude and respect from their fellow American and British countrymen.

Ironically, gratitude is something they really do not value. They have no use for it. Not that they are antisocial or rude introverts, they just consider themselves to be professionals, and they shun fanfare and glory as a practice. They walk away from the photographer's camera or a journalist's pen. They most certainly deserve more pay for the security they provide our great nation. But the only thing they really crave, more than anything, is to not be left behind on the next mission.

Most remain on active duty as I write this and still serve in the ranks of Delta or other special operations units. Many of the men found inside this story were in the northern city of Mosul, Iraq, in July 2003 to help in the killing of Saddam Hussein's two horrible and murderous sons.* Many are fighting in Iraq as this story goes to press. Most have been wounded in action at least once, many twice, and it is not uncommon for them to return to the fight missing fingers, toes, or feet. Some still carry bullets and shrapnel deep inside their bodies. And will for life.

Moreover, I can't think of a single former mate who has not been decorated for valor—most of them multiple times. Because many are still operational it's necessary to preserve their anonymity. Pseudonyms or nicknames take care of this, mine included. For other personalities, folks like publicly recognized senior military leaders, true names are used in the interest of continuity with previous writings and when it's obvious no foul is committed. The Delta operators and others who were there know who is who.

Unfortunately, the names of most of the SBS commandos, the CIA operatives, and the Special Forces A Team members have escaped my memory, and the ones I do recall also must be protected. It was an honor to have served among them.

This ad hoc group of commandos was not perfect, but in the interest of accuracy, flaws and missteps are shared herein as well.

I have wrestled with the idea of sharing this account for years. I eventually justified my willingness to write publicly because this is post-9/11. The world has changed significantly. We ignore the lessons learned at Tora Bora at our own peril.

Moreover, because this was Usama bin Laden, the most wanted man in the world and public enemy number one in all but the most fundamentally Islamic and extremist places, I believe the world is interested.

---

* Authors Michael Gordon and Bernard Trainor recount these events in the book *Cobra II* on pages 561 and 562. *Newsweek* first recounted the event just a few weeks after the raid in "See How They Ran," *Newsweek*, Aug 4, 2003, pp. 22–29.

KILL
BIN
LADEN

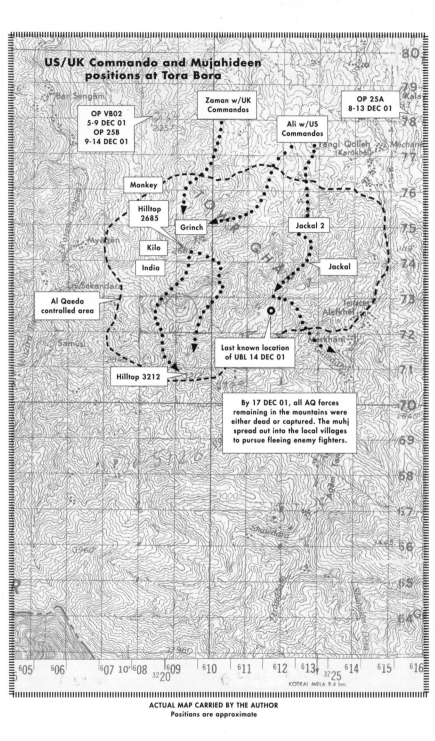

US/UK Commando and Mujahideen positions at Tora Bora

OP VB02
5-9 DEC 01
OP 25B
9-14 DEC 01

Zaman w/UK
Commandos

Ali w/US
Commandos

OP 25A
8-13 DEC 01

Monkey

Hilltop
2685

Grinch

Jackal 2

Kilo

India

Jackal

Al Qaeda
controlled area

Last known location
of UBL 14 DEC 01

Hilltop 3212

By 17 DEC 01, all AQ forces
remaining in the mountains were
either dead or captured. The muhj
spread out into the local villages
to pursue fleeing enemy fighters.

ACTUAL MAP CARRIED BY THE AUTHOR
Positions are approximate

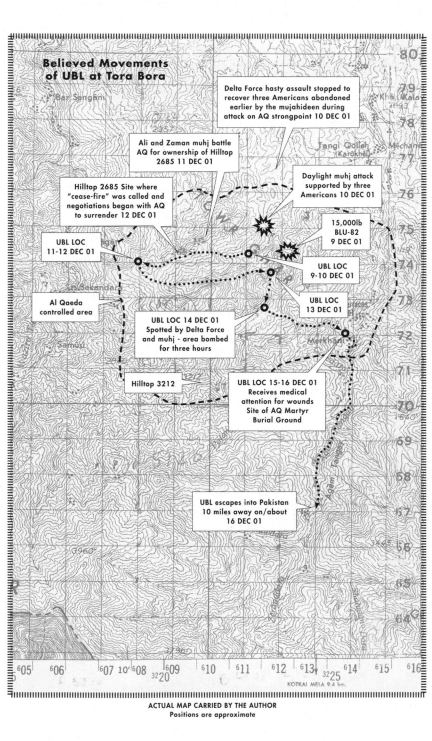

Believed Movements of UBL at Tora Bora

Delta Force hasty assault stopped to recover three Americans abandoned earlier by the mujahideen during attack on AQ strongpoint 10 DEC 01

Ali and Zaman muhj battle AQ for ownership of Hilltop 2685 11 DEC 01

Daylight muhj attack supported by three Americans 10 DEC 01

Hilltop 2685 Site where "cease-fire" was called and negotiations began with AQ to surrender 12 DEC 01

15,000lb BLU-82 9 DEC 01

UBL LOC 11-12 DEC 01

UBL LOC 9-10 DEC 01

Al Qaeda controlled area

UBL LOC 13 DEC 01

UBL LOC 14 DEC 01 Spotted by Delta Force and muhj - area bombed for three hours

Hilltop 3212

UBL LOC 15-16 DEC 01 Receives medical attention for wounds Site of AQ Martyr Burial Ground

UBL escapes into Pakistan 10 miles away on/about 16 DEC 01

ACTUAL MAP CARRIED BY THE AUTHOR
Positions are approximate

1

Unfinished Business

Only those who will risk going too far can possibly find out how far one can go.
—T. S. ELIOT

By December 2001, only three months after America was attacked on September 11, Delta Force was already on the ground in enemy territory, an elite group of American commandos cutting their teeth in this new war on terror by rampaging from cave to cave in Afghanistan's snow-covered Tora Bora Mountains, hot on the heels of Usama bin Laden and laying waste to scores of Taliban and al Qaeda fighters.

The vicious fighting did not last long, however, and by December 17, our frustrating allies, the Afghan mujahideen, felt they had done and seen enough to publicly declare victory. The muhj looted some conquered caves, pillaged the dead terrorists, and came down from the rugged mountains for a triumphant return to the ancient city of Jalalabad, where they licked their wounds and took stock of their hard-earned treasure.

Of course, the main objective of the attack had been to kill or capture bin Laden, and despite the optimistic claims of the muhj, we were not sure that had been accomplished. His body had not been recovered from the rubble in the mountains after the fighting. Could he have been buried alive in one of several hundred caves? Did his most loyal fighters secretly remove his remains from the area?

If bin Laden survived, nobody was saying so. Maybe a helicopter belonging to the unreliable Pakistani Inter-Service Intelligence, a longtime Taliban supporter, had scooped him up and ferried him across the border. Perhaps he put on a woman's burkha and slid into the back of a taxicab for a drive southwest to his old stomping grounds in Khost? Or did he ride bareback on a white stallion through the high mountain passes and trot safely into Pakistan? Did he just sling his AK-47 comfortably over his shoulder and simply walk out under his own power, helped by nothing more advanced than a wooden cane? And if bin Laden did happen to survive, was he wounded? If so, how bad? Was there a doctor who tended his battle wounds? A lot of questions and no answers. No one knew.

As the months slowly passed, Usama bin Laden's disposition–dead or alive–remained a mystery to even the most advanced intelligence services. Not a single acronymed agency could say for sure. The CIA, NSA, FBI, DEA, DOD, DOJ, MI5, and MI6 knew little more than the general public. No videos or authentic audiotapes of bin Laden had been released during that crucial time, and every possibility was examined at one time or another in scores of newspapers, magazines and online postings from all corners of the globe. In the absence of proof, it was all complete speculation.

So a year later, as the winter of 2002 approached, Delta theorized that the answers to the unanswered questions might lie in retracing our steps in Tora Bora, where someone still in the area might be holding the secret to how he escaped. Maybe by backtracking, we could finally put the jigsaw puzzle together and provide some actionable intelligence. Someone still in the area might be holding the secret that would provide us with some clue, some trace of bin Laden.

Delta Force had never left Afghanistan, and less than a year after the original battle in the mountains, our squadron found itself rotating back into the country, just in time to hunt the elusive, ghostlike leadership of the Taliban and al Qaeda during the Christmas and New Year holidays. If we could not be with our families for that special season, what possible better alternative was there to being in a war zone with Delta teammates? To a man, we were proud to be there.

Unfortunately, the operational pace had not improved much from the previous year, because intelligence was still so scarce on our high-value targets. Usama bin Laden remained HVT no. 1, and his right-hand man, the Egyptian terrorist Dr. Ayman al-Zawahiri, was HVT no. 2. Unfortunately, both still wear those designations at the time of this writing, and continue thumbing their noses at the international community.

We spent many days and nights looking for a golden nugget. For countless hours, we studied satellite imagery of suspected bad-guy compounds, patiently watched hour after hour of live video from the Predator drone aircraft, and analyzed stacks of classified military intelligence reports or CIA cable traffic. Everything required close attention if we hoped to discover some inkling or HVT signature that would show that our targets were indeed down there.

That was not enough, because if we found something, we had to be ready to move instantly. We spent long stints on the local pistol and rifle ranges and worked out hard in a gym that looked like a circus tent, where we pumped iron and burned calories on the treadmills. To hone the fine edge that Delta demands, we repeatedly rehearsed various mission profiles with the expert flyboys from the 160th Special Operations Aviation Regiment (SOAR). Some of what little time was left over was spent doing things like enjoying DVD miniseries movies like *The Sopranos* and *Band of Brothers*.

Finally, a nugget was turned up through hard work by the CIA and a bunch of rough-and-tumble, tobacco-chewing good ole boys with thick beards, Green Berets with a Special Forces Group of the Alabama National Guard.

The neighbors of an Afghan gentleman whom we will call Gul Ahmed had dimed him out to CIA assets. He lived in the large Agam Valley, a dry and rocky riverbed that sprawled along a north-south axis thousands of feet below and to the east of bin Laden's Tora Bora sanctuary. A single-lane road had been cut through the valley by the bulldozers and earthmovers of the construction company owned by Usama bin Laden's family in Saudi Arabia during the jihad against the Soviet Union. Legend had it that a young bin Laden himself rolled up his sleeves and worked that land from the seat of a bulldozer.

The suspect, Ahmed, was not only a well-known local supporter of al

Qaeda, but also managed an elaborate weapons cache operation up and down the strategic valley that leads directly across the border and into Pakistan.

Besides his propensity for dealing arms to terrorists, insurgents, and the highest bidders among area tribes, the dossier said, Gul Ahmed also was a key figure during the previous year's fighting, which took place almost within earshot of his backyard. The turncoat neighbors said that Ahmed and his sons provided logistical support—food, water, medical supplies, firewood, and ammunition—to al Qaeda during the battle.

These acts alone made him a personality worth targeting, but not necessarily important enough that the gig had to be executed by Delta. The Green Berets from Alabama were more than capable of rounding up Gul Ahmed and his relatives. However, there was something special about this cat.

One key piece of information threw the ball into Delta's court. Ahmed allegedly had hidden a severely weakened and wounded Usama bin Laden in his home for three days the previous year, while hundreds of mujahideen and forty or so Western commandos painstakingly searched the mountains for the al Qaeda leader. The intelligence packet also claimed that toward the end of the battle, Gul Ahmed's hospitality and tribal contacts were reported to have been good enough to smuggle the terrorist mastermind through a snow-swathed mountain pass that was just seven miles to the south, and out of our reach.

Well, well. That changed things a little bit and made it a little more personal. Mr. Ahmed was given the moniker of a "known al Qaeda supporter," a designation normally accompanied by a mission statement of "kill or capture." Again, that alone was no big deal, but pulling it off would have a rather pleasant spin that would make the assault troops tighten our chinstraps a little tighter and affix our olive drab Velcro American flags a little straighter on our shoulders. If this intelligence on Gul Ahmed was true, it would provide the first viable lead on anyone that could help us piece together the puzzle of how bin Laden escaped from Tora Bora.

The thought of going back into Tora Bora was exhilarating. We couldn't have been happier to visit this gentleman's family and pay our respects.

We needed to know if the HUMINT—intelligence gleaned from humans—of bin Laden finding a refuge, even for a short time, in this al Qaeda facilitator's house was factual. It would have been nice for everybody if we could have simply dropped in to see the man during the day. Sit around cross-legged on a colorful Afghan rug, sip some lukewarm tea, and grub on nuts and dried dates while we asked a few questions.

Somehow we felt that would not work. This gentleman probably would respond only to a little more aggression.

The first order of business was to locate Ahmed's bedroom, and one of the best reconnaissance operators in the business volunteered for the job. He was known in Delta as Shrek, affectionately named after the movie cartoon character with whom he shared a similar large and muscular build. He sported a deep bronze tan from the sun's glare off the snowy peaks in northern Afghanistan, and much of his face was covered by a thick brown beard that he had grown over many months. Shrek might draw notice on a street corner in Iowa, but would fit in well among the Afghan locals. He had proven his skills time and again, and as much as any Delta operator, Shrek had developed a good feel for the people of the area and understood the very different culture in which honor, hospitality, and revenge are valued like Americans cherish baseball, hot dogs, and apple pie. He had been decorated for valor while chasing bin Laden through the mountains almost a year earlier, and in my opinion there was no better man for this job.

We had a lot of information, but Shrek would hopefully provide us with actionable intelligence we needed to present the situation for a strike to our higher command. Intelligence had to be *actionable*. Not a guess, not too sketchy, and not too old to receive approval to execute a mission. No actionable intelligence equaled no mission launch and typically would send the whole lot of us back to sliding another movie into the DVD player or pumping more iron under the big tent.

We were asking Shrek to hang it all out, to undertake the sort of mission that most American men can only experience vicariously through

Tom Clancy novels or Tom Cruise Hollywood thrillers. On his own, he would have to burrow into a dangerous haystack that was made up of dozens of log-and-mud-walled adobes jammed together on a steep, terraced ridgeline, and discover the needle that was the home of Gul Ahmed.

"Oh, yeah," I added during the initial briefing, putting one more big task on his broad shoulders. "While you are there, we also need you to confirm that Mr. Ahmed is at home and not shopping across the border in Pakistan."

As Shrek made his final preparations, I stopped by his tent and found him dressing for success with a well-worn Afghan mujahideen outfit, including the baggy drawstring pants and a shirt down to his knees. The one thing wrong with his attire was that a red and green baseball cap with the emblem of the Hard Rock Café—Washington, D.C., a souvenir he had picked up when we were in the nation's capital six months earlier, was perched on his hairy head. He replaced it with an old, floppy wool hat of the kind worn by the muhj.

Both of us were on our third tours in Afghanistan, and although we had discussed and briefed back the plan several times, we felt more comfortable with the mission when we could look each other in the eyes one last time. It was important that he understood exactly how we expected to communicate, what was critical to report immediately, and what could wait. More important, I wanted to give Shrek that warm and fuzzy confirmation that, should shit go wrong out there, the boys would pause *The Sopranos* and come to the rescue. He might be working alone, but he was Delta, part of the team. However, we both knew the truth was that we would not magically appear at his side whenever he rubbed the magic bottle. From Bagram, we would need two hours in a helicopter traveling as hard and as fast as the pilots could push it. Nothing we could do to change that.

Into a small bag, the meticulous professional delicately placed a mini video camera that he needed to capture critical information for the assault force; the structure of the walls, type of doors, location of the door hinges, height of window sills, high wires, possible approach routes, the locations of armed guards, possible escape routes, and a dozen other things. He added a small handheld global positioning system, or GPS, that would provide the exact coordinates that would be critical for any surgical clandestine operation. Last in the bag was a small satellite phone that would serve as his only link to us, the lifeline to his teammates and safety.

Finally, Shrek picked up his most precious weapon, his baby, a 7.62mm German-made H&K G3 assault rifle topped with a HOLOsight red dot scope, IPTAL infrared laser, and a high-powered CQB light. He rubbed it warmly.

"Hey, brother, aren't you gonna have a heck of a time hiding that weapon from curious locals and the muhj you come in contact with?" I asked.

Shrek looked at me sideways, with those piercing eyes almost hidden behind all that thick hair. He looked scary. He carefully placed his prized H&K rifle under his sleeping bag to protect it from the horrendous fine dust that inevitably covered everything. "Dalton, I'm only saying good-bye for a few days, but like some of our old ladies back home, she would be pissed at me for leaving her behind." His personal protection on this trip would be a folding-stock 7.62mm AK-47 assault rifle, which could be easily hidden under his robes.

Shrek was happy. I wondered if we would ever see him again.

In the city of Jalalabad, Shrek caught a ride for the long trip south to Tora Bora on what might be considered a bus, but was only a clunker of a foreign-made minivan from the 1980s. The other passengers were a dozen Afghan men who ranged in age from seven to seventy, and it was crowded and stuffy. He adjusted his uncomfortable position because the hidden AK-47 was jabbing him in his lower left side.

Growing bored, his thoughts drifted to home and his old pickup truck. That beat-up beast looked strange enough by itself, but its driver, a big, bearded man in ragged civilian clothing, resembled a terrorist on ste-roids. After 9/11, when all military posts upped their gate security and started strict checks on suspicious vehicles and people, even the greenest military policeman could not resist pulling it over, and Shrek would be stopped three out of five days a week. But now, as an American com-mando on a singleton mission, his truck seemed like heaven compared to the bus, and home was very far away.

He didn't dare to speak to the other passengers, since he was trying to pass as an Afghan. When the jitney crossed tribal lines, he had to contend with armed checkpoint guards who were hungry for whatever booty for passage they could draw from the unsuspecting and unprotected strangers on the little bus. Discomfort and danger he could handle. It was the stench trapped inside the small minivan that was his worst problem. As he jolted along, Shrek prayed for a head cold and a stuffy nose, and wondered: *Don't these guys ever take a friggin' bath?*

The rest of us set up back at the air base to plan the hit, and we would spend days reviewing possible courses of action, throwing out ideas or techniques we knew would be useless for this particular mission.

There were about three dozen buildings in the general target area, and just to the south, four more buildings were built into a 60-degree slope that ascended to the west behind them. Ahmed would be in one of those four. Below the houses was row after row of damp, terraced farm fields that stair-stepped down to the rocky valley floor.

Recent satellite imagery showed hundreds of bomb craters that were still recognizable, even a year later. Several days were spent conducting a detailed terrain study that led to a big decision: We discarded the use of helicopters for insertion. After weighing the risks versus gain and the chance of compromise, we decided to go with our own version of the Trojan horse. Of course, it was not a new idea.

In 1400 B.C. at a place called Troy, the Greeks built a large wooden horse as a gift to the Trojans, who had proven to be a formidable foe after two deadly engagements. The Trojans accepted the strange present and hauled it through the gates of the city wall. That same night, following several hours of strong drink and feasting, the Trojans fell into a deep sleep, allowing Greek warriors Achilles and Odysseus, along with a couple of dozen commandos, to silently slip from the horse's belly and attack. The legendary impregnable city of Troy was sacked.

Delta had first contemplated using the Trojan horse concept back in 1979 while developing courses of action to rescue the fifty-three American hostages seized by Iranian militants in Tehran.* During the months of planning for Operation Eagle Claw, one option was to drive across the border from Turkey and into Iran hidden in the back of trucks. The overall option was discarded as being too risky and providing zero flexibility, but the idea remained.

The final plan for that Iran raid was to go in by helicopter to a rendezvous point roughly fifty miles from Tehran, load onto civilian trucks stashed at the hide site, and drive to the target area under the cover of darkness. Once at the embassy compound, the bearded operators in blue jeans and black dyed army issue field jackets planned to scale the ten-foot wall and rescue the hostages. That entire mission, of course, was aborted when a sudden sandstorm intervened, wrecking helicopters and costing lives.

At this point, I must preserve some details of our own updated Trojan horse scheme in Afghanistan to protect the tactic for future operations. Suffice it to say that if a bored Afghan militiaman at a roadblock separating tribal lines looked in the back of either truck, the farthest thing from his mind would be that the actual load was a dozen American commandos on a business outing.

We procured a couple of standard Afghan cargo trucks that suited us just fine. White tarps with large innocuous lettering stamped on the sides were tied to rusty metal rails along the truck beds. It was critically important that the trucks appear normal to casual or curious eyes. They had to appear boring, but simultaneously also be obvious, and appear as large, loud nuisances that needed to be quickly moved out of the way so things could be brought back to normal at any checkpoint. We would be hiding in plain sight.

But to make it work, we also had to surrender some advantages. There would be no sandbagged floors to protect us from the blast of a land mine, tossed grenade, or roadside bomb, and no armored plating to provide

---

* Derek Leebaert, in his book *To Dare and to Conquer,* discusses when and where Delta planned to use the Trojan horse option during the eventually aborted rescue attempt of American hostages in Iran. The June 2006 edition of *Tip of the Spear,* a monthly magazine published by USSOCOM, discusses former MACV-SOG Dick Meadows's participation in Operation Eagle Claw. Already retired from the military, Meadows was pressed back into action, and along with a few others infiltrated Tehran, Iran, to prepare for the arrival of the rescue force and confirm the location of the hostages. See http://www.socom.mil/TOTS/2006/TOTS_web-200606.pdf.

360-degree protection from gunshots or shrapnel. That sort of heavy protection would add a lot of weight to the trucks and make them sag on their axles, and therefore draw unwanted attention.

Twenty-two Delta operators donned desert camouflage fatigues kitted up with black or green Kevlar helmets and green, black, or tan vests with ceramic plates to provide basic lifesaving protection against the thundering velocity of a 7.62mm round fired from an AK-47 rifle.

All of us wore custom-sewn web gear that resembled souped-up Batman belts more than anything military. These vests provided a pocket or clip for everything imaginable—various explosive grenades, flash-bang stun grenades, six thirty-round magazines of 5.56mm ammunition, six spare pistol magazines, quick-tie tourniquets, flex cuffs, Spyderco or Horrigan special knives, handheld infrared pointer, Garmin GPS, spare batteries, tubular nylon, snap link, Leatherman tool, mechanical breaching tools, explosive charges, and fuse igniter systems. Finally, we also had one item that none of us ever wanted to use—special medical kits to stop a buddy's bleeding, or your own.

Each helmet was adorned with state-of-the-art flip-up ANVS-9 night vision goggles, or NVGs. Peltor ear protection, of the type worn by shooters and hunters, was connected to each operator's interteam personal radio. Each operator was armed with personalized suppressed M-4 assault rifles and the sidearm of choice—M-1911 or Glock variant—all professionally tooled and pampered by the best gunsmiths in the world. The year before, we had dressed for battle in garb indigenous to the country. This time we carried a lot more bells and whistles.

Most guys wore a subdued three-and-a-half-inch-by-two-inch American flag velcroed on their shoulder, chest, or helmet. Some chose a full-color flag and others chose the patches of the New York City Fire Department or the Washington, D.C., Metropolitan Police Department. A few mavericks had patches that I have no idea what they represented. All wore black and luminous yellow call sign patches on their shoulders—a common practice in every special operations unit and since adopted by many conventional units.

In Delta Force, the uniform standard is largely personal choice. Sure, some things are required, such as the color of fatigue top, needed to recognize friend or foe while moving through dark back alleys and shadowy hallways, or the specific equipment that must be carried by each team member. But comfort and efficiency are the most important factors in dressing for close combat. Bloused pants, shined boots, and starched fatigues are hard to find inside Delta. As long as an operator can do his job on target—slide down a rope from a hovering helicopter, enter the breach, eliminate the threat efficiently, and dominate the room—why should I care if he wears a Mickey Mouse patch or one from his local hometown bail bond service? Time is precious and we spend it on the important stuff and take great care not to get run up a tree by the proverbial Chihuahua.

In Delta, big-boy rules apply.

As things came together, we broke another operator, Ski, away from a staff job he had been assigned to do at Bagram to go down to the Jalalabad safe house and give Shrek some company. Ski was more than happy to get away from the computers in order to have the possibility of some action. A Green Beret in his previous life, Ski's jet-black hair hung unevenly from under his wool hat, reached his collar in the back, and hid his forehead and even his eyebrows in the front. His beard was so thick that it ran up his cheeks to just below his eyes. When he spoke, it almost seemed as if a ventriloquist were nearby, because if you were hard of hearing, the only indication that he was talking was the jerky up-and-down movement of the Marlboro cigarette between his lips.

Shrek and Ski sent back photos and exact grid coordinates of Mr. Gul Ahmed's residence, and our intelligence shop confirmed it was the same building we originally suspected based upon our conversations with the CIA and the Alabama Green Berets. With that information, it was time to launch.

Shrek also had solved the mystery of a strange and eerie monument that had defied identification by our imagery analysts.

Standing just to the east of the Ahmed home was a large rock formation that appeared naturally left after thousands of years of flowing river water following centuries of melted winter snow snaking down from the mountains. The large rock was roughly the size of eight tractor-trailers all turned on their noses, with their tails straight up, and glued together at their sides. It appeared on the imagery as a giant rectangular cube with rounded edges.

A worn footpath wound around the rock and ended at the top, where a small mosque was under construction. The doorway was visible on the east side, a design that allowed an entering Muslim to face to the west—toward Mecca, birthplace of the Prophet Muhammad—to perform his daily prayers.

Outside the square mosque were the mounded, rock-covered graves of al Qaeda fighters killed during the previous battle of Tora Bora. They were at peace in paradise now, exactly what they wanted. There were at least fifty individual graves, complete with individually carved tree trunks and makeshift limbs of various lengths pointing skyward. Six to ten feet high, these staffs were adorned with red, green, white, tan, or blue scarves, flags, or torn pieces of clothing that the fallen warrior had worn in battle. The colored banners and pennants fluttered and waved peacefully in the wind.

It crossed our minds that Usama bin Laden might actually be buried in that graveyard, which was already well known locally as an al Qaeda monument and was becoming a popular stop for Muslims desiring to pay their respects to the martyrs.

It was logical that if Ahmed had provided shelter for bin Laden, and if the ailing al Qaeda leader had succumbed to his wounds and expired, then moving his body several hundred feet to this memorial was not out of the realm of possibility. We pulled out photo imagery from the past year that showed the mosque was constructed several months after the battle.

This thought, however intriguing, quickly moved into the too-good-to-be-true category. It would have been virtually impossible to hide a burial site of bin Laden that was so accessible to tourists and the faithful.

Nevertheless, the place was a stark reminder of the cost of war. We were happy that these Tora Bora fighters had paid the ultimate price.

First blood was spilled on our mission before it really got under way. At midafternoon, we piled into some pickup trucks for the short drive out

to the MC-130 Combat Talon aircraft that was waiting for us on the asphalt runway, with her engines already turning. When one of the pickups
took a sharp turn, a large piece of equipment shifted in the cargo bed,
smacked a young operator named Rip square in the nose and catapulted
him out of the bed of the truck. His Kevlar helmet and body armor protected him upon impact with the runway.

Our medic, Durango, went to work to stop the facial bleeding and
mend the wounds enough to get him on the plane, although I think Rip
did not know where he was for a few minutes. After we loaded and took
off, I made my way over to Rip, who was staring straight ahead, stoic as
ever, and holding a bandage on his nose. His dark beard was matted with
the thick red blood, adding even more menace to the long wavy hair and
piercing eyes. I bent over to his ear and yelled to be heard over the engine
roar. "You gonna make it?"

Rip nodded vigorously in the affirmative, clearly in no mood for small
talk.

"It's no big deal if you can't go on. We can leave you on the plane
and they'll bring you back," I yelled.

Rip snapped his head up, locked on to my eyes and yelled, "I'll be
okay, and I'm good to go!"

His manner said more than his mouth. I did not need to hear the
words, because his look had delivered the message loud and clear: *Do not
dare to leave me out of this mission! I'm going all the way to the target.* It was
exactly what I expected. I slapped him on the shoulder, smiled, and let
him be.

It was still daylight when our Combat Talon touched down in Jalalabad,
where Ski and Shrek waited at the end of a secluded taxiway. We off-
loaded our gear and moved it immediately to the cargo trucks, then Shrek
and Ski gave the team leaders a final intelligence dump. We arrived at the
airfield with the assault plan, but were depending on Ski and Shrek to figure out how to get us there.

They told us that we would have to negotiate three known roadblocks to reach our destination in the mountains. The first two were expected to be relatively benign, just several militiamen and tribal thugs shaking down commuters for whatever tolls they could get. This assumption came from some local Afghan militiamen hired by the CIA, who believed we could move through those two points if we just held our breath. The checkpoint guards would not act as long as there were no indications that our trucks contained anything more than ordinary supplies being hauled to the needy somewhere in that region. Even with these assurances, we remained concerned. In commando-speak, such locations were referred to as "friction points," and caution was required.

Shrek and Ski had come up with some ingenious planning to get through the third roadblock, which was more complex. A small sedan would travel with us but stay far enough from our convoy to keep the signature low. In the car would be four Afghan militiamen who were on the payroll of the CIA and had been trained by the Green Berets. Once the trucks were two thousand meters short of the roadblock, the sedan would speed around us to the checkpoint, the militiamen would jump from the car with their guns raised, and demand the guards drop their weapons or else. If a gunfight broke out, we would reinforce them. If, instead of gunfire, we saw three flashes of a red lens flashlight, it was safe to proceed. Sounds simple, doesn't it?

Ski and Shrek would be in the truck cabs because they looked more local than the rest of us. We wanted them not only to look local but to also smell like filth because they would need every bit of that indigenous charade for this to work.

With the plan in place, we had no worries.

The ever-thoughtful Ski amazingly had found about twenty thick foam mattresses in a variety of colors, which were welcome additions to our tricked-out cargo trucks. We expected a good amount of bouncing and jerking from side to side on the trip as the trucks navigated streambeds studded with boulders the size of basketballs, washed-out pathways, and gigantic potholed sections of war-ravaged roadway.

Another addition came from our new troop sergeant major, Stormin', who obtained a half-dozen cases of bottled water and several empty five-gallon water cans for use as portable urinals during the trip. The guys were always thinking.

By the time we were ready, we reckoned that our trucks were at least as comfortable as the Trojan gift horse.

While we had discussed the final plan, the boys positioned the equipment and inspected the rigging of the tarps. We couldn't afford any light holes that might compromise us as we drove through busy downtown market streets or crossed through the few expected rural roadblocks and checkpoints that defined tribal lines, for a Trojan horse operation is all or nothing.

If compromised, the gig is up right then and there. One has little choice but to come out swinging and hope for the best. If this happened, we would unass the truck as quickly as possible, eliminate any threat, and hightail it to the nearest building and own it. Once inside, we would turn it into a stronghold by occupying the roof and covering all windows and doors. Then a radio call to our teammates and Rangers back at Bagram would bring us the beautiful, thundering sound of the 160th SOAR birds.

Regardless of what we did after being compromised, if we weren't within sprinting distance of the target, we were likely facing mission failure, something that we and our commanders did not look upon too favorably.

One thing was certain. We would not come out of those trucks with our hands up in surrender.

We settled in for a long trip as our little convoy made its way south from the airport and left the city limits, packed like sardines in a can, moving only from one ass cheek to the other to ease the discomfort. It was impossible not to think of how many of us would be hit if a burst of AK-47 rounds stitched the side of the truck and ripped through the protective walls that had been cobbled out of thin metal and cloth tarp. Enemy bullets aside, we were at the mercy of our Afghan driver's total lack of off-road skill. He consistently seemed to aim for the dark spots in the road and drop two tires into every pothole in the broken asphalt or intentionally bounce over every big rock.

After the first of an expected seven hours traveling at the pace of a one-legged snail over the severely rocky roads, we were certain that we were developing lower back pains for life. Some of the guys fiddled with pieces of their weapons, and the bottled water went quick because we all knew to hydrate for the expected climb that night. The urine cans were wrestled back and forth.

The boys, focused on the mission, could spend but a few moments thinking of their wives and kids back home before automatically switching back to mentally review the various mission contingencies briefed and rehearsed during the planning phase. I'm sure some of them took time to secretly curse me for getting them into this, but I ignored that, keeping my attention glued to the map that I held in one hand and the Garmin GPS in the other.

As we approached the first checkpoint, our communicator, Gadget, manipulated his satellite antenna to the appropriate azimuth and angle, then whispered into his mike. "Wrangler Zero-One, this is Rascal Zero-One. Checkpoint one, over."

His call was monitored by the Joint Operations Center back at Bagram, where our current location was plotted. Important information should we run into trouble. Help was several hours away, and the Ranger cavalry could only fly to the rescue if they knew where we were.

As expected, the first checkpoint proved fairly simple to pass. The guards stopped us and questioned the Afghan driver as to where the supplies were headed. We glanced at each other as the white beams of several flashlights danced over the tarps and supplies while our driver awaited permission to proceed. Beside him in the front passenger seat, Ski held his breath, as did all of us hiding back in the belly of the horse. In less than a minute, we were on our way.

Several uneventful hours later, we arrived at the second checkpoint, which separated two tribes that had been feuding for centuries in Nangarhar Province. These guards probably would be more aggressive and might decide to help themselves to a small portion of our cargo, which would reveal our perfidy.

As we approached, we reached up with our nonfiring hands, lowered our NVGs, and the world went lime green. With weapons at the ready, we sat as still as bronze statues when the trucks slowed to a halt.

Afghans scuffled around both sides of our truck and several voices barked orders or directions in deep native Pashto. From the front seat, Ski keyed his radio and whispered, "It appears some local commander is here, and they went to ask him if the truck can pass. Stand by."

Long minutes passed as we attempted to regulate our breathing while listening intently for anything out of the ordinary, for there was cause for concern. The flashlights outside had become steady beams on the tarps and the supplies in the back. Suddenly, the truck rocked as a guard leaped up on the tailgate, squatted, and spoke to the others. There was no need for me to alert the boys that we were moments from a major showdown and possibly a gunfight. The situation had everyone's undivided attention.

Risking being overheard by someone unseen in the darkness outside the truck, Ski keyed his radio again and softly whispered, "Sounds like we are okay. Local commander told them to let us through."

I could feel the collective silent sigh of relief and relaxing of muscles as we eased an inch or two back into our sponge mattresses. We pressed ahead. Hydrated more. Wrestled the cans.

We reached the final checkpoint five hours into the trip, and things picked up. The sedan of militiamen zoomed around us on the shoulder of the dirt road and we stopped and waited inside our trucks tense with anticipation as the empty minutes ticked away. After about ten minutes of waiting, Ski saw red lights blinking the okay signal in the distance and we continued forward.

As we went by the checkpoint, only Ski and Shrek, in the truck cabs with the drivers, had the luxury of seeing the guards wrapped up snugly in blankets the militiamen gave them as gifts. Everyone was sitting around a small warming fire while one of the militiamen brewed up some hot tea to cut the sharp edge of the cold Afghan winter. They looked like one big happy family at a hometown cookout.

Three checkpoints behind us, so far so good, but we were not clear yet. It was imperative that the trucks continue looking innocent and routine because we had been warned of a heavy machine gun emplacement a few hundred meters above the mouth of the valley. We had to pass right under its nose, and once committed on that road, places to bang a U-turn would be scarce, particularly while being shot at. The trucks rolled on, unmolested. Our cover was holding.

Ski came up on the net. "Ten minutes."

I folded my map, shoved it in my chest pocket, powered off my GPS, and stuck it in its pouch. I wouldn't need either item because Shrek and Ski had coordinated for a CIA source, a local carpenter's assistant, as a guide, and he was to be waiting for us.

I reached up to manipulate my NVGs, as I had done hundreds of times before, and the goggles fell off my helmet. "Shit! Of all the times, not now," I whispered. A close look showed that the screws that attached the mounting bracket to the helmet had vibrated loose during the roller-coaster ride, and in the darkness the tiny screws were nowhere to be found. Coming to grips with the idea of having to rely on my own vision, on a hunch I sent out a net radio call asking if anyone had a roll of tape. A moment later a gloved hand appeared in the darkness clutching a roll of black electrical tape. Four wraps around my helmet and the goggles held like a charm.

The trucks finally stopped, end of the line. After seven brutal hours crammed in the trucks it was time to drop from the belly of our Trojan horse and, we hoped, catch the enemy sound asleep.

We quietly spread out along the valley floor, awed by the breathtaking sight of the large boulders in the valley and the steep walls of ridgelines to the east and west. As seen through the uneven shades of light green produced by the NVGs, the ridges seemed to extend as high as Jack's beanstalk and we could not make out where the ridgelines' highest peaks ended. As we took a knee and gained our bearings, it was obvious that our guide wasn't going to simply walk us down the valley floor to the target building. No, we were going to have to climb a steep wall to get to Ahmed's residence.

It took Shrek ten minutes to locate our guide, who wore a faded olive drab army jacket and a black facemask to protect his identity should a local happen to be awake and see us through a window or doorway. He had to live here, and protecting his identity was crucial. We followed him over rickety single-log bridges, in between tight adobe homes where both shoulders rubbed against the walls, up precarious ledges, and over large rock formations. He knew exactly where he was going. No doubt that this was his hometown.

The route was physically exhausting. We had started this journey at the Bagram Air Base, which was 5,000 feet above sea level. By the time we reached the target house we would have gained another 1,500 feet in elevation, and the steep climb was made more difficult because we were all carrying loads—weapons, ammo, water, radios, explosives—weighing anywhere from sixty to one hundred pounds. As the troop commander, I typically carried the lightest load, but even my chest was screaming for oxygen as we moved up the near-vertical slope, softly picking up each foot and delicately placing it in front of the other. The boys seemed to be handling the ascent with ease. I'm a mere mortal, but they were animals.

About two hundred meters from the target, Shrek and the guide moved to the far side to provide security. At fifty meters, we paused to catch our breath, give Shrek time to get into position, and radio our location back to the base.

A distinct humming sound rode the night air, the familiar buzz of an AC-130 gunship that was burning holes in the sky directly above us. Gunships make us happy, but this time the presence of the aircraft caused a worry because it could be easily heard by anyone on the ground. By circling around the target area too soon, the aircraft risked compromising us and also alerting Gul Ahmed, and either development might prompt him to squirt. He was not stupid. This time, the services of the gunship could wait.

Our U.S. Air Force combat controller, Jeff, raised the AC-130 and directed it to clear the airspace and to go loiter a few miles away. As the plane faded from earshot, we once again settled back to dead silence.

Still, there was another bird stacked up there. A Predator drone circled 9,000 feet over our heads, out of hearing range, but with its infrared camera locked on the target buildings. The images flashed back to the JOC and gave the Delta commander and the entire task force staff seats almost as good as ours. On a large screen, they could easily make out twenty dark figures around the four structures.

Shrek made a final radio call. "Be advised, the guide thinks Mr. Ahmed will attempt to jump out a window and run for another home." The guide's timely reminder was no big deal, since that is always an obvious possibility. We stood and departed our last covered and concealed position, and moved up the hill to introduce ourselves to Gul Ahmed.

The home was typical of a middle-income Afghan farmer, and through our NVGs we saw chickens scooting calmly around the dirt yard, several goats that were frozen in confusion about the intruders, and a big donkey that stood dead still, as if it were trying to hide its presence.

We had chosen for this mission to employ mechanical breaching to gain entry; we would simply open an unlocked door or use a sledgehammer or ax, but refrain from using explosives. No need setting off a loud boom that would announce our presence to everyone in the area. The doors were expected to be of the standard, flimsy type and were likely only secured with a light chain. They were there mostly to keep prying neighbors out and animals in, and we breached them by a quick manipulation of the loose chain or a simple mule kick.

Charlie Team silently entered the front door of the main residence without anyone the wiser, but just inside the door stood a large water buffalo that knew these specters did not belong there. The big animal spooked and made a beeline for the front door, with the big horns nearly impaling a Delta operator.

After clearing that immediate room, the team flowed through the open doorway to the left. Inside was a large bed fashioned from tree trunks and rope, and the unmistakable outlines of two humans beneath a blanket. One of the boys kicked the bed and both figures quickly bolted upright, a confused man and a naked woman staring into the darkness. The man was our target, Gul Ahmed, and the boys easily subdued him, but his partner began screaming uncontrollably, and her keening wails started a chain reaction of shouting throughout the entire two-story log structure and then spilled to the other structures.

Within two minutes of the breaches, the sweet sound of victory squawked through my earpiece. "One-One, this is Charlie-One, PC [Precious Cargo] secure," reported Grumpy, the Charlie Team leader.

I called back, "This is One-One, I understand PC secure, over."

"Roger, we got him, building three, bottom floor secure. I need some assistance on the second floor."

Grumpy was mature, quiet, and unassuming, a no-bullshit kind of guy who had been in Delta for seven years and had a general disdain for the chain of command. He told it like it was and didn't pull any punches, not even for me. Normally unflappable, his calm request for "assistance" was his way of telling me to send another team to help him—*now!*

In fact, at the time, he was locked in a hand-to-hand struggle with a pissed-off, twenty-something Afghan male. Grumpy was not in much danger, but his opponent believed that he was fighting for his life. Grumpy somehow had held the guy at bay with one hand, protecting both his M-4 assault rifle and his M-1911 .45-caliber pistol from his opponent's frantic grasping, and found a moment to squeeze the push-to-talk button on his radio. Nobody would have blamed Grumpy if he simply ended the fight with a single ball round to the man's forehead. The rules of engagement clearly authorized lethal force in this situation, but the seasoned Delta sergeant knew this guy would be of no intelligence value dead. Besides, the loud report of a gunshot would attract unwanted visitors from around the neighborhood. So the wrestling match continued.

Two of Grumpy's teammates charged up the outside wood and mud stairs toward their next breach point, moving fast toward their designated portion of the target area. They jumped over the two brawlers without breaking stride, confident that Grumpy, an expert in jujitsu, could handle one unruly Afghan who weighed maybe 150 pounds.

They kicked a dilapidated door to the right off its hinges. Grumpy was proud that his boys were acting like trained professionals. Sure, they cared about their team leader; they simply had assessed the situation and moved on to the next door, just what he had taught them to do.

All of the structures were clear and secure within five minutes without a shot being fired.

The incessant wailing and screaming of the twenty-five to thirty women and children in the small group of buildings woke up the neighbors. We didn't expect so many women and kids. They outnumbered us. We collapsed our northern security team to help in calming and controlling them. From the south came the distinct rattle of an AK-47, but no shots landed near us.

From the north, two adult males slowly approached, apparently more out of curiosity about the screaming family members than with any idea that American commandos had caused the ruckus. One had a weapon slung over his shoulder, and with no northern security to intercept them, I leveled my M-4 at him and placed my infrared laser on his forehead. An instant decision was necessary: *Armed? Yes. Displaying hostile intent? No. They live.* I eased a bright green laser line a few inches above his head and squeezed off two suppressed rounds to get their attention. They had come far enough. Message received, the two men turned about and beat feet back the way they came.

In addition to Mr. Ahmed, four of his sons and brothers were found and secured. We had zero time for sorting out who was who, so they also would be taken with us and turned over to the Joint Interrogation Facility in Bagram. Even if some were completely innocent, they still had value, for their stories could be used to determine whether Ahmed was telling the truth or not during his own interrogation sessions. They could also be played one against the other or to corroborate each other's stories.

Gadget relayed to the Delta commander. "Wrangler Zero-One, this is Rascal-One. One-One sends PC secure. No casualties. Request exfil in ten minutes. Leaving with PC plus four crows. Over."

The JOC exploded in applause and high fives and smiles flowed around the tent. They all had worked many long hours to make this happen. But we were far from being mission complete—essentially with all friendly personnel safely back at our sleeping tents and the precious cargo turned over to competent authority.

As the troop sergeant major, Stormin', prepped to get everyone out of Dodge, I moved down the ridge to our primary helicopter pickup zone with Jeff, the combat controller. The spot had been chosen from studying recent imagery and we knew it would be tight. Jeff stepped off the dimensions of the area until he reached the end of the terrace, where he was looking down a ten-foot drop to the next terrace. He shook his head, unhappy with what he saw. It was going to be extremely difficult to get the black MH-47 Chinook helicopter into such a tight spot, and he walked over and asked my opinion.

"Hey, brother, this is your ball game," I replied. "Is it going to work or not? If you don't think it is, we'll move to the alternate. Trust your instincts."

"Roger that," Jeff coolly responded. "I'll bring her in here."

As we waited for the distinct thumping sound of double rotor blades, Stormin' moved the teams down the hill, closer to the pickup zone, along with the five captives, who were barefooted and hooded, with their arms flex-tied behind their backs. A few were noncompliant, requiring the boys to use a few come-along techniques. A little well-placed pain goes a long way.

When they were seated on the ground, Crapshoot, our Alpha Team leader, approached Ahmed, grabbed a handful of the black cloth hood and raised it high enough to clear the eyes. Crapshoot leaned to within inches of the Afghan's face and peered directly into his eyes.

"*You are Usama bin Laden!*" Crapshoot barked in the face of the middle-aged Afghan.

Ahmed's eyes went wide with astonishment and he protested, "*No! No! No! Me Gul Ahmed!*"

"Thank you. Just checking," Crapshoot dropped the hood over the man's face and grinned. Instant positive identification.

The big Chinook helicopter approached low toward the landing area with its big twin blades whoop-whooping in the night. The bird made a test pass to size up the tight space that we had designated for a landing. Jeff talked to the pilots, advising them to orient the ship's nose to the valley floor and, from a hover, slowly descend roughly 150 feet to make a lip landing above the damp terrace. The maneuver required that the aircraft lower until the tail ramp kissed the ground and we would rush aboard as fast as possible.

Under the circumstances, it was a risky and difficult maneuver for any helicopter pilot and crew, and we wouldn't have even considered asking anyone but our brothers from the 160th to attempt it.* The rotors would be spinning precariously close to one of Ahmed's stone farm houses, and any blade strike would likely prevent our exfil and force the bird to limp back to Jalalabad. If it didn't fall out of the sky first. In addition, two high wires drooped dangerously close, and the crew chief and door gunner had to ensure they could be cleared during the descent.

The MH-47 pilots did a super job, but the danger mounted by the second, and when the helicopter was actually lower than the high terrain on three sides, it is a wonder that it was not shot out of the sky as it held in a long hover. It would have been an easy shot into the cockpit for even a novice marksmen sitting on his back porch with a slingshot.

When the rear rotor blade actually came within inches of striking a rock wall, Jeff aborted the landing and narrowly diverted a catastrophe. The ship pulled up and out of the area to reposition and acquire the alternate pickup zone on the valley floor.

We breathed sighs of relief, probably never happier in our lives that a landing was called off. I keyed my radio mike to let Stormin' know to shift the boys to the alternate pickup site, but he was way ahead of me and already had them moving.

There was no further need for stealth. If the earlier screaming by the women and children had not awakened everybody within a mile or so, the racket of the helicopter certainly had gotten their attention. Everybody knew we were there.

We took off for the alternate pickup zone, slipping and sliding down each terraced piece of terrain, happy to be going downhill and not up. Jeff still needed to look over the alternate site to be sure it was clear of all obstacles. Three terraces below the original site, the MH-47 slowly came over the ridgeline from above and behind us, and I winced as it slowly de-

---

* The flying heroics of the 160th are well known throughout the world and several books cover their selection process and derring-do accomplishments. Retired CW4 Mike Durant, of *Blackhawk Down* fame, had authored two books on the organization. The first, *In the Company of Heroes,* covers his personal experience in Somalia. The second, titled *Night Stalkers,* recounts several previously unknown secret missions of the 160th. Also, David Tucker and Christopher Lamb describe the talents of the 160th in their book, *United States Special Operations Forces.*

scended toward the alternate site. It seemed as big and slow as the Goodyear blimp above a Little League ball field. I couldn't help but think that we were putting the aircraft and crew in great danger by asking them to come into pretty much a similar location twice. It was discussed during the planning, and although it was not smart tactics, in this case we didn't have much choice. Our Trojan horse trucks would never have made it back on a return trip with five detainees through alert and insulted neighborhoods.

Then the MH-47 pilot noticed that one terrace seemed to be larger than the rest, and instead of going straight for the alternate site, which rested another two hundred meters below, in the middle of the valley floor, the pilot decided to try this new area.

The aircraft descended about one hundred meters, again with its tail to the ridgeline and made a textbook tail-wheel landing, beautiful flying that saved us at least twenty or so more minutes in the area.

As soon as the ramp touched down, four or five of the Alabama Green Berets piled out onto the grassy terrace and fanned out to secure the area. Following them were a couple dozen Afghan militiamen from the same group that had provided us with guides and drivers, and had taken care of the third tribal checkpoint on the way out. They would now secure this area after we left, and calm the excited masses. Afterward, they would talk to the locals and Ahmed's wife and children to see what could be gleaned about his association with bin Laden and his participation in the battle of Tora Bora.

Should Mister Ahmed not be forthcoming, his wife's testimony might help his amnesia, encouraging him not to be so coy. Maybe she would be worried about his safety and want him to cooperate, or perhaps proud of his notoriety and willing to tell us all about it.

As the boys crested a four-foot berm just beyond the landing zone, one of the detainees began to resist. Unfortunately for him, his escort was one of the Alpha Team boys known as Body Crab, who had been a long-time Army Ranger before coming over to Delta. The Body Crab stood about six two, had deltoids that looked like football shoulder pads, and although he had an awesome sense of humor, he was not in a playful mood. He executed a perfect face plant on the struggling detainee, which motivated the young man to stop struggling and come along nicely.

Within a minute or two, we were loaded and heading back to Jalalabad airfield where our squadron commander, Lt. Col. Jake Ashley, and squadron Sergeant Major Jim, a.k.a. the Grinch, awaited.

The air mission commander, Clay Hutmacher, was sitting in the jump seat just behind the two pilots. Although not actually flying the ship this night, he was in charge and could have aborted the pickup for a dozen reasons and none of us would have questioned the decision. Standing in the rear of the helicopter, I scribbled a note on my small light board and passed it to him. "Thanks for being the best pilots in the world tonight." We were happy customers.

The trip back was much shorter than the trip out, and we were soon enjoying some hot chow the cooks had prepared, a much-appreciated and long-standing Delta tradition. For some strange reason, the food always seemed to taste a whole lot better when the missions were successful.

Ahmed was given a bottle of water, a Quran, and a new set of pajamas, then was introduced to his new home and personal interrogator.

Shrek, Ski, and Nuke, our appropriately named explosives ordinance disposal expert, had stayed at the site to update the Alabama Green Berets on what had taken place before they arrived and to interview Ahmed's wife. But only a few minutes after our helicopter cleared the area, something else required their attention.

Several armed groups of locals were spotted moving toward the Ahmeds' home, some of them testing the waters by firing their AK-47s at our guys. Mistake. Instead of wasting their own small-arms ammo, our boys remembered the AC-130 that was still on station overhead and called it in to do some work. In this case, bigger was better and the threat evaporated before it could gather momentum.

After a few hours sleep, we gathered for a full hot wash with representatives from every group of folks that had played some part in the mission. Among them were the intelligence analysts and staff operations wizards who did the lion's share of work just to get us out the door. The helicopter pilots and crews from the 160th and representatives from the Combined Joint Special Operations Task Force, who owned the Alabama Green Berets, and CIA analysts and operatives in civilian clothes rounded out the guest list.

These hot washes are critical to Delta's success and are always run by the senior noncommissioned officer involved in the mission. Officers usually sit in the back, but participate just the same.

Similar in many ways to the U.S. Army's formal after-action review, hot washes are used to identify what went right, what went wrong, what needs to be sustained, and what needs fixing. However, it is quite unlike a standard after-action review, where a sacrosanct rule is that nobody should be individually identified for having done something wrong. In a Delta hot wash, if you messed up, you certainly hear about it, and although it's nothing personal, thick skins are required, regardless of rank or service.

Once the overall review was complete, a few minutes were spent exchanging handshakes, slaps on the back, and a few laughs before all of the external folks depart the area. As soon as the room was cleared of anyone who was not part of Delta, a second, internal hot wash was conducted, best characterized as a no-holds-barred commando confessional.

Every operator is expected to pony up to anything he did wrong during the mission. Whether it was poor judgment, a mental lapse, or a physical slip-up, you could bet it would be discussed. No infraction was too small, and any operator worth his salt would man up to not meeting the Delta standard. If he didn't, you could bet someone would bring it up before the meeting adjourned. It always impressed me how a Delta team leader with six or seven years in the unit could tactfully tell a new troop commander—an officer—how screwed up he had been during an assault. Of course, some were more tactful than others, but it all had to be said. If you kept an open mind, you could really improve your performance. If you did not, then you weren't long for the Unit.

The mission to capture Ahmed was the first successful capture mission for Delta since the start of combat operations in Afghanistan. Delta was responsible for killing scores of enemy Taliban and al Qaeda in places like Shah-i-Khot and Tora Bora, and on dozens of raids across the country, but this marked the first time the targeted personality in the mission statement was actually found on target and captured.

This statistic was indicative of the small number of al Qaeda terrorists or Taliban leaders on whom the intelligence community had actionable intelligence. This fact alone accounts for why we spent an awful lot of time looking for the special piece of information that would provide insight into the location of bin Laden, al-Zawahiri, or Mullah Muhammad Omar.

When the raid was all over, I could not help but think that here we were in Tora Bora a year after our first violent attacks in these mountains, but instead of having bin Laden within reach, as we did back then, we were now grabbing any little person who might have spoken to him at some time. Gul Ahmed was just another piece in the puzzle. We would not be informed of what, if anything, he gave up, and we went back to work. But the intel on Usama bin Laden remained dry.

Nonetheless, one of the most memorable comments of my career in Delta came from the Unit command sergeant major, Iggy, who remarked as we entered the hot wash after snatching Gul Ahmed, "That's one for the books, sir!"

Well said, sergeant major!

2

Welcome to Delta

Don't be late, light, or out of uniform.
—DELTA SELECTION AND ASSESSMENT CADRE
MEMBER, SPRING 1998

I am an army brat. My father served two tours in Vietnam, including time with the 173rd Airborne Combat Brigade, and spent months hospitalized in a body cast while his wounds healed. In the early 1970s, he was assigned to a new post in Frankfurt, Germany, and I attended a military community elementary school, played baseball, shot marbles, traded comic books and bubblegum baseball cards, and fought a thousand G.I. Joe battles. For cheap thrills, I enjoyed playing combat dodge ball behind the three-story whitewashed apartment building with my twin brother and the other kids.

It was there that I gained my first recollection of terror. The violent, left-wing Baader-Meinhof gang terrorized Germany in those days. In 1972, radical members of the group operating beneath the banner of the Red Army Faction bombed an American military headquarters building in Frankfurt, killing an American officer and wounding a dozen other people. I remember my mother coming around the corner of the apartment building to interrupt our sandbox battle and save the G.I. Joe with his lifelike hair from being crushed by a flying Big Bertha marble.

"Get inside," she said. "The radio just announced some of the Baader-Meinhof gang have escaped from prison and may be in our neighborhood."

Terrorists were nearby, she said, and I, at eight years old, wondered "What's a terrorist?" I begged her to let me stay outside, hoping that I might see one of those mysterious gang members skulking about, perhaps wearing a long, dark trench coat. No chance.

Dad was reassigned back to the States a short time later and we settled in a townhouse in Alexandria, Virginia, while he held assignments at Fort Belvoir, Virginia, and the Pentagon. My adolescent love of G.I. Joe dolls waned, but my hunger for adventure accelerated as I grew older and I craved the excitement of competition, particularly the victory side of things,

We rode bicycles with banana seats and monkey handlebars, replayed Super Bowls with neighborhood buddies using Nerf footballs, rode skateboards around the lake in the summer and skated on it in the winter, and swam in the community pool. In a few years, we graduated to tunneling around the large labyrinth of an underground sewer system from one side of the neighborhood to the next, where old *Playboy* magazines were tucked away in a dry crack.

It was another magazine that had a critical impact on my young brain. I had always considered the U.S. Army to be just my father's employer, and was too young to understand what it was really about. Like many who grew up after the Vietnam era, I viewed the military as a dead-end profession. The army was the path taken by the rejects, the last guys chosen during neighborhood pickup games, or by deviants who were "encouraged" to sign up by small-town judges offering a venue other than jail, and by those uncertain of where they would fit into corporate society.

That attitude had begun to slowly change along with my weird affection for risk taking. One day as I browsed the magazine rack of a local 7-Eleven while sucking on a cherry-flavored Slurpie through a curly straw, I saw the cover of a *Gung Ho* magazine that featured a full-color picture of retired U.S. Army colonel James "Bo" Gritz. His dress uniform, heavily adorned with the shiny medals and colorful ribbons of a modern warrior, was propped on a chair near him.

After leafing through the periodical, I bought it, went home, and read how Colonel Gritz was in the fight of his life as he tried to explain a botched attempt to rescue American prisoners of war believed to have been left behind in Laos after the American withdrawal from Southeast Asia in 1975.

The journey that took Gritz and his small team of former commandos and adventurists through oceans of bureaucratic red tape and over administrative walls had ended without success. Regardless of one's personal opinion of those raiders, their personal sacrifice and commitment were intoxicating.

The magazine remained in my small personal library over the years, unofficially filed under What I Want to Be When I Grow Up. But I was only about thirteen years old, and my career choices also still included professional football and baseball.

Before seeing that magazine, I honestly had not paid much attention to what my father did for a living. But now, when I occasionally looked into Dad's closet, I noticed that some of his honor ribbons looked the same as those that Gritz had: Purple Heart, the Vietnam ribbons, and a Bronze Star with a V for valor. Still, that was not enough to make the military seem attractive to me as a profession.

I was not talented enough to be any sort of professional athlete, but I loved sports and, like all kids, dreamed of making the all-star team, scoring the winning goal, or sinking the buzzer shot. When I was fourteen, I returned a kickoff for a touchdown, and when I hit the end zone, I launched into a flamboyant dance like the pro wide receiver Billy "White Shoes" Johnson. My hips gyrated like a cheap pop star as I repeatedly thrust the ball into the air. My dad, who had volunteered to work the chains on the sidelines for that game, watched the whole pathetic display and was not amused.

His disappointment in my self-serving actions frustrated and confused me. *C'mon Dad, lighten up a little. I just scored a touchdown here. What harm can a little victory dance do?* His reaction and comments seared me to the core, but it would take a few more years for the lessons to fully register. Teamwork was more important than individualism, and selflessness was better than selfishness. The greatest lesson my father taught me was of humility.

In high school, my teammates voted me captain of the football team, and I thought it would be pretty cool to walk to midfield for a coin toss each Friday night. Other than that, how hard could this team captain stuff be? Again, my dad was there to puncture the selfish bubble. Being team captain meant that I was a leader, he said, so simply playing hard and fair, basic blocking and tackling, no mental mistakes, and enjoying the game were no longer good enough. More is expected of a leader. I didn't understand that lesson for a while, either.

It was not until well into my army career that I realized that my personal success hinged much more on the performance of my fellow soldiers than on my own. If one hopes to be considered a leader in deed more than in just a word, he or she had better learn to deliberately and consciously shun the spotlight and embrace the humility of selfless service. After a while, learning to turn credit outward rather than inward begins to feel natural.

I entered college, but quickly determined that it was not for me. I dropped College Physics 102 and turned in my ROTC pickle suit after barely three months' use. Armed with my Dad's critical lessons in humility and teamwork, knowing a little bit about leadership, and having the distant memories of West German terrorism and Bo Gritz's selfless adventures, I joined the army. Under no pressure at all, I simply chose to serve. I was not drawn to duty to defend Mom, the flag, and apple pie, but the lure of the risks involved, the possibility of going into harm's way, was intoxicating. It was 1983 and I was nineteen years old.

I had found a home, and would serve for twenty years.

By the middle of October of that same year, just a week before the United States invaded the tiny Caribbean island of Grenada, Pvt. Dalton Fury found himself packed with about fifty other Airborne Rangers in the back of an MC-130 Talon aircraft, running an exercise.

I was part of Charlie Company, 1st Battalion, 75th Infantry (Ranger) and making the space even tighter was a pair of modified M-115 black gun jeeps strapped bumper to bumper along the centerline of the aircraft's floor. Four 125cc olive drab green motorcycles were strapped near the tail ramp of the aircraft.

As we waited at the departure airfield, I looked out the back of the plane and watched two late 1970s pickup trucks hurrying toward us. The men in the trucks were strikingly different than the uniformed Rangers all around me. Some were much older, some had short, well-groomed hair, while a few had very long hair that blew in the wind. Others wore long and thick mustaches or goatees.

I was curious, but resisted the urge to wake up my team leader, who was catching a quick nap next to me. I knew better.

One of the trucks pulled up to the ramp of our plane and four men deliberately stepped down onto the tarmac. All wore blue jeans, one had a dark sweatshirt, another a tight T-shirt, and the remaining two wore plaid western-style shirts with big collars. In their hands were .45-caliber grease guns.

The mystery men grabbed small black bags from the truck, walked on to the plane, and took seats on the cold metal flooring without a word, a gesture, or even a simple hello. They didn't check in with anyone. No, they just went about their business and pulled out a small tube of black cream. A few dabs on their palms, they slathered it all over their faces, as if applying sunscreen lotion. Two of them work black balaclavas—skintight thug hats that hid their faces while showing only the eyes and lips.

It was my introduction to Delta.

The very existence of Delta is officially classified by the Department of Defense. No open discussions of the Unit's existence are entertained with the media. Very few former operators have chosen to violate the unwritten code against speaking about the Unit publicly, and very few unofficial sources are available.

Ironically, the first member of Delta to break the code of silence was the man responsible for its birth, and its original commander, Col. Charlie Beckwith, in his book *Delta Force,* written in the early 1980s. It provides factual insight and describes in tremendous detail the exhausting selection process that is used to find the *right* guy for Delta.*

Although published just seven years after the unit was officially

---

* The history, importance, and uniqueness of Delta's selection process is discussed in detail by both Colonel Beckwith in his book *Delta Force* and CSM(R) Eric Haney's book *Inside Delta Force.*

established, Beckwith's comments about the extensive training program to mold an individual, to hone and maintain his war-fighting skills to a razor's edge, and teach him "how to think" and not "what to think" are characteristics that have stood the test of time. Above all else, Beckwith told the country what can be expected from someone who earns the right to call himself a Delta operator.

Opinions still vary as to just how factual Beckwith's story was. Did he reveal sensitive information that could heighten the danger of already high-risk operations? Did Beckwith unnecessarily endanger future unit members? Or did he inform terrorists worldwide of the phenomenal abilities of the unit and what it can do to protect America?

As an insider, I'm convinced that Beckwith revealed no important secrets and that the Delta operators fighting the ongoing war on terror today, many years after his book was published, are still of the high standards that Beckwith demanded.

In the spring of 1998, I found myself with 121 other officers and sergeants at a remote camp in the steep hills and mountains of the northeastern United States. We had been especially recruited and had already survived numerous pre-tryout physical and psychological tests. For the next month, we would be further assessed mentally, psychologically, and physically for "potential service with Delta."

I was by then a captain in the Rangers, and had decided before arriving that my definition of success was to make it through the entire month without getting hurt or quitting. If I was not selected, then okay. It would be a blow to my ego, but simply representing the Rangers as best I could and returning with my head held high would be my bottom line. I think most of those around me harbored similar feelings, because the odds of being around at the end of tryouts, and actually being selected for Delta, were extremely slim. We knew it would be difficult. We had no idea.

By the time I reached the final event, after enduring twenty-five days of hell, I was happy that I had not gotten my hopes up too high, for my performance so far had been sketchy.

It had rained all day and showed little sign of letting up. Huddled in the back of the covered truck, unable to see outside, we waited for our assigned code name to be called. Once it was, we scrambled out as gracefully as possible with minds and bodies already at their limits from twenty-five days of hell, and moved toward a nearby area that was faintly lit.

That night, we individually faced what we hoped was the last land navigation event. The lucky ones would cover roughly forty miles of mountain trails, pock-marked asphalt roads, and densely vegetated terrain that covered the hundreds of meters of elevation change. The unlucky would cover more distance as they self-corrected their march after a sleep-deprived wrong turn or two. The really unfortunate would either move too slow or fail to recover from their error in time to finish within the unpublished time frame. I fell into the middle category, the unlucky.

For the past three and a half weeks, our individual assigned code consisted of a color and a number that was changed daily. This night, however, the smooth-talking Delta assault cadre member named Hoov barked at us from the back of the camouflaged truck. "There are only two colors left—Blood and Guts!" he said. I became Blood 36.

I was the fourth of six candidates in our truck, and was called out just past 2200 hours, taken to a small shelter tarp tied to the trees, and given a short, scripted set of instructions. As the officer spoke, my mind seemed incapable of registering what he was saying. I was too pumped up, or too exhausted, and ready for the entire nightmare to be over. When he finished his short brief, he turned me around and pointed me in the initial direction.

It was pitch-dark, no moon yet, and the ground was soaked. Had I not been steered in the right direction, I might easily have walked off the edge of the earth. Armed with a rubber M-16 rifle, eight different map sheets, and a compass, and toting a sixty-pound rucksack, I was away on the first of what would soon seem like a lifetime's worth of steps.

Trying to jog the trails at night was stupid. After three weeks of assessment, this was not the time to twist an ankle or blow a knee, both easy to do in the blackness on an unknown trail. I maintained my own desired pace for an hour, maintaining a good pace count so as not to miss a turn in the trail. One wrong turn could spell the end.

Incessant pain in my upper back helped keep my mind off the weight of the rucksack digging into my shoulders during the hour that passed before I came into contact with any other humans. Four or five candidates were whispering to each other as they huddled around the white light of a candidate's flashlight that illuminated a rain-soaked map case. The trail had gone cold because heavy rains had flooded the low areas and deep pools of rainwater hid what I thought was the desired footpath.

The discussion centered on whether to go through the water in hopes of picking up the trail when the terrain rose, or steer around it by taking some other trail that was not seen on the map. I had stopped for a breather close by and tried to listen in to the verbal logic train. Just then, a Ranger candidate stepped from the darkness, breathing heavily. He was soaked up to his chest, and his rucksack still dripped water. His compass dangled from around his neck as he held his map and flashlight in one hand and weapon in the other.

He silently signaled to the huddled group that trying to ford the flooded trail was not an option. The Ranger then approached me and said, "No way, man. It's too deep." I recognized him them. Nitro was a seasoned Ranger squad leader from Savannah, Georgia, home of the 1st Ranger Battalion.

We were under strict orders not to talk to anyone during the exercise, but taking risks is what this business is all about anyway. Delta was not looking for choirboys. "How far did you get?" I asked.

"About twenty meters or so. It's hard to tell."

I looked at my map again, my hand wiping rainwater off the plastic case, but preventing me from seeing the important fine brown contour lines telling elevation and the blue dotted lines that showed an intermittent stream.

"I'm going for it," I said quietly. "Can't afford to go around. It will take twice as long to get back on the right trail."

"I don't know, man. I don't think you can make it." Nitro's opinion was not to be underestimated, but time was our enemy.

I glanced over at the group. Some were still debating the issue while others had already taken off to find an alternate route. Their flashlight beams could be seen faintly in the distance. *We're wasting time here,* I thought.

"You can always go around if you want, or you can come with me," I offered, "We'll strike some high ground not too far past where you turned around."

Nitro looked at me for a second, shifted his heavy rucksack around on his back and shoulders. "Alright, I'm with ya," he said. Years later in Aghanistan, I saw Nitro's courage firsthand in the face of enormous odds and ambiguous surroundings.

By now I was completely soaked, except for one area, and a few steps later, the icy water finally reached my groin, too, giving me a frigid reality check. I don't exactly remember when Nitro and I eventually split up, but once we lost each other, another twenty-nine hours passed before I saw him again.

The rain worsened over the next few hours and my body temperature was dropping fast. I had only eaten a single bite of a chocolate Powerbar. I felt nauseous and lost my appetite, a sure sign that I needed to keep re-fueling my body, both with water and food. I ignored it. My rucksack was soaking up rain like a giant sponge, adding at least another five pounds to my load and making each step much more labored. To refill my Camel-bak water container, I would have to take off the rucksack, but I was too cold and miserable to do so.

I was simply too focused on succeeding, too focused on moving forward one step at a time, and too stupid to stop for a few moments to refuel my body.

When the morning sun finally began to break over the horizon, about six hours into the march, I decided to get rid of the batteries in my flash-light to shed a few ounces of unneeded weight. The two D batteries were part of the load slowing me down, so I threw them into a fast-running creek, hoping I would finish the march before darkness fell again. It made some sort of fuzzy sense at the time.

I was continuing down the waterlogged trail that paralleled the creek when my mind told me I might have made a big mistake. Somewhere along the way I had allowed rain to seep into my clear plastic map case, probably when I had stopped to don my camouflage wet-weather jacket to prevent losing any more warmth in my body. I had waited until after I was thoroughly drenched from the rain to do it.

The map case is used to shield your map from inclement weather, and works well until you have to switch out map sheets as the trail leads you off of one sheet and picks up on a different map. My maps got soaked while I was swapping them, and from then on, with each slight tug inside the map case, the papers disintegrated. Figuring I was about thirty miles into the movement, with an assumed ten miles still to go, I knew I had big problems.

I crossed a footbridge that spanned a swift-running river to get to my next rendezvous point and saw another candidate, a blond and muscular Green Beret, standing beside a cadre vehicle. His map also had deteriorated from the rainwater, and he was piecing it back together like a child's jigsaw puzzle. Luckily, the two portions of the map I needed to reach the next rendezvous point were still intact. I showed the cadre member sitting in the driver's seat where I currently was on the map and the point to which I was going next. Those were the only two required pieces of information a candidate had to present before he could continue the exercise. Fortunately, we were not required to point out the exact route we planned to take, because that portion of my map had turned to mush. I also had a good hint because other candidates who had done a better job keeping their maps dry were moving in what I figured had to be the correct direction.

I set off again, physically and psychologically spent, moving one step at a time on some untapped fuel reserve that few men ever push themselves hard enough to experience. It's so much easier just to quit.

Only a hundred meters along, I found myself staring at a massive hill. Without the details of the map to help me make a decision as to which way to go, or if an easier way existed, perhaps a small trail to get me to the top quickly, I just stepped off. Straight ahead.

Thick, intertwined, nearly impassable underbrush of wait-a-minute vines and trees slowed me to a snail's pace. I worried, sniveled, and felt sorry for myself. *I'm losing too much time. I will never make it in time. No, don't quit, keep moving, the terrain can only get better. Maybe it's less dense near the top.* Fortunately, it was.

I broke free of the thick vegetation about ten yards from the crest of the mountain and a trail appeared, giving me a shot of adrenaline that I desperately needed. *Maybe I can still make this. How long have I been walking? Twelve, thirteen hours?* My pace quickened and my legs thanked me for finally stumbling onto flat land, and I was wondering if I had passed the rendezvous point or not. In fact, I was not even sure which direction to head on the trail but I soon found the answer.

To my amazement, someone was actually walking the same trail, but approaching me. He was in civilian clothes, and his blue rain jacket contrasted heavily with the dark browns and greens of the thick trees and bushes. Odd. *Who in his right mind would be out here for a stroll in this weather?* The answer hit me like a breath of fresh air: Only a Delta selection cadre member would be out here! That's it! If I was correct then he must have just come from a rendezvous point somewhere up ahead. Then I hoped he was not moving toward a point that I might have missed.

As we neared each other, I tried to stand a little straighter and hide my physical and mental anguish. The hood was pulled over his head, but I recognized him. It was not just any cadre member; it was the longtime unit command sergeant major. As we passed each other I said, "Hello, sergeant major." He responded only with a half grin, half smile, which was all I needed to pick up my pace.

The euphoria soon passed. It had been hours since I had seen another candidate and I was pretty much resigned to the belief that I wouldn't make it. I was certain this would prove to be my last day, but there was no option other than to press on.

It began to rain harder and I was sure I was nearing hypothermia, and darkness was on me, a man who had disabled his own flashlight! I started looking for a dry place to stop for the night. I wanted to end it, but except for the sergeant major, way back, there was no one around to whom I could say, "I quit!" Any cadre member would have done, but I couldn't find anybody at all.

I saw a small derelict cabin off the beaten trail, and I thought of building a fire to warm my tired bones and muscles and get some sleep before resuming my march in the morning. I was disappointed for failing. Lost in thought, the cabin was well behind me before I could decide whether to stop. *Turn back? No, keep going. You can always find another spot to quit.*

I reached another rendezvous point and my mind was arguing with itself—the devil telling me to jack it in and the angel whispering words of encouragement and strength. I pressed on.

Another hour and another rendezvous point. I had completely lost the ability to determine time or distance, even while wearing a perfectly good wristwatch and with a compass around my neck. My mind was numb to even kindergarten math.

As I went through the standard procedure of preparing to show the cadre member in the truck where I was and where I thought I was going next, the selection course commander, wearing bright and colorful civilian clothing, suddenly appeared from behind the truck. *This is it. I'll bet he enjoys seeing us at our most vulnerable and weakest state.*

My camouflage Gore-Tex rain jacket was zipped all the way to the bottom of my chin, and a soaked black wool cap hung barely above my eyes, giving me the look of a tired and wet gangster. I was a pathetic sight for sure, and didn't feel I deserved to call myself a soldier. My muscles, cramped as tight as a bear trap, screamed for mercy. Physically and mentally, I was finished.

The commander extended his right hand and said, very formally, "Captain Fury, congratulations on successfully completing the stress phase of selection and assessment. Your evaluation for potential service as an officer in Delta begins now. Good luck!"

I had made it.

The evaluation for potential service with Delta continued another four days before I finally found myself standing before the commanders' board, wearing the best set of four torn and tattered camouflage uniforms I had and a pair of brush-shined and -scarred jungle boots.

I reported to the Delta commander, Col. Eldon Bargewell, a special ops legend. As an enlisted man during the Vietnam War, Bargewell served as a team leader in the Special Operations Group. Years later, having become an officer, he commanded Delta operators in Panama and was part of a handful of operators who rescued American citizen Kurt Muse from the Modelo prison. He led his squadron in Desert Storm, served as a key figure in the Balkans, and was a general officer in Iraq.

At his right was the unit command sergeant major, the same man I had passed on the mountain trail a few days earlier, and about fifteen other Delta senior officers and sergeants also were in the room. The "docs," the unit psychologists, were in the back of the room, dissecting every candidate's mannerisms and responses. They already had taken their pound of flesh when I spilled my guts to them and allowed the shrinks full access to my closet of skeletons.

For roughly an hour now it was open season on Dalton Fury. Nothing was off limits as the personal and professional questions came at me like darts. Tell us about your run-ins with the law. What were you thinking when you ordered your company out on a twelve-mile road march on Christmas Day in Korea? How do you explain this? Can you be trusted? Why should we select you, an average officer?

Any fear of personal embarrassment was subordinate to their desires in the brutal interrogation, and at the end of the hour, I was totally confused and mentally exhausted. Colonel Bargewell stood, stepped forward, and extended his hand. "Captain Fury, welcome to Delta," he said.

Next only to my wedding day and the births of my two children, it was the proudest moment of my life.

Yet it would still be some time before I would be considered a full-fledged Delta operator. Soon after the commander's board, the would-be Deltas attend the six-month Operator Training Course, a finishing school where finer points of killing are taught, along with other unique skills required of a covert commando.

Finally, I was declared ready, and was put to work.

With the required operator training behind me, I was fortunate to land in Lt. Col. Gus Murdock's squadron. I had met him only once before, when he had appeared in the rain at the end of the endurance course, sizing up the candidates, but knew him by reputation, which could be the base for a multivolume nonfiction action series.

Murdock had been associated with Delta since the early 1990s, had been on the ground in Mogadishu, was a key player in running down Colombian drug kingpin Pablo Escobar, and had hunted war criminals in the Balkans. Twice wounded in action, he would give up his command just before 9/11, then to no one's surprise, was one of the first special operations officers inside Afghanistan. He spent several years in Iraq commanding a Joint Special Operations Task Force, and was there when Saddam Hussein was captured. Murdock eventually became the overall commander of Delta Force, and was the most phenomenal officer I ever served under.

Gus took a personal interest in the mental and physical conditioning of his subordinate officers, and on Officer Day he took pleasure in pitting fellow officers Serpico, Bad Chadio, Super D, and me against each other in man-to-man, winner-take-all commando competitions. Of course, Gus never was a good spectator and would usually be found in front of the pack during these adventures.

I'm convinced that Murdock was hiding gold or moonshine down the hill at the Delta obstacle course because he was always there. At least once a week Gus would show up unannounced in our office wearing a dull green flight suit and grab all the officers to "run the O course." We learned to make ourselves scarce around the squadron area just before lunch.

Not to be outdone, Sergeant Major Ironhead and my second troop sergeant major, Jim, dreamed up masochistic events of their own. The events had to be painful, unique, and involve some analyzing of a problem. Simply thinking wasn't enough to be successful. Climb four flights of stairs at the sniper condo and come down carrying a 150-pound dummy over your shoulder; drag a wounded teammate one hundred yards as fast as possible; put on full fighting kit, close to forty pounds of gear, and use a long rope and simple snap link to get your team up an elevator shaft.

All these exercises were tailored after real-world expectations and designed to break up the monotony of the standard days of close quarters battle, running, shooting, lifting, and swimming. Guys in Delta typically possess type A personalities so each event was very competitive. Nobody liked to lose, including me, but I was just too average among these elite men to ever win. And I knew it.

In Delta, as in the most successful Fortune 500 companies like GE, Microsoft, and Cisco, the organization makes the individual its number-one priority. It teaches, nurtures, and implements bottom-up planning. That is the direct opposite of the U.S. Army's structured and doctrinally rigid military decision-making process, which is too slow and inflexible for fast-paced, high-risk commando missions or minds, and one undeniably driven from the top down.

The Delta technique is a modification of the Delphi method of estimation or prediction that was developed by the RAND Corporation. In Delphi, groups of experts are elicited for combined judgments. We apply this method to planning complicated direct-action assaults.

The sergeants in Delta typically stay in the Unit for eight to twelve years, which provides a continuing institutional memory. Their collective longevity ensures that most good ideas have been proven as "best practice" methods and can be expected to serve the Unit well again. They also remember mistakes that must not be repeated. The senior officers in Delta have spent multiple tours in the Unit, some ten years and counting. The obvious experience base is priceless and it would be foolish to exclude any of those men from the process.

Still, there is no confusion that bottom-up planning also means bottom-up leadership. Leadership can't be abdicated. But the practice of bringing in these quick minds on decisions is one of the greatest virtues of Delta. Shared knowledge and the cultivation of organizational strength must be fully understood and embraced by everyone selected for the service. Individuals are subordinate to the group.

I refer to this as the Delta problem-solving process, in which a group of experts, say fifteen operators and five experts in critical support skills (communications; nuclear, biological, and chemical warfare; medical; explosives; etc.), are presented with a problem (hostage rescue, kill-or-capture mission) and interact face-to-face in a combined session. After hearing the problem, the group breaks up into their respective assault or sniper teams to develop solutions. Unlike the normal Delphi method, Delta encourages an adversarial process and exploratory thinking.

My job as a subordinate commander was not to have all the answers but rather to guide the process, keep it moving, and as Gus Murdock consistently cautioned, prevent groupthink from taking over. Then, what the experts conclude needs to be cross-checked with the intent of the higher two commanders before the final decision is made.

My three troop sergeant majors had more than three decades in the commando business, which shored up my personal inexperience in the counterterrorist trade. Their knowledge and camaraderie, tested in battle, was an enormous combat multiplier. Who could blame me for wanting to work with men of such caliber? Together, we formatted and packaged the product at the end of the process, synched it with the other moving pieces in the big picture, then briefed it back to the experts as a group to allow for any changes of opinion and to ensure we all were in as we moved toward launch time. In Delta, egos need to be checked at the door.

Strangely, the greatest benefit of this bottom-up process is saving precious time. Conventional units doctrinally prepare three courses of action, then undergo a lockstep process to decide which course presents the most promise of success, based on what the enemy is believed likely to do in a given situation. A conventional staff scrutinizes each option and ultimately recommends the one most likely to succeed.

This can waste an enormous amount of time and it is unsuited to the fluid, ambiguous nature of the war on terror. Minutes count. By the time a conventional planning process has been completed, Delta is already typically "mission complete" and back in the chow tent for hot soup and crackers.

The positive value of our organizational culture and the uncommon sergeant-to-officer relationship cannot be overestimated or matched in any other military organization. By way of example, our squadron's troop sergeant majors already were living legends inside the Delta community when the attacks of 9/11 took place.

Jim and Bryan were both decorated for valor for leading small teams in the Tora Bora Mountains in 2001, awards that were pinned next to the Bronze Stars for Valor they had won during a little-known firefight on a rocky outcrop in western Iraq in 1991. Jim eventually became the squadron sergeant major and retired from Delta after being wounded in Iraq and earning his third Bronze Star for Valor. His new job would be no less dangerous.

The third one, Pat, was wounded and decorated during Operation Acid Gambit, the rescue of hostage Kurt Muse at the beginning of the invasion of Panama. Pat survived three helicopter crashes during his time in Delta, and was again wounded during the first combat raid into Afghanistan before retiring several months later.

A fourth troop sergeant major, Larry, was also on the Muse rescue in Panama and is one of the best pistol shots in the world. Soon after retiring, Bryan, Pat, and Jim took their skills back to Iraq and Afghanistan, as part of an organization with the mission of protecting our troops from improvised explosive devices—IEDs. Résumés containing the words "Delta Force" rise to the top of the heap in a hurry in today's security-conscious world. Dozens of former Delta operators have moved into the security industry, while others have taken their skills to the CIA, and they provide progressive leadership, organizational ingenuity, unique expert training, and unparalleled vision in helping protect the United States.

Having retired from the army, many of Delta's world-class shooters have chosen to carry their skills to the civilian, law enforcement, and military markets where they teach the finer points of combat marksmanship and urban battlefield tactics. Delta Force legends like Paul Howe of Combat Shooting and Tactics Inc., Larry Vickers of Vickers Tactical Inc., Brian Searcy of Tiger Swan Inc., and Kyle Lamb of Viking Tactics Inc., can't only teach you how to shoot a gnat off a bull's ass at fifty yards while on the move but they will actually show you how it's done first. And they will teach you the combat mind-set so important to develop to do this task while someone is trying to kill you first. If you truly want to see the best of the best in action and are serious about dropping the bad guy before he gets the drop on you, then give one of these guys a call.

What makes Delta so intriguing to the average American? Delta operators are intuitively winners, and although many folks openly cheer for the underdog, deep inside, we secretly prefer being with the winners. And there is something about Delta specifically, and special operations in general, that is very attractive to the typical male adult.

Many red-blooded American men want to be special operators, just as many young boys want to be professional ball players, because it is arguably the highest achievement in the military profession. Of course, just as in professional sports, only a relative handful of men possess the desire, commitment, or God-given ability to reach that pinnacle. I used to add luck to the equation as well, but I heard numerous times over the years that "Delta makes its own luck."

It is gospel in the U.S. Army that noncommissioned officers, the sergeants, are the backbone of any outfit. Nowhere is that more true than inside the special operations community. They are remarkable men.

The typical Delta sergeant, from the youngest staff sergeant to the unit command sergeant major, possesses an incredible command of the English language. Most have little, if any, college training but own remarkable vocabularies. After having briefed you on the finer points of a sensitive situation, you usually have to grab a dictionary to look up a few words that they used. I'm not sure that the power brokers look for this quality during the assessment and selection process, but it is a common trait.

That hones them as polished and confident public speakers. These sergeants are equally at ease briefing congressmen, senators, general officers, ambassadors, and senior administration officials. A Delta sergeant is hard to intimidate and equally hard to impress.

When Vice President Dick Cheney and President George W. Bush visited the Unit compound after 9/11, they were briefed by Delta sergeants. That stands in sharp contrast to most conventional military units, where senior officers typically do the talking while the rank and file remains safely corralled in formation at a distance. Over the years, I observed these refined supersergeants frighten officers and officials of all types, time and time again. Present company included.

Another shared and rare quality is the care with which these men tackle tough problems. Regardless of the risk involved or the high-profile personality targeted, each problem is given the same attention as the next. It's business, but business with a passion and a deep commitment to fellow man and teammate.

So, how does an organization fill itself with so many first-round draft picks? The credit certainly rests with the unique selection and assessment process, in which a candidate with Rubik's Cube instincts might be more attractive than a marathon runner or bodybuilder.

I think retired U.S. Army colonel David Hunt summed up a Delta Force operator best in his book, *They Just Don't Get It*:

> Here is the recipe for Delta. You start with an already spectacular soldier who has a proven service record of, say, five years, usually as a part of Special Forces or as a Ranger. He volunteers to go to the mountains of West Virginia, where he must run forty kilometers over mountains with over sixty pounds on his back plus his weapon. He must pass a series of mental and physical tests. Only one in fifty will make it through this process. Once you make it through this "selection," you then spend almost a year learning the "deadly arts" in a training program that is designed for masochists. And there you have it, a Delta warrior! These guys shoot 50,000 rounds of ammunition a year per man. They train attacking trains, planes, and automobiles. They train in tunnels, in sewers, on high wires, and even in trees. They actually run with 60 to 100 pounds on their backs. They jump from airplanes carrying more than 500 pounds. These super soldiers can do amazing things.

But such supersoldiers are a hard crop to grow, and because it takes a great deal of time to make them, a new threat has formed for the special operations community, an interior danger that might bring down the entire edifice.

Retired major general Sid Shachnow created the fundamental Special Operations Forces principles—"SOF Truths"—and former Special Ops four-star general Wayne Downing chiseled them in cement. The first rule is: *Humans are more important than hardware.*

Unfortunately, the "SOF Truths" seem to have been mislaid somewhere along the way since 9/11 and a sudden push developed to expand the entire special operations community. If these guys are so good, then let's put more of them in the field! Congressional authorization to increase the manpower is one thing, but money alone is not a magic wand. Simply issuing conventional forces black commando gear covered with fastek buckles and Velcro will not transform them into special operators. The very idea is utterly naïve and dangerous.

Regardless of the spin, any widening of entrance prerequisites, changing grading systems, or "relooking" previous SOF failures is the same as lowering the standards. You still must find just the right type of American to meet the highest standards, not revised and lesser tests, before he can join the ranks, and another SOF truth remains unassailable: *You cannot mass-produce commandos.*

Within a few months of my joining the squadron, Gus Murdock sent me on a real-world mission to the Balkans, and there I had the opportunity to see the unique skill, talent, and commitment of a typical Delta sergeant. Again, it made me feel pretty average, for although I was qualified in every way as a Delta officer, I was still a rookie. Murdock would not team me up with anyone who did not know the ropes.

My partner was Jamie, a longtime clandestine operator who truly enjoyed stalking humans, and I knew enough to take my lead from him. Jamie had started off as an assaulter and was wounded in Somalia before moving on to more advanced stuff. I discovered that he had the mind of a criminal and the free spirit and awareness of a fugitive. Jamie could have made a fortune as a crook in the outside world.

He grew up in New Mexico, where he spent his time racing dirt bikes, four-wheelers, go-carts, and eventually professional BMX racing bicycles. His favorite toy was a Z-28 with a nitrous oxide kit, and he outran the local police more than fifty times with his bikes, trucks, and cars. But he was smart enough not to flee the authorities unless he was certain he could shake them.

When Jamie first arrived at Delta as a young assaulter, he took the initiative to check out all the squadron's motorcycles, adjusting all the controls so they were ergonomic to the rider, replacing all the spark plugs, checking the wiring, and putting fresh gas in the tanks. Then he did the same thing to all the mechanical breaching tools. He was a master me-chanic, meticulous about routine things, and fanatical about ensuring the little things were done well above standard. Okay was never good enough. He tuned those machines like fine concert pianos.

He took great pleasure in focusing on things like ensuring that our operational vehicles ran perfectly. It was a daily chore that the rest of us were happy to avoid, and it captured his attention like nothing else, al-most to the point of being annoying, as he sought perfection. Watching him tinker with perfection was like listening to fingernails being scraped across the chalkboard.

Jamie was a serious driver, but aren't we all? Only he was unique with his seriousness about driving under duress, at high speeds, on uneven ter-rain, in rain and snow, on sand and on gravel. Perfection was the goal. One day the unit brought in a *professional* motocross rider to upgrade their skills and Jamie skipped the first two days of training. He came on the third day after a teammate asked him to check the guy out.

It didn't take long for Jamie to recognize the special instructor was not all he advertised, and he challenged the guest to a race. The guest hopped on the fancy and expensive race bike he brought with him while Jamie just picked one of the squadron bikes. Well, the guy was good, but Jamie kicked his ass.

Shortly after arriving in the Balkans, we took off for a downtown outdoor market to purchase several props and clothing to support our urban re-connaissance mission. We tried to buy a rusted bicycle with bald tires and a tattered seat for one hundred dollars cash from an old lady, but she wouldn't let the bike go. A hundred bucks wasn't enough? It was a sweet piece of junk, at least twenty-five years old and exactly what we needed, but we let it go. We found another one an hour later and threw it in the trunk.

We bought some fishing poles and tackle, buckets, street brooms, con-struction helmets, soccer balls, Adidas workout suits, and other gear that would provide us "cover for action" near a potential target site long enough to take some video or snap a photo.

Then we drove around checking the atmospherics of the cities and smaller townships, conducting route reconnaissance for future missions, and servicing safe houses that were scattered throughout the country. Jamie had been to the Balkans so much in the past few years that he didn't need a map. Mine stayed in my lap and out of sight as I kept a forefinger on it to follow the roads.

On one summer day, we were conducting a low-visibility urban reconnaissance in a small, rundown city that had seen better days. We didn't shower or shave for two days so we would match the unclean men who lived where running water was scarce, and we dressed in local mismatched and baggy soccer sweats. Our mission was to locate a specific casino restaurant that intelligence reports said was frequented by an indicted war criminal who often used it as a meeting place. This food joint, though, was different than most of the others, because it was floating on a river.

Driving a silver Volkswagen Jetta with all our props in the trunk, I dropped Jamie off several blocks from the restaurant and headed to a nearby park. Jamie set out on foot reconnaissance carrying his fishing pole, tackle box, and a bucket, while I settled in to reading the local paper, which might as well have been in Chinese or upside down, since I can't read Serbo-Croatian. I chain-smoked locally made cigarettes to complete my midmorning masquerade. Both of us carried concealed M-1911 handguns.

Jamie turned the corner and headed down the street until the restaurant was a few hundred meters to his front. Crossing a bridge, he noticed some fishermen down on the riverbank, so he stepped over the wooden guardrail and descended the bank to the edge of the water with his own fishing gear. Just like that he was in a perfect position to observe the boat. If the fellow we were looking for showed up, Jamie was sure to make a positive identification. A guy fishing nearby with his daughter began shouting at him, and Jamie just stared straight ahead. If he ignored him, perhaps he would leave him alone. Unnecessary talking is a commando sin because it can alert locals that you are different. Jamie knew the language well enough, but his foreign accent would be a dead giveaway.

The other fisherman was persistent. He could see that Jamie wore a wristwatch and he wanted to know the time. Jamie frowned and gave some crude hand signals, tapping his hand with a closed fist several times, pointing at his ear, and cocking his head as if he wanted sympathy. He tried to make it so uncomfortable for the stranger that he would just leave him alone. It worked. The fisherman lowered his head, raised his hands, palms at waist level, and apologized to the deaf-mute before turning away with his daughter and heading up the riverbank.

After an hour and a half, Jamie approached the park and we made eye contact, the signal for me to depart and conduct another foot reconnaissance while he took over watching our car. My job was to see if I could spot the target's vehicle and confirm it through the license plate number.

I took a different route, and as I turned a street corner in the bustling business district I found myself near a U.S. Bradley fighting vehicle, part of the Stabilization Forces (SFOR) that had been sent into the country. Several more were spread out at about hundred-meter intervals, but I had to brazen it out and continue walking. As I approached one, I noticed a soldier up in the turret and another sitting near him. I stopped and stared at them for a few seconds and they stared back. I took a puff on my cigarette, raised the folded newspaper that I could not read, and said, "*Dobro SFOR!*"

The young soldier in the turret asked the other, "What does that mean?"

"It means 'SFOR is good,' you dumb ass," the second soldier responded with sarcasm. "How long have you been here, anyway?"

I walked away confident that my orange and blue sweat jacket, seventies-style sunglasses, and greasy hair obviously were appropriate for the mission. Fellow Americans had not recognized me.

Within an hour, Jamie and I linked up, loaded the car, and headed back to our safe house, stopping along the way for some fresh bread and fruit. It was Saturday and our intelligence people said the guy who was our target liked to party and hold meetings on the bottom deck of the boat. We decided to return to the restaurant that same night, when money was changing hands and the busy nightlife would provide perfect cover.

Trading our soccer rags for some stylish local clothing of black slacks, collarless shirts, and old black leather jackets, we headed out after dark for the forty-five-minute drive back to the city. It was a beautiful night, with a sky full of stars and a slight breeze off the river, and we parked and went into another restaurant believed to be frequented by the target.

Right away, we saw a small group of Green Berets at a nearby table, out partying for the evening themselves. They were part of the American commitment of Joint Commission Observer teams assigned to ensure that both the Serbs and the Bosnians upheld the Dayton Peace Accords and assist in the relocation of refugees. The Green Berets had no idea who we were and that we could understand every word they said. After nursing a beer apiece and with no sign of our target, we returned to the car and drove to the parking lot outside the casino boat restaurant.

We sat in the lot observing the place for several minutes. It was busy. The parking lot was full, too many vehicles to check for tag numbers, but after watching all the activity and hearing the live band, Jamie figured we could get inside for a closer look. If our target was a true party guy, he very likely was in there.

But how to get in? We watched the line of customers cross a long and rickety plank bridge with a rope handle rail on each side, then up an angled walkway to a second-floor bar entrance. Women were admitted without much more than a look and a smile from the two bouncers, but the guys handed over a couple of bucks for a cover charge, then were given a pat-down search. That meant we would have to leave our pistols, holsters, and spare magazines behind and venture inside with only Jamie's Spyderco knife and a Surefire flashlight. Not a lot of weaponry when facing the Serbian Mafia.

Jamie looked more local than the locals as he walked up, paid the bouncers, calmly took the pat-down and slipped through the door. A few minutes later, I followed. We did not get any change back from the doorman.

The place was jam-packed on the upper level with young adult and middle-aged Serbians. The booming band was a perfect working atmosphere, since we would not be expected to talk. Jamie ordered two beers by sticking up two fingers, pointing at another beer bottle and flashing some money. We were inside, blending, perfectly camouflaged for the environment and hiding in plain sight.

Having a drink while on duty was an ironic part of doing the job professionally. In war-weary Bosnia, telling the bartender you are the designated driver and hoping to be given a Coca-Cola on the house would have been way too American. I enjoyed the excitement of the moment. We were on the target, but completely invisible. The experienced Delta operator, Jamie, was as comfortable as the other several hundred nightclubbers. The new guy, me, was a bit more amped.

In the farthest two corners of the club were some tables set up on a loft. Anyone of importance probably would like that location, so we left the bar and moved toward the back of the club. We tried not to bump into too many people as we edged closer to the band and the dance floor.

We stood around for a few minutes as the music blasted, trying to get a discreet look at all of the men who matched the general description of our target: dark hair, big beer belly. Lots of those were around.

Everything seemed cool, so Jamie headed for the pisser. Normally, leaving another operator alone was a violation of principle, but there are few hard-and-fast rules in this type of work. Every decision is based on what an operator thinks he can get away with. For Jamie, after taking stock of the situation, taking a quick trip to the pisser was no big risk. What could happen, anyway? It was just a nightclub full of people having fun and giving the finger to the rest of the world. A drunk in the crowd started yelling at the band's lead singer, who was getting irritated but continued to strum his guitar.

After leaving the bathroom, Jamie went back to the bar for two more beers. So far, all was good. As he made his way back toward me, there was a sudden and thunderous rumble of human voices and pounding feet, and the crowded dance floor erupted in chaos. Within seconds, a wave of people were stampeding toward the door, giving the feeling that the party boat was capsizing.

Is our cover blown? If it is, these folks sure ain't happy about it. Trying to avoid being trampled, I stood still and tried to make eye contact with Jamie. He was no longer blending in, since he was the only one moving upstream against the crowd, toward me. Jamie also thought it was the worst-case scenario. He wondered what could have happened to cause the panic and concluded: *It must be Dalton.*

In a few seconds, we linked up and found the real cause of the problem. One of the bouncers had just beaten the crap out of a uniformed Serbian police officer. The bouncer seemed seven feet tall and thick as a refrigerator and moved past us holding on to the cop as if he were carrying a lunch box home. The cop was out cold, his arms and head hanging limp and feet dragging behind on the floor.

Even in the Balkans, a bar fight is usually soon followed by police sirens, handcuffs, and paddy wagons, which also usually means trouble for unfortunate innocent bystanders—like us. But another immediate concern was that if these guys didn't respect the local police, they sure as heck wouldn't think twice about offing us. If the cops are scared of this place, maybe we should be, too.

Any chance of identifying our target that night slid to nothing in a hurry, and it was time, in military terms, to exfil the site immediately. In other words, we had to get the hell out of there.

We made our way through the door and into the outside air, only to find that police flashers had filled the parking lot and a few cops had already reached their roughed-up partner, who had regained some consciousness. Other cops were trading heated words with the bouncers while several more officers had men pressed up against the squad cars and private autos parked in the lot. Jamie and I could not risk being swept up with the crowd. Our car was only about thirty feet away, but getting there was not going to be easy.

We walked to the end of the boat as calmly as possible, attempting to not draw attention. Then we jumped over to the steep and soggy embankment and managed to flank the parking lot and approach our vehicle at a crouch before slipping inside. One of the first things a Delta operator does when handed the keys of an operational civilian vehicle is disable the interior lights that shine when a door is opened. That routine procedure allowed us to enter the car without alerting the nearby cops.

I was happy to let Jamie drive. He was back in his element as he cranked the engine, looked at me, and smiled, then calmly reversed out of the parking lot. He hit the gas and left the party in our rearview mirror.

We were going just over the speed limit on a major two-lane highway toward the safety of our house when we came upon an unexpected Republic of Serbska police checkpoint near the zone of separation, or ZOS, a mile-wide curvy line drawn on the ground to separate Bosnian Christians from Bosnian Muslims.

It was too late to turn around, and we had no choice but to approach the checkpoint and hope for the best. Police officers signaled Jamie to stop, and he put on the brakes and rolled down the window. Just as three uniformed policemen approached, flanking the car, Jamie hit the gas and burned rubber out of there.

After a hundred meters, we saw the police flashers come on behind us and several squad cars begin to chase. Jamie immediately found a cutback road a few hundred meters after rounding a small bend. He killed the headlights and simultaneously stepped on the brake, pressed down the clutch, and snapped the steering wheel hard left. The front tires grabbed the asphalt while the rear wheels slid around in a 180-degree arc, a perfect high-speed evasive maneuver executed in complete darkness and without night vision goggles. It scared the shit out of me.

Jamie gassed it and the car sped back toward the oncoming police, but with no overt lighting on our vehicle, which made it momentarily invisible to them. Once again at the turn, Jamie went sharp right, onto hard dirt and eased up about thirty meters before stopping. A few seconds that seemed like a lifetime crawled by before the police cars with their flashing lights came along and drove right past us.

I could tell our young hell-for-leather driver from New Mexico had done this kind of thing before. We were both smiling. "Damn, Jamie, that was scary shit but some excellent driving," I told him, trying to regulate my heartbeat and not advertise my inexperience.

"Yeah," he replied, already thinking of any errors he might have to admit in a hot-wash debriefing. "I think I gave it too much brake and not enough torque on the wheel, but it worked."

The moment emphasized for me the importance of the Delta selection process in choosing the right kind of guys for the Unit and giving them unique training and skills. Delta operators know how to work in small teams, miles and miles away from any friendly American military unit . . . even when a routine mission turns to crap.

3

Nine-Eleven

"Billy Fish," says I to the Chief of Bashkai, "what's the
difficulty here?"

— *THE MAN WHO WOULD BE KING,*
RUDYARD KIPLING

We awoke inside a large white and yellow striped circus tent on September 11, 2001, our Delta squadron having been deployed to a foreign country to sharpen our joint war-fighting skills. It would be another day of prepping our equipment for the upcoming mission, scrubbing vehicle and helicopter loads, reviewing contingency plans and scouting and studying intelligence reports and recent satellite photos.

A few discreet operators, trained in the delicate skill of close urban reconnaissance, were already in place near the target area. To help us refine the assault plan they would send back to us via small satellite radios digital photos of key breach points—roofs, doors, and windows. In different corners of the tent, the staff sergeants and sergeants first class were talking about the type of explosive charges needed for this door or that window.

That practice mission remains classified, but the real mission might certainly happen within the next few years. Typically, once these training exercises are complete, they are put "on the shelf," filed away but ready to roll in an emergency. Should some terrorist organization or criminal gang execute their end of the action at that site, Delta would trigger a response that had already been planned down to the last detail.

Super D, our squadron operations officer who never let stress or a crisis overtly raise his heartbeat above normal, and I also were up early that day, hard at work in the guarded hideaway located at an obscure end of an old European military air base taxiway. We had to put our plan for the upcoming mission before the commander for his approval soon, and were finishing the briefing slides. Eyes fixed on the laptop screen and forefinger ready on the mouse to make any minor adjustments, Super D asked, "What do you think?"

"Looks great. Let's get past this briefing and get out there and execute this thing," I answered.

"Yeah, good enough," Super D said. "I'll get the boss over here and run through it and make any changes so we can brief the general this afternoon."

Bart, the squadron operations sergeant, walked in from another tent about fifty meters away to relay some information from our squadron sergeant major. Then he casually commented, "Hey, a plane just crashed into the World Trade Center in New York."

We looked up at Bart, curious. "No shit?" said Super D.

I added, "No shit?"

Bart was a muscular, strong guy, a master at jujitsu and a champion-caliber boxer, but he also was friendly and had a unique sense of humor. Was he joking? "Can you believe that shit? They think it was a small private plane. Geez, there you are checking out the new secretary near the water-cooler and a plane comes crashing through the boss's window."

That day, September 11, 2001, may have started like any other, but within an hour of first call, the events taking place in America, several time zones away, would change our lives forever. They would change the lives of almost everyone in America.

Bart walked away across the grass infield, back to the other tent. Super D and I jaw-jacked a little. We gave little real thought to the airplane crash in New York, subconsciously chalking it up to mechanical failure or perhaps a heart attack overcoming the pilot above bustling lower Manhattan. We remembered that the World Trade Center had been the target of Islamic terrorists back in 1993, but no one was considering that terrorists might also be behind this new situation. Anyway, we were deep in our own business.

A few minutes later, Bart was back, moving much quicker this time, his eyebrows raised and a look of disbelief on his face. "Hey, get this. Another plane just crashed into the other Trade Center building. Now they think it's terrorists!"

Super D and I were dumbfounded, afraid to believe it was true. We knew how hard it would be for a terrorist to crash just one plane into a skyscraper, but two different planes hitting the side-by-side Twin Towers within fifteen minutes of each other was more than astonishing. What pilot would ever freely fly into a building if he knew the action would likely kill hundreds of people more than just his passengers? We tried to put ourselves in the mental state of the pilot, wanting to believe that, even with a gun to our heads, we certainly would let the bullet rip through our skulls before knowingly killing more innocent people.

I remarked, "If it's terrorists, I wouldn't doubt it if they cancel this training exercise immediately."

Super D nodded agreed. "Yeah, kind of makes what we're doing here a lot less important than it was a few minutes ago. Let's get over to the head shed and see if they have the news on."

The Tactical Operations Center, or TOC, was wall to wall that morning with concerned soldiers, staff officers, commanders, Rangers, army helicopter pilots, air force officers, and a few Delta operators. All eyes were glued to the CNN reports as we tried to make heads or tails out of what was happening back in our country, thousands of miles away.

Everybody thought not only of their own family's safety, but also the families of the reportedly tens of thousands of people who were believed to have been killed after both Trade Towers collapsed, on live television. As the death toll grew, we were back inside our circus tent, and intelligence analysts were posting hourly pen-and-ink updates. What we were reading was beyond belief:

American F-15 fighter jet deliberately downs American Airlines
flight 1089 over the Atlantic Ocean.

American F-16 shadowing United Airlines flight 283, believed
heading toward Washington D.C., not responding, lethal force
authorized if plane reaches U.S. airspace.

F-15 downs Delta Airlines flight 766 over northwest Virginia. U.S.
Capitol and White House struck by jumbo jets. Both on fire.

The enormity of what we read jerked us into action. Retrieving our weapons from the metal storage containers, we upgraded our perimeter security. One thing was for certain: We weren't going to be surprise victims of a terrorist truck bomb or a rocket attack without returning the violence in spades.

The father of one of our mates worked in the Pentagon and was there during the attacks. Sergeant First Class Brandon Floyd called his mother to make sure his dad was okay, but she had not heard from him either. We were all worried for Brandon and tried to keep his spirits up, silently praying and hoping his dad was at a coffee shop downtown or still stuck in traffic—anywhere but at his desk that morning. As darkness fell, another call home turned up good news. Thankfully, the former army colonel was okay, but was knee-deep in the twisted steel and burning rubble at the Pentagon, helping the injured and recovering the dead.

By the morning of September 12, twenty-four hours after the attacks, the makeshift scoreboard in the tent tallied thirteen jets hijacked, with four deliberately engaged and blown out of the sky by American fighter pilots over American soil or waters. The other nine successfully struck targets in New York and Washington, D.C. What in the world was happening? How could this be? Who could coordinate such a complex operation like this? Is this war?

It was the second day, September 13, before we learned the actual toll from that horrible day of infamy. An uncanny phenomenon of the crisis business dictates that a first report is always suspect. Miscommunication, manifested in multiple reports by various news agencies of the same event, the jammed telephone lines and cell towers bulging from maximum usage, and the fact we were on the other side of the world had contributed to the fantastic and inaccurate reports.

It didn't matter, though. Whether it had been thirteen or only four hijacked jets, to a man we wanted to pull those target folders off the shelf, kit up, lock and load, and hop a plane to wherever we might execute some quick and pure revenge for this unparalleled attack on our homeland. Whether we were at war seemed largely irrelevant.

E ven years later, it is hard to imagine any Americans not having the fireball images or the dual collapsing of the Trade Towers ineradicably engraved in their minds. Over and over again, for days on end, television ensured that caustic morning would be remembered as vividly as the jumpy black-and-white footage of the Hindenburg disaster or the Japanese attack on Pearl Harbor.

The attack had taken one hour and twenty-four minutes from the first strike on the North Tower to the crash of an airliner in a Pennsylvania field. Nowhere near the time it takes Mom to prepare a typical Thanksgiving meal, and less time than it takes to trim the hooves and shoe a couple of stubborn horses.

Although what had actually happened inside America remained cloudy to us, one thing was absolutely clear. It was time for America to stand up and be counted. Somebody would pay; Americans would accept nothing less than old-fashioned vigilante justice on this one.

The feeling we had at the time is indescribable as I sit here now with my pen, so many years after the event. But in that awful moment of national uncertainty and irrefutable vulnerability, one thing was a given: This was a good time to be in Delta—and we knew it.

4

Molon Labe

Calamities are of two kinds: misfortune to ourselves,
and good fortune to others.

—THE DEVIL'S DICTIONARY, AMBROSE BIERCE

It would have been an understatement before the Twin Towers fell to say that senior American government and military officials were hesitant to send Delta to far-off places to resolve sensitive problems. "Too risky," they said. "Not your mission," they said. "It's a police action and does not require your unit's unique skills."

Delta operators are well known inside the Special Ops community as being excellent decision makers in action, but first you have to get to the target. The decision to deploy the Unit seemed to be controlled by folks who were echelons above the Almighty himself, and the political will prior to 9/11 to do anything more than peacekeeping efforts simply was not there.*

Strategically, the recommendation to deploy American troops,

---

* The political will to use Special Operations Forces prior to 9/11 is well documented in a January 2004 edition of the *Weekly Standard*. In an article titled "Showstoppers," author Richard Shultz provides nine reasons why US officials never sent our Special Operations Forces after al Qaeda before 9/11. See http://weeklystandard.com/Content/Public/Articles/000/000/003/613twavk.asp.

particularly Delta Force, is made by a very small crowd in Washington, with the final decision being made by the president. If the commander in chief's key advisors consistently tell him Delta's services are not required or necessary, then Delta stays home. These key advisors take their cues from various general officers located both inside and outside of the Washington Beltway.

One former Special Operations commander likened the Clinton administration's hesitancy to use Delta to never putting a Super Bowl–caliber team into the game. The former operator added that our nation's leaders were risk averse, with former secretary of state Madeleine Albright being the most aggressive.

Delta apparently was only to be used for fine carpentry work. That did not change until nearly three thousand innocent citizens died on 9/11.

Back in Europe, before the World Trade Center dust had time to settle, we could feel the hands of fate reaching down and tearing the shackles of timidity loose from our nation's decision makers. The aversion to risk displayed up our chain of command, particularly since the Mogadishu misadventure eight years earlier, was a character flaw that the American people would no longer accept. This new challenge was so much bigger, so much more important.

President George W. Bush's aggressive response to 9/11 seemed like a relief to us, but it did not mean we were finally in the game.

Unfortunately, Bush's offensive mind-set didn't trickle down through the ranks of the military's general officers with the speed one might expect. Even though President Bill Clinton left office in January, 2001, our nation was still hamstrung in September by the same timid senior military officers he had confirmed.

Over the next year in Afghanistan, my men and I were continuously shocked to see the national security apparatus still sluggishly displaying the same reluctance to take risks that existed before 9/11.

The operational kid gloves did not come off until the invasion of Iraq in March 2003.

Delta operators had stopped shaving after 9/11, knowing that sooner or later, we likely would be working among men with long beards. Our squadron returned home and was bustling with anticipation and activity, but one of our sister squadrons was already on standby and well into the planning phase. It would lead the Unit, and the nation, into Afghanistan to begin to right the colossal wrong.

Waiting for our number to be called was tough. For those serving in an elite military unit, the idea of being left behind when a fight looms is utterly devastating. We clung to the belief, however, that our country was on the verge of a total war with terrorists, so if our sister squadron was served the main course in Afghanistan, then we would be happy with the global leftovers.

We spent our days developing new or reviewing the shelved courses of action for numerous unique and politically sensitive target sets. In fact, while our senior military commanders on Capitol Hill were desperately searching for answers and appropriate response methods, Delta already had a playbook for this very eventuality. Over the years, Delta intelligence analysts had amassed a priceless encyclopedia of who's who in terrorism, and it was filled with information about what makes them tick, and was updated daily according to the twist and turns of their evil minds.

Only a month after the attack, down at MacDill Air Force Base, Florida, the home of SOCOM, talented covert operatives, intelligence officials, and Special Forces commanders gathered to author the nation's way ahead to destroy terrorists and their infrastructure around the world.* The men and women in Florida were also to figure out what could be done to

---

* Authors David Tucker and Christopher Lamb in their book, *United States Special Operations Forces,* discuss this Way Ahead meeting.

kick off the campaign of vengeance and to give the president viable and re-
alistic options.

Among this galaxy of professional and experienced commandos was
our Delta squadron commander, Lt. Col. Jake Ashley. A tall and lean man,
Ashley had a vocabulary the equal of an Ivy League law professor's, and I
often thought he would be more comfortable as a congressman than as a
commando.

Although a little short on personality and pleasantries, his ability to
package data and collective insight before smoothly presenting the goods
was extraordinary. When it came to briefing and putting the decision
makers at ease, he had few peers.

Our frustration at not yet riding into the fray was compounded by what
we were seeing on television. Every major network was spotlighting
politicians and self-advertised military experts, few of whom had any idea
about what role Delta would take. One of the silliest suggestions was that
we should be put aboard civilian airliners as federal air marshals. Granted,
a Delta operator could do that job, and just prior to 9/11, several recently
retired Delta warriors had been hired as primary instructors in the air
marshal training program. But this was not how the nation needed to use
the sharpest knives in the drawer.

There were lengthy discussions of the harebrained idea on the news,
during which government officials who should have clearly understood the
importance of operational security were freely tossing about our Unit designation, which remains classified to this day.

As our sister squadron moved into the final days of rehearsals before
leading the charge in Afghanistan, our squadron was handed two interesting and challenging missions. The first cannot be discussed in this

book because it remains strictly compartmentalized. In fact, some of my men likely still don't know that sensitive target location or the person targeted. That short-notice mission, however, kept some of us planning around the clock for several days before the intelligence dried up.

It only increased our frustration. We were used to scrapped missions after being put on short standby, but this latest word to stand down reminded us of pre-9/11 days. We were hungry. Hell, where were all the terrorists?

The second mission was to rescue Shelter Now International hostages being held somewhere in Kabul, Afghanistan, which was under Taliban control.

We went to work studying photos from the intelligence shop and reviewing Predator footage of the major hardball and hard-packed dirt roads. Some photos taken by the unmanned aerial vehicle also had been sent via satellite from some of our guys on the ground with the CIA north of Kabul, and near Kandahar in the south.* All routes in and out of the capital city were controlled by sporadic and intermittent Taliban checkpoints.

We decided our only way to reach the hostages, short of fighting our way in, was to look like a bunch of ragtag Taliban or al Qaeda fighters ourselves.

Only small groups of Taliban and al Qaeda fighters enjoyed freedom of movement inside Kabul after nightfall, and for that the Taliban favored imported Toyota pickup trucks. There you have it: We would become terrorists for an evening.

The unit acquired a dozen Toyota 4×4 pickup trucks and while our mechanics modified them to fit a dozen specific mission parameters, we gathered Taliban-like turbans, mujahideen wool *pakool* hats and other Arab and Afghan clothing.

Higher headquarters needed some prodding to appreciate the tactic we were setting up. One afternoon, troop sergeant major Jim and I sat around brainstorming how we might garner more support for our plan to hide in plain sight.

We pulled a recent photo of some Taliban fighters in a pickup truck near

---

* Former CIA official Gary Shroen, in his book *First In,* discusses the Delta advance party sent to Afghanistan to develop rescue plans for the Shelter Now International hostages.

Kabul. We then outfitted one of our assault teams with similar clothing, RPGs, and AK-47s, loaded them in a similar pickup, and took their picture.

The two photos were almost identical and we packaged them in a short PowerPoint presentation. To the slide with the two photos juxtaposed, we added the caption, "At less than 10 percent illumination, what does the enemy actually see?" The unit operations officer was convinced and he took it over to higher headquarters. A few hours later, we had approval.

The options for a successful rescue inside Kabul were still limited. Sure, the 160th SOAR pilots could deposit us wherever we wanted, but that was only half the performance. The idea was not just to get out with the hostages; it was to bring them home alive.

The basic idea was to pass ourselves off as an al Qaeda convoy moving through the city at night, taking advantage of bombing that would be going on north of the capital. We had no illusions of being able to pass any close inspection or talk ourselves past a sentry, but all we needed was just to avoid being recognized at a distance by the brief look of a sentry.

If our ploy worked, we would continue to roll toward the hostage location. If not, we would eliminate the guards with our suppressed weapons to keep things quiet from neighborhood ears. We did not want a Mogadishu-like confrontation.

Then we had some very good intelligence from the CIA about the hostage building, right down to which rooms they were in. Unit engineers constructed a mock-up of the building so we could rehearse the assault dozens of times.

The cover-for-action theory looked good to us, and maybe the rescue of the hostages in Kabul might have worked, but it all became moot because the Taliban collapsed so fast. When Kabul toppled on November 10, the Taliban ran for their lives, and some sympathetic Afghans spirited the hostages out of the city to a point where they were safely picked up by helicopters.

In late November 2001, Secretary of Defense Donald Rumsfeld visited the Delta compound and my troop was tapped to demonstrate the Unit's unique skills.

These capability exercises, or CAPEXs, occurred every other month or so for various VIPs, and most were just a pain in the ass, since they took away valuable training days in preparation.*

However, times were different now; we wanted to show this wartime secretary of defense more than we would unveil to an average visiting ambassador, congressman, or even a general officer. Since my troop was putting on the demonstration, the responsibility for most of the briefing fell to me. We wanted to impress the hell out of Rumsfeld, for our goal was to hear him tell us that we were going to Afghanistan.

The day of the CAPEX, a teammate approached me roughly thirty minutes before the secretary's arrival. Cos had been wounded in action in Somalia in 1993 and again was wounded during the October 19, 2001, raid on the home of Taliban leader Mullah Mohammed Omar in Kandahar, Afghanistan. Cos was now back in the United States, nursing his latest wounds, and asked if I minded introducing him to Secretary Rumsfeld.

Here was an operator who had spilled blood fighting for our country, and I thought the request totally reasonable. Cos had earned an introduction, but that didn't mean I should not pull his chain a bit. "Well, Cos, I don't know. That's not part of the approved itinerary," I wisecracked. "Hmmm, I wonder how high the approval authority would be for a last-minute request."

He knew that I was kidding, but I quickly changed gears. "Absolutely, Cos, I'd be honored to do it. Be outside standing in the background. As soon as the secretary is turned over to me from the Unit commander, I'll break the script and call you over."

"I'll be there. I owe you one, Dalton," Cos replied.

"Easy day, Cos. Easy day."

It was an unusually warm day in North Carolina and Sergeant Major Ironhead and I squinted into the sun as the VIPs approached through the Delta garden.

---

* Author Derek Leebaert, in his book *To Dare and to Conquer,* discusses these capability exercises performed by Delta for visiting VIPs.

Flanked by several dozen uniformed officers from various higher head-quarters, the secretary and his party made their way toward the bus. I recognized Steven Cambone, the special assistant to the secretary, and Pentagon spokeswoman Torie Clarke, who was walking with a cast on her foot.

After shaking Rumsfeld's hand and asking about the weather in Washington, I motioned Cos to come forward. The looks on the faces of some of the senior officers present was incredulous. *Who does this major think he is breaking the rehearsed itinerary for this type of shenanigans?* Sergeant Major Ironhead shot me a smirk.

Rumsfeld was clearly enthralled as I described Cos's dedication and explained his convalescent status. He was genuinely appreciative of the operator's sacrifice and commitment. The whole episode lasted less than a minute and was more than worth the slight change in schedule. A few days later, Cos was back in Afghanistan. Two days after that, he was wounded while fighting in Kandahar. Again he recovered. Again he went back, and in November, 2003, he was wounded for the fourth time, in Baghdad. Who would not shake up a VIP schedule for that kind of operator?

Further into the CAPEX, Rumsfeld listened to Pope, a Delta sniper team sergeant, describe the dozen or so modifications to the Toyota trucks that our guys had made. It was more of a diversion, and while it was going on, another Toyota pickup slowly made its way up behind the visiting party. Four operators armed with AK-47s and RPGs, adorned with healthy beards and dressed in Afghan rags, were propped menacingly in the bed of the truck as it rolled to a silent stop roughly forty meters away.

Pope asked Secretary Rumsfeld to turn around and take a look at how we planned to use these new vehicles that had been bought out of his budget. A wide smile lit Rumsfeld's face and he marveled about how authentic the boys looked.

After an hour or so of discussion and demonstrations that included a show by special helicopters and a free-fall parachute demonstration by Navy SEALs, I climbed aboard an old school bus with the secretary and a bevy of generals from the Special Ops community and senior Delta officers to move to still another demonstration site.

Rumsfeld had a slight look of angst, and he said to me, "What we really need is small groups of folks, say two to four people, that can go anywhere in the world and execute discreet missions against these people [al Qaeda]."

I was shocked! Did the secretary of defense, a month and a half after 9/11, still have no idea what Delta offered our nation? Was Delta's operational security so tight that not even the secretary understood the Unit's capabilities?

I didn't have to worry about answering because various generals and senior Special Ops officers nervously showered him with answers, buzz words, and reassurances that the capability he had just described was exactly Delta's job! Those unique abilities he described had already existed for many years.

Throughout the exercise, we emphasized that we were capable of operating alongside Afghan warlords, infiltrating hostile areas, conducting long-range helicopter assaults in extremely cold weather, and fighting in dangerously unforgiving mountain passes.

As the CAPEX came to a close, we had shown Don Rumsfeld, the cleanup hitter for the world's only remaining superpower, that Delta Force, the most versatile, lethal, and trustworthy tool that he had, was ready to be pulled out of the toolbox and put to work.

In fact, our sister squadron was already operating secretly inside Afghanistan. Delta was the United States' premier counterterrorism force, and it was high time that someone treated us that way, and gave the taxpayers their money's worth.

Little did we know at the time of Rumsfeld's visit, but our squadron's fate was being determined some 7,000 miles away in northwest Afghanistan.

On a sunny but cold day at Bagram Air Base, about thirty-seven miles north of the capital city of Kabul, four men were gathered around the hood of a Humvee outside the headquarters of Task Force Dagger, home of in-country Special Forces operations at the time. Gary Berntsen, the lead guy on the ground for the Central Intelligence Agency, was paying yet another visit to barrel-chested colonel John Mulholland, the commander of Dagger, to lay out fresh intelligence sources on the where-abouts of Usama bin Laden.

It was not the first time the CIA had approached Mulholland on the issue, and the first request had been unequivocally rejected. To increase his chances this time around, the CIA man had brought along more fire-power, in the persons of Lt. Col. Mark Sutter of Delta Force, and a Spe-cial Forces officer we will call Lieutenant Colonel Al, who was attached to the CIA.

The three visitors felt so strongly about the new intelligence that they would not discuss it by phone, even over secure lines. But to do anything with the vital information, they needed more than just to share it; they needed an army. Short of that, they would settle for a Special Forces A Team or two from Mulholland.

To Gary Berntsen the new details were hot enough to be "actionable intelligence," by definition something that could be acted upon. In the past week, credible sources had placed bin Laden in the historic city of Jalalabad, close to the Pakistan border and the entranceway to the Khyber Pass. Locals had reported scores of vehicles loaded with al Qaeda fighters and supplies moving south, toward bin Laden's old fortress, the caves and secure positions nestled high in the Tora Bora Mountains.

There already were numerous Special Forces A Teams working in the western part of Afghanistan, and that put these highly skilled soldiers at the top of the CIA wish list for assistance. Mulholland voiced his concern that bin Laden held well-prepared defensive positions up in those moun-tains, as well as a significant terrain advantage.

But there was something else going on, too, for the colonel's Special Forces teams had been burned already by Afghan warlords who had per-sonal vendettas and agendas that were counter to the United States objec-tives. The warlord the CIA was now backing to hunt down bin Laden was a relative unknown, and had not yet been vetted to Mulholland's satisfaction.

Gary Berntsen continued his hard pitch, placing the Green Beret com-mander in a dilemma. For a few uncomfortable moments, it looked like a stalemate.

Then Lieutenant Colonel Al, who had been friends with Mulholland for a long time, looked the colonel in the eye and promised that any Green Berets that Mulholland could spare would be used only under Al's personal guidance and within their capabilities. He promised to watch over them like they were his own.

Mulholland wanted bin Laden dead as bad as the next guy, probably even more so if the death of the terrorist might get him out of godforsaken Afghanistan a little earlier. He reluctantly agreed to commit some Green Berets, but not before leveling a few veiled threats at his friend Lieutenant Colonel Al: Don't get my guys killed in some harebrained reenactment of Custer's last stand.

Once they had Mulholland's blessing, Lieutenant Colonels Sutter and Al, along with the operations officer of the 3rd Battalion of the 5th Special Forces Group, went to work developing a plan that would pass muster by the various decision makers back at the CIA in Langley, Virginia, and at Fort Bragg. A gentlemen's agreement made over the hood of a Humvee in a country that was one big battlefield is quite different from appeasing the senior leaders managing the war from the United States.

In a rare display of unity, during that single afternoon, the three planners cast aside all politically correct barriers, or the stovepiping of information, embraced a united front, and developed a viable interagency plan. All parties involved had to wipe the snot from their noses and sing from the same sheet of music. It was a bonding not often achieved among senior levels of the intelligence and the military communities.

That agreement was nice, but whether this hunt for bin Laden would turn out to be a great success or a complete goat screw was yet to be seen.

Based upon that meeting at Bagram, our squadron's luck changed, and a day or two later we received deployment orders to Afghanistan.

We spent a couple of days tying up loose ends, spent time with our families, and studied the available intelligence reports on potential targets. Then we walked out of the Delta building in North Carolina and loaded the buses for our long journey to war.

We were going off one man light. Former Ranger and Delta assaulter Scott had wanted to go to Afghanistan as much as the rest of us, but a civilian job had been aggressively recruiting him. He stalled as long as possible and even pushed back his end-of-service date, hoping for the deployment orders to come through before he had to make the final decision. The timing was all wrong, and he had dropped the paperwork that ended his military career just before we got the word to move out.

It was a disappointment for everyone, including Scott, but he came out to meet us at the bus, in civilian clothes with his long hair blowing in the wind, to shake hands and wish the squadron luck.

A couple of C-17 Globemasters hauled us across the Atlantic Ocean, long and tiring flights to the ISB, our intermediate staging base near the Arabian Sea. The change from the chill of North Carolina to the searing heat of the Middle East hit us hard. We stowed our gear, dressed down into brown T-shirts and black running shorts, and got down to preparing to enter Afghanistan.

Intelligence remained painfully scarce, since very few friendly forces were inside Afghanistan at that early date. The whereabouts of bin Laden and his stubborn and faithful Afghan host, Mullah Omar, were unknown. Anyone's guess.

Then we were slammed by a silly deception plan that had been dreamed up by parties unknown. The majority of the Rangers and our Delta teammates were being sent home! Somebody had decided to try and fool Usama bin Laden, al Qaeda, and the Taliban into thinking that the Joint Special Operations Task Force had left the theater of operations, so the bad guys would let down their guard. The naïveté of that idea still boggles my mind today.

"Aren't we at war?" we asked. Why were we not pouring all available assets into Afghanistan, rather than withdrawing our strength? What about helping the 5th Group Green Berets deliver the coup de grâce to the Taliban? Moreover, what about the deadly and dangerous business of hunting and killing terrorists in their rugged mountain redoubts and desert lairs? Why were we drawing down just as we were about to embark on what was arguably the most important mission ever given to our organization?

Fortunately, a couple of hundred Rangers would be arriving at Bagram eventually and could form a potential quick-reaction force should we get into big trouble. None were yet in the country, however, so the key word remained only a "potential" QRF, not a real one. Still, it was a bright spot in a sea of ambiguity. No helicopters or air assets were yet based in the country, but some of those stationed within flying distance also were being sent home. Crazy stuff.

Ours not to reason why. Our sister squadron was at the ISB for another few days, heading back to the States after a busy month and a half, and we picked their brains for lessons learned. During their brief stint, they had raided Mullah Omar's house in Kandahar on October 19, conducted mounted reconnaissance missions south of that city, and executed in-and-out missions that destroyed fleeing Taliban convoys. Their most striking mission involved the first nighttime combat HALO (high altitude, low opening) parachute jump since the Vietnam War.

Another friendly face at the ISB was that of Gus Murdock, who had been our squadron commander until just a few months before 9/11, when he had been corralled to head a new organization. Gus was now in charge of a mix of sister-service operators, support personnel, fixed- and rotary-wing aircraft planners, and some top military and civilian intelligence geniuses, and they would fight deep in the shadows and along the seams of the war on terror.

Within a day or so, a small advance party from our squadron flew ahead to Bagram, dubbed FOB Yukon. They were to determine whether Yukon could be suitable as a staging base for us, and what they found was not exactly a fixer-upper.

Built by the Soviets during their own Afghan war, Yukon had plenty of real estate, buildings, and a runway, but was in terrible shape. Derelict Soviet jets and rusted airplane parts littered the area, and years of bombardment had left the old runway severely cratered. Most windows were shattered in the gutted buildings and there was no running water or electricity. Hundreds of unmarked land mines were hidden beneath an inch or so of fine brown dust.

Still, Yukon could be made workable, and our unit engineers assumed the monumental task of turning it into a long-term station that could support combat operations for an indefinite period. They worked miracles.

In his book *Against All Enemies,* former White House counterterrorism expert Richard Clarke recounted a tabletop exercise by intelligence officials and analysts conducted in 2000. The participants were divided into two groups, one playing the role of al Qaeda and secretly developing weapons of mass destruction to be used against the United States. That group also was asked to determine where in the world al Qaeda might likely hide the weapon. The second group countered the first and began with the assumption al Qaeda had already developed a weapon.

It didn't take long for the al Qaeda role players to determine an excellent place to hide their nefarious activities. From studying satellite imagery, topography, and safe havens, the choice was obvious. Clarke referred to the place as a "valley in Afghanistan called Tora Bora" and it was such a logical place for terrorists that U.S. assets began to photograph it from the air continuously and map the numerous cave entrances.

I can assure you that Tora Bora is much more than a single valley. Indeed, it is a vertical no-man's land, a hellish place of massive, rocky, jagged, unforgiving snow-covered ridgelines and high peaks separated by deep ravines and valleys studded with mines.

What Clarke's experts were not tasked with determining, nor were they even capable of doing so at the time, was how this mountainous redoubt might look if bin Laden had prepared it for an assault by foreign troops.

However, any student of mujahideen tactics in the Soviet-Afghan war could make a pretty good assumption that it might have become impregnable, both from the air and ground. During the twelve years since the Soviet withdrawal, the defenses in the Tora Bora Mountains had matured and expanded significantly.

The hardworking guys in the intelligence shop didn't get much sleep and didn't have as much to work with as did those tabletop teams Clarke described. Where were the satellite photos? Where were those maps of cave entrances? I don't know, but they weren't with the men who needed them most. Our intel people were reinventing the wheel by having to study the forbidding Tora Bora area from scratch. Things looked pretty bleak.

The fortress was densely pocked with well-built bunkers that were cloaked from ground and air observation by remarkable camouflage. Al Qaeda used a defense-in-depth concept to impede an attacking force at various points while allowing defenders to reposition farther back in other prepared and well-stocked positions.

An attacking force had two basic approaches from which to choose. They could stick to the low ground in the valleys and ascend steadily while moving deeper into the mountains. Or they could take the well-worn footpaths used by drug smugglers, goat herders, and generations of mujahideen and outside warriors dating back to Alexander the Great.

But modern enemy weapons now overlooked those ancient foot routes—DShK-38 12.7mm heavy machine guns and 82mm mortar tubes, SVD 7.62mm Dragunov rifles, RPGs, AK-47s, and PKM machine guns. Any force attacking uphill, already tired from the climb and with limited lateral space in which to maneuver, would certainly face an unfriendly welcome. Once committed to a particular avenue of approach, the decision to continue or turn around would require great caution.

The helicopter option was quickly ruled out for Tora Bora. At least two camouflaged ZPU-1 14.5mm AAA guns and several dozen SA-7 SAM rockets were waiting down there, and the low-flying birds would be fat and easy targets. The last thing we wanted was another Mogadishu, with a helicopter shot down. Such a tragedy always seemed to shift the mission away from its original objective and into recovering friendly forces.

Lieutenant Colonel Ashley, our squadron commander, knew the muhj had been very successful in shooting down Soviet helicopters with shoulder-fired rockets in the 1980s, and he also was a veteran of Somalia and vividly remembered that disaster.

The restrictions that would limit helicopters in such terrible mountain battlefield conditions further dampened hopes of getting any quick reaction force to a trouble spot in a hurry.

The more we studied how to tackle those mountains, the more the situation started to display many of the trappings of a modern siege.

Centuries ago, a commander typically could surround the stronghold, sit tight, and wait for the defenders to starve themselves into capitulation. Sieges of castles or towns usually began in the spring or summer, when the attackers could retain some level of personal comfort, and dry weather supported the use of fire and heavy siege engines.

Or the ancient commander could choose to attack the fortified position, which was obviously more hazardous. So far, everything we had seen about Tora Bora tilted us toward the latter and riskier method.

In the modern year of 2001, our snipers would serve as archers and our bullets as fire-tipped arrows. Our pickup trucks would be the war chariots, and rusty but usable Afghan tanks and black-market mortars would stand in as ballistas and bombards. Our fighters and bombers could rain down JDAMs and BLU-82s like ancient Greek fire.

There was another intriguing option, and we liked it enough to plan it out. What about going in the back door, across the 14,000-foot mountains on the Afghan-Pakistan border? What if several teams could insert safely by helicopter into Pakistan, on the far side of the highest Tora Bora peaks. They would have bottled oxygen and acclimate themselves as they ascended even higher, and once they crested the peaks and found any signs of al Qaeda, they would be in business.

The commandos would own the high ground and could accurately target bunkers or cave openings with lasers for U.S. warplanes to strike them with relative impunity.

A tactical plan drawn up by the Delta experts is rarely denied, and in fact I cannot remember anyone ever saying no once Delta determined what it needed to do to accomplish its assigned mission. This one worked its way up through our various commanders, but somewhere way, way above us, it was denied. We would not be allowed to infiltrate through Pakistan.

Any plan has negatives, including this one. Just resupplying such recon teams with water, ammunition, and radio batteries would have been a tall order. That did not mean, however, that we should not do it. We were Delta and we could overcome such things. Having Delta guarding the far side of the mountain passes, closing the ring, would have made a huge difference. But our plan was shot down.

Over the years, it has come to be believed that Pakistan president Pervez Musharraf refused permission for us to have the staging access we needed for a cross-border infiltration and that Central Command decided the issue was too sensitive to press. This is only partly true.

Author Ron Suskind, in *The One Percent Doctrine,* replayed an event that unfolded deep inside the White House. As President Bush and Vice President Cheney watched, a senior CIA operative laid a map of Afghanistan out on the floor and argued for an immediate commitment of American troops to seal Pakistan's side of Tora Bora, thus cutting off a potential al Qaeda escape route.*

He displayed satellite imagery to prove that Pakistan's military was not yet in place to accomplish the task. Further, the CIA man strongly suggested that Pakistan could not be counted on to fulfill their promise of troops to secure the area.

According to Suskind, President Bush was not completely swayed, and opted to trust our Muslim allies in the new war on terror. The back door would remain wide open to the enemy. We were not pleased.

With their southern flank secure, al Qaeda could focus on the west, north, and east, and they built their defenses accordingly, around the assumption that those big border mountains were inviolate.

On the ground, we knew that back in 2001.

Even our huge advantage in air surpremacy was not going to work in our favor, at least for a while. Those valuable air assets were not yet even

---

* In *Cobra II,* authors Michael Gordon and Bernard Trainor recount the meeting between representatives of the CIA, Vice President Cheney, and President Bush.

based inside Afghanistan. Bagram airfield and the Kandahar airport, dubbed FOB Tahoe, were not ready to accept aircraft. For the present, the planes were still bedding down well to the northwest in Uzbekistan and to the southeast in a remote stretch of Pakistan, and the air fleet was being downsized in a strange attempt to fool the terrorists. It was not difficult for us to envision how the great distances could hamper air support during a gunfight in Tora Bora, with us out there at the tip of the spear.

Aware of all of the things that were not likely to be successful, or were disapproved by some higher levels, the squadron boss Ashley, operations officer Super D, and the rest of the staff went to work to identify things that might make our mission work.

Recent satellite imagery and pictures from high-flying reconnaissance planes allowed the analysts to measure what was happening in the mountains. The information was packaged into a color-coded PowerPoint slide show. Winter temperatures were frigid, the mountain range was sheathed in low and lingering clouds, and deep snow was stacking up in various valleys and passes.

The clear conclusion was that those vital passageways were so clogged that al Qaeda and bin Laden could not be leaving the mountains anytime soon, which meant they would have to make a major defensive stand.

Ashley wanted to make those possible exit routes even more dangerous by dropping some CBU-89 GATOR mines into the passes. The GATORs would spread a minefield that would both deny enemy foot soldiers their escape routes and also knock out vehicles, leaving the enemy trapped and shaping the battlefield more to our liking.

Even this logical request was disapproved at some higher level, most likely even above the four-stars at CENTCOM. Later, after the battles were done, we learned that indeed there had been a political twist to it because some of our allies threatened to opt out of the fighting should the GATORs be employed.

Multiple sources still said that bin Laden was in the mountains and reported that he was still alive, well protected, and moving continually on horseback from cave to cave. Additionally, we learned that he enjoyed widespread support among the local population.

That was no surprise. Since at least 1985, he had been providing jobs and jihad opportunities for many residents during the construction of the trenches, bunkers, and caves that comprised the mountain redoubt. Either his fellow Muslims in the area genuinely believed in him or bin Laden had simply bought their allegiance. This is not meant to suggest that all Muslims support bin Laden or are the enemy, for they clearly do not and are not. It's very likely many were just too scared to turn on him.

Save for the big intelligence coups that it was winter in the Afghan mountains and bin Laden could ride a horse, neither we operators nor our commanders had much to go on. We knew our ability to move cross-country mounted in the Toyota pickups was limited, so the only remaining solution was for us to just walk up the mountains.

A final piece of bad news was that our first-line quick-reaction force, or QRF, would not be made up of American Rangers after all, but of Afghans. We all initially overestimated the ability and willingness of the Afghan muhj, but for the time being, we were going to bet our lives on them. Thinking the muhj could do as well as the Rangers was a complete pipe dream.

One limitation was the inability of the muhj to fight at night, a deficiency that was originally chalked up to their not having much night vision capability. We would soon learn that the muhj did not really need any night vision equipment; they had no desire to fight in the dark.

It was a friction point that would get even uglier when the shooting started.

Things were shaping up for an interesting next couple of weeks.

Bin Laden's major assumption, as well as personal desire, was that the United States would introduce massive numbers of conventional troops, just what the Soviets had done in this same terrain. He figured that large numbers of Americans would face the same challenges as Russians. In his mind, it all added up to another opportunity for his guerrillas to inflict large-scale casualties on another superpower. After our turn-tail-and-run withdrawal from Somalia, he had to believe that hard and costly combat might invoke an American or even worldwide outcry to withdraw from Afghanistan.

Of course, details of al Qaeda's defensive disposition remained unknown while we were planning at the ISB. Satellite imagery is nice, but clarity, confirmation, and documentation of the al Qaeda fortress came only after American boots had walked the ground.

A small cluster of task force planners, commanders, and Delta operators gathered inside a makeshift briefing area at the ISB. White sheets of target cloth served as walls, and we took seats in rickety chairs. It was a pretty dilapidated feel for a place in which such an important mission was being finalized.

A laptop computer sat on a large cardboard box next to a small projector that threw the image of a slide with black letters on the wall: A SQUADRON MISSION BRIEF, 2 DEC 2001.

Our sister assault troop would continue the hunt for Mullah Omar in the south. Our teammates had been in that fight since the beginning and were well versed in the Taliban order of battle there.

Meanwhile, the majority of our Unit would focus on bin Laden in eastern Afghanistan. As close as I can remember, it went something like this: On order, conduct linkup with the Eastern Alliance Opposition Group in the vicinity of Jalalabad, Afghanistan, to facilitate killing or capturing Usama bin Laden.

That was a pretty simple and direct set of orders. Meet and greet some local Afghan mujahideen, then go find bin Laden and kill or capture him.

Placing the word "capture" in the mission statement was standard practice, because some targeted personalities are more valuable alive than dead. They might have valuable information that can lead to someone higher up the food chain or reveal critical information that might disrupt a planned terrorist operation.

The fact is that the live-or-die decision is not complicated for a Delta operator. When an operator enters a room, his first task is to eliminate all threats in his designated sector. If the targeted individual happens to be standing there, he determines his own fate. If he is unarmed and not displaying hostile intent, then he lives and is chalked up under the capture category.

Delta does not waste time looking at the face, but takes an instant snapshot of the entire person before focusing on what is critical—the hands. If the target has a weapon, well, he is a dead man with a one-way ticket to martyrdom with carry-on baggage only.

Usama bin Laden was different. Simply put, he was more valuable being dead. It was made crystal clear to us that capturing the terrorist was not the preferred outcome. The president had already signed a memorandum of notice that authorized killing the terrorist mastermind on sight.*

Bringing a captured bin Laden to trial in the United States would surely have created a media frenzy that would make the O. J. Simpson trial look like a catfight between mothers at the local PTA. Other nations would be undoubtedly drawn into the ugly mix.

Biting their fingernails at the idea of such a trial was our critical ally, the Saudis. Bin Laden was a native of Saudi Arabia and part of a huge, rich, and important family in that country. A major trial of bin Laden in a Western court of law would expose and embarrass members of the Saudi royal family and our double agents inside Saudi intelligence and perhaps put the entire regime at risk.

Following the short brief, Maj. Gen. Dell Dailey issued the commander's guidance. He was adamant that we stay focused on bin Laden and not get swept into sideshow firefights. Once bin Laden was killed, we were to give his remains to the Afghans.

He voiced concern about our ability to operate at such high altitudes in extreme winter weather, and he queried the intelligence officer about the minefields. The general also tried to temper our natural offensive mind-set with caution not to outpace our ability to resupply as we pushed into the al Qaeda stronghold. The general went on and on. He seemed to have a hundred concerns, and his staff could provide very few answers.

All good stuff, but somehow I got the impression the general was not too keen on Delta venturing up into the mountains. There was an impression of hesitancy, almost as if some folks still hoped the problem would somehow solve itself before we entered Afghanistan. Then we all could return to our normal training routine at home.

---

* See article on "Targeted Killings" published by The Foundation for Defense of Democracies. See http://www.defenddemocracy.org/publications/publications_show.htm?doc_id=218872.

The general seemed concerned that we might stage a massive uphill frontal assault against an entrenched enemy who owned the high ground. He had to be aware that Delta doesn't march single line abreast into automatic weapons fire.

Dailey also told us that we were not going to Tora Bora to support the friendly Afghan mujahideen. That was an odd statement because it was exactly what the 5th Special Forces Group had been doing with the Northern Alliance for weeks.

We appreciated the general's concern for our health and welfare, but his comments were out of synch with our mission statement. After all, just a few minutes earlier, one of the slides specified that we were to link up with a warlord to kill Usama bin Laden.

As assault troop Sergeant Major Jim and I listened to the comments, we shot each other curious looks: *Can you believe this shit?*

Bottom line, it was not perfect, and nobody ever said it had to be. We couldn't rewrite the script to our liking.

Bin Laden was up in Tora Bora waiting for us, and we had no problem obliging him, regardless of the strategic or operational limitations.

Still, I didn't leave that briefing with a warm and fuzzy feeling.

Only a few minutes after the briefing broke up, Dailey approached Jim, Ski, and me. He still wore that look of concern, but then he paused, focused, and very general-like gave us all the command guidance we had ever really needed.

"Fellas, kill bin Laden . . . and bring back proof!"

That was more like it.

At midday on the fifth of December, we loaded several MC-130 Talon II aircraft for our four-and-a-half-hour journey into Afghanistan. In addition to several dozen operators, each aircraft contained two pickup trucks strapped to the floor and loaded down with supplies and combat gear. I took up a seat on the passenger side of a white Toyota that still smelled showroom new.

I plugged in a laptop computer so it was powered by the vehicle battery and called up the FalconView software. On the screen, I began sorting through layers of satellite imagery and maps, including a Russian-made 1:50,000 of Afghanistan.

A cable snaked out of the truck window to a circular GPS antenna behind one of the aircraft's window blackout screens. That linked us with several airborne satellites that gave life to a tiny royal blue airplane icon that represented our plane. That little image crept over the map on my screen as our aircraft crossed the Arabian Sea.

We hugged the Pakistan border just east of Iran and bent around the southern and eastern side of Afghanistan. Somewhere above the Northwest Frontier Province of Pakistan, the pilots banked hard to the west and we entered Afghan airspace, heading toward Kabul.

Bart, the squadron operations sergeant who had given us the first word on the September 11 attacks, was there to meet us on the runway at Bagram. He led us to an old, bombed-out rectangular building, our new home away from home, where we dropped our gear. To keep the frigid air away, the advance party had boarded up the windows in the hard clay walls, acquired kerosene space heaters, and covered the cold concrete floor almost wall to wall with crimson red carpet.

The building, and one just like it sitting roughly forty meters away, was among the very few where the land mines had been cleared outside. Only enough space had been cleared to allow us to walk around the perimeter by staying close to the buildings and to pull up a few pickup trucks in the front.

Within thirty minutes, we were summoned to the Joint Intelligence Agency Task Force building a couple of hundred yards down the street. With land mines in our thoughts, we walked to the building, which was a little larger, a little warmer and had more divided rooms. This was the austere home of the Fusion Cell, the relatively new designation given to an ad hoc faction of professionals charged with collating, analyzing, and making heads or tails out of the various intelligence collected by multiple means; hence the name Fusion. Their task was daunting, even for such a talented bunch of men and women, and it did not take long for some jokers to add a prefix to the name, changing it to the Confusion Cell.

Gus Murdock had beaten us into town from the ISB, and was in charge of joint advance special forces operations, as part of the Fusion Cell. After some quick handshakes and dirty jokes, we sat down to get our former squadron commander's take on our next move. The news was not good. Gus said the intelligence community was estimating that between fifteen hundred to three thousand enemy forces were currently inside the Tora Bora Mountains.

That was when we started to realize Delta was being asked to do something clearly outside our Mission Essential Task List. We were quite certain that Delta had never before been tasked to tether their combat operations to a tribal opposition group. Moreover, we were to conduct military operations while relying on indigenous security and guides, local quick-reaction forces in lieu of Americans, and do so with an extremely untimely and weather-dependent casualty evacuation support plan. It was most un-Delta like. General Dailey's vagueness began to make sense.

The CIA had passed word while we were still in the air that Gen. Hazret Ali, the head of the Eastern Alliance, was ready to receive us immediately over in the border city of Jalalabad. We were looking forward to it, because we had zero information about the Afghan warlord with whom we were to link, other than the basics of his biography. Ali, a Sunni Muslim, had come from the Pashai tribe in Nangarhar Province, and distinguished himself as a field commander in the war against the Soviets. Beyond that, we knew zilch.

But the CIA in Jalalabad, Team Jawbreaker Juliet, said Ali was ready to help, and that was good enough for us. Anyway, we had been told the Afghans must *appear* to be a part of any action. We did not think that was any big deal, but it sure became one.

We were to drive down from FOB Yukon to Kabul, link up with a few advance force operators and CIA folks, and receive a quick intelligence dump. From there we would proceed under the escort of a dozen or so CIA-funded mujahideen over to Jalalabad, where the Afghan warlord kept his headquarters.

Gus told us it was all set and we needed to move out soon. While I briefed Jim and the boys on the situation, Sergeant Major Ironhead, and reconnaissance troop Sergeant Major Bryan, code-named B-Monkey, our communicator Bernie, and Shag, a Pashto speaker, loaded two trucks. Jim elected to stay behind to coordinate things and oversee preparations to eventually move the rest of the boys forward once the details were worked out with the CIA and General Ali. We figured it would be a day or two at most.

We were under strict instructions that we could only "borrow" the linguist Shag for a few days and would have to send him back to Bagram very soon. Somehow, once we reached the shadows of Tora Bora, we forgot that order.

After packing, we went back inside to try to get warm while we waited to leave. We were too amped up to sleep, so we just sat on some cardboard boxes, tapped our feet on the floor to keep our blood flowing, huddled close to take advantage of one another's body heat, and crossed our arms to cut the chill.

Bernie, our communicator, who was checking his laptop computer, called out with a hoot. "Hey, Dalton! You just got promoted!"

Higher headquarters back at the ISB had become nervous because I, the senior man representing the task force in this important meeting with General Ali, was only an army major. After all, in the American military, a general officer does not typically deal with lowly majors, and having someone of such menial rank handling the delicate high-level meeting might suggest to the Eastern Alliance and its venerated commander that we were not serious.

To alleviate the problem, they authorized me to masquerade as a lieutenant colonel for this particular mission, as if being one step higher on the ladder would make a difference.

Just like that, while sitting in a cold, cold room, I became make-believe Lt. Col. Dalton Fury: No promotion ceremony, no extra pay, no fanfare, just 100 percent unofficial. In fact, the only thing I got was a lot of sharp wisecracks from the boys around me.

The phony promotion was totally unnecessary. Field marshal, lieutenant colonel, major, or Private Gomer Pyle would have made no difference to General Ali, as long as whoever it was didn't impede the cash and arms flowing in from the good ole United States of America.

In fact, if anything would have helped me impress General Ali, it would have been a thicker beard.

But our thoughts soon returned to what lay ahead and the unforgiving enemy that controlled the treacherous terrain where we would be fighting. We would be outnumbered, and intelligence analysts were saying that our new Afghan allies did not think anybody, including us, could win in the Tora Bora Mountains against the al Qaeda fighters who had been part of the massive guerrilla uprising that had already faced, and beaten, another superpower, the Soviet Union.

Ironhead, cool as ever, spoke the squadron motto: "Molon Labe."

That was the challenge given by the Spartan king Leonidas at Thermopylae when Persian king Xerxes I offered to allow the outnumbered Spartans to surrender, if they would just drop their weapons. The defiant term means—*Come and get them!*

5

Running Guns

We drove our pickups down the safe lane to the Joint Intelligence building to meet the escort that would lead us through the mined airfield perimeter and then some thirty miles to the south before handing us off to a second escort near the outskirts of Kabul.

Parked and waiting was an ominous-looking, dark, two-door sedan with a couple of men wrapped in Afghan clothing sitting in the front seat. I peered into the driver's window to make sure my eyes were not playing tricks.

You have got to be shittin' me. We were not sure who our guides were supposed to be, but I was shocked to find Doc and the Judge. *I must be still sleeping, in the middle of a bizarre dream. Had to be, because no way in hell can these men be our guides.*

Two former Delta Force staff members: one was the Unit lawyer and the other the Unit psychologist. "How's it goin', Dalton? Good to see you. Ready to roll?" Both officers had left the Unit months earlier, following Brigadier General Gary Harrell to his new assignment at CENTCOM.

"Uh, yeah, good to see you guys, too," I stumbled, trying to conceal my surprise. Both were well known in the Unit, and totally trusted, but they just seemed a bit out of character, a lawyer and a psychologist suddenly appearing in their Afghan duds and in a car, out here in the middle of nowhere, when we thought they were back in Florida. "We're ready when you are. Give me one of your radios and lead the way," I said.

We pulled out of FOB Yukon several hours before dawn broke. Besides the headlights of our three vehicles, only the stars gave off any light and an eerie, thick darkness shrouded the land. The tops of the towering mountains to the north were not visible, but we could feel their presence.

Sergeant Major Ironhead drove while I rode shotgun in the lead Toyota, and Bryan drove the trailing truck, along with Bernie and Shag. The long ride gave me some time to consider the man behind the wheel. I was a thirty-seven-year-old army major masquerading as a lieutenant colonel, riding through the Afghan night next to a man who was one of the most talented, trustworthy and skilled noncommissioned officers to ever walk the halls of the Delta compound.

The squadron sergeant major was a good-humored, well-read, humble, and courteous former Ranger who was loved and respected by us all. Now in his early forties, he had spent fifteen years as a Delta operator, stood an inch over six feet tall and had a confident gait. He played by the rules—after they had passed his commonsense test.

Ironhead loved running the high grassy mounds that separated one shooting range from another in the Delta compound, for beneath his calm and polite demeanor hid a masochistic demon of discomfort. No tight silk shorts and fancy lightweight and expensive running shoes for this guy. No, when Ironhead stepped out of the back of the building, he didn't bother to change out of his boots, or flight suit, or battle dress uniform. He would stop by the team room only to grab his protective mask and put on his body armor so the tough run would be even harder. Ironhead had a much higher tolerance for inconvenience than the rest of us.

His choice of hairstyle was typical. He wore a close-cropped flattop haircut which was now hidden beneath his brown Afghan wool hat. It was practical. Peacetime counterterrorist operations were one thing, but long hair in ground combat made little sense to him.

Months later, after Tora Bora, he chose to return to the Rangers as a battalion command sergeant major. In the early days of the invasion of Iraq, he went on a Ranger raid at a place called Haditha Dam. After taking the five-kilometer-long objective with only a single company of men, some of the young Rangers asked Ironhead when they would be getting some backup support.

"Listen, you're on a classic Ranger mission." he sharply reminded them. "You're deep behind enemy lines, seizing a target that's way too big for a company of men, and being told to hold until relieved."

That was all that was needed. The Rangers yelled "Hooah" and went back to work, even though they were on the receiving end of several 155mm artillery barrages that lasted for hours.

Ironhead grabbed an SR-25 long-range rifle and made his way to a nearby water tower. Working as a sniper, the former Delta operator personally delivered dozens of Iraqi fighters to their maker. His performance that day won him a Silver Star, but did not surprise anyone who really knew him.

Then there was Bryan, who was driving the second truck. Like Ironhead, he had been around the unit for more than a decade, and absent an official troop commander, he was the ranking operator in the reconnaissance troop.

The master sergeant was a former Green Beret and a natural leader, one of the better pistol shots and long-gun shooters in the building, and a master climber. Bryan was calm and cool under pressure, and had a knack for dissecting a contentious issue completely before speaking out. Then he would pick out the decision that had been the least thought about by everybody else, but the one that would be collectively agreed upon as the best.

We had a great team going up the road.

T hirty minutes into the drive, the sun rose in the distance to expose a landscape straight out of the ninth century. High snow-covered peaks dominated the land to our west and north. Dry streambeds and deep wadis cut the vast rolling and rocky desert floor. Colored foothills featured uneven splotches of tan and gray, while green painted the countryside, and the dirty skeletons of burned or rusted Communist-era armored vehicles stood dead and abandoned. Long forgotten village ruins and adobe tan compounds completed the scene of desolation.

Rocks the size of softballs, painted red on one side and white on the other, lined the road edge to mark mine fields: Proceed no farther or risk blowing yourself to smithereens.

Halfway to Kabul we noticed an unexploded bomb just off the road, with its nose buried a foot or so in the ground and the fins sticking out. The dud looked fairly new, and no doubt had been delivered by an American bomber within the last couple of weeks and intended for some fleeing Taliban troops during the Northern Alliance's big push on Kabul.

Our next escort waited in a lone vehicle parked to the side of the road. It was another old friend, Lt. Col. Mark Sutter, who had been commanding the Northern Advance Force Operations team, or NAFO. By the time Iraq rolled around, Sutter had succeeded Jake Ashley as squadron commander and was the best combat leader in Delta: fearless, out front, and possessing a remarkable ability to audible away from a briefed plan to make quick and timely decisions in the thick fog of war.

After quick handshakes and some backslapping, we said goodbye to Doc and the Judge and followed Sutter on a fifteen-minute drive through the back streets of Kabul. We slowed to ease through an Afghan security checkpoint, then entered a parking lot behind a large guesthouse in the center of town. In the past few weeks, it had become the home of Jawbreaker, the CIA's lead headquarters. From here, Sutter commanded and controlled, or "C2ed," the advance force cell. It was the same building that the CIA had used during the 1980s to monitor and support the Afghan war against the Soviets.

It was instantly clear that security was very, very tight. Standing guard, wearing black North Face clothing and with a new AK-47 at the ready, was none other than His Majesty, Sir Billy Waugh. Now well into his silver years, Billy should have been rocking in his favorite chair watching the war unfold on television, but instead, he was standing smack-dab in the thick of things . . . *again*.

His reputation in the special operations and intelligence communities, including multiple tours in Vietnam, was the stuff of legend. Anyone up for an exciting ride should read his memoirs, *Hunting the Jackal*. Time and again, we were bumping into some of the best operators in the business, already on the ground over here, but Billy was special.

With his usual growl, he and Ironhead and Bryan immediately began swapping yarns from other third world shit holes, European urban sprawls, and the Sudan. Bryan had done some Delta work there in the early 1990s while Billy was undercover for the CIA, snapping photographs of bin Laden's comings and goings in anticipation that the pictures might come in handy one day.

Luck is Billy's ally, I thought. Stay close to him.

Inside the guesthouse, the first person I met was Gary Berntsen, the CIA's point man in Kabul and the instigator of that fateful meeting around the Humvee at Task Force Dagger. On this cold December morning, Gary was upbeat, slapping backs like a proud sandlot football coach, obviously eager to get things moving. He offered us his complete support. "Anything you need," he said.

Gary shared his own account of the CIA's mission in Afghanistan and his tough take on the Tora Bora situation. Several years later, Gary got around to publishing his own book, *Jawbreaker,* but, unfortunately, the CIA heavily censored out much of the interesting stuff.

Gary did not have much more information than Gus had given us the night before, but his estimate of enemy manpower matched exactly. "We believe fifteen hundred to as many as three thousand fighters are there," he said, then added, "Kill them all."

The CIA nerve center had the look of a spy movie set. Numerous compartments were abuzz with folks hacking away at laptops, thumbing through stacks of classified documents, talking on cell phones, or conducting secure radio calls. Armed guards seemed to be everywhere. Every box was padlocked and every door was outfitted with a push-button cipher lock.

Out of that crowd emerged Adam Khan, an unlikely but invaluable warrior in this new war on terror.

The Afghan-born American citizen, a former marine with an impressive commanding personality, was standing at Ground Zero the day after 9/11, helping another government agency deal with the aftermath of the terrorist attack. His cell phone rang and some former colleagues were calling. They needed his help. More accurately, they said his nation needed his help and asked if he was interested in inserting into Afghanistan as a liaison officer with Special Ops units. "Do you want to read the news or do you want to make the news?" they asked.

Adam Khan accepted the challenge and was now back in his hometown of Kabul for the first time in twenty years. Danger did not bother him.

He was fluent in numerous dialects of the two key battlefield languages, Pashto and Dari, and although his current orders were only to ferry us safely to General Ali's headquarters, he was to become much more than just our travel guide. Adam Khan would be the critical nexus between the CIA forward headquarters in Jalalabad, General Hazret Ali's command, and Delta.

He did whatever it took to help us, including tasting the local food or tea before any American commando dug in to make sure it was not poisoned. I know that sounds a bit Hollywood, but it's true. Over the next two weeks, many a Delta operator would owe an awful lot, including some lives, to Adam Khan.

We hit it off right away, and I sent up a silent prayer of thanks that this American would be with us.

As Adam Khan tidied up a few things inside the building, the rest of us were outside, shivering and talking smack with Billy while we helped load a few trucks with supplies for the Northern Alliance in the Panjshir Valley. There were crates of new AK-47 rifles, Chinese Communist vests, bags of blue-dot special tennis shoes, U.S.-issue camouflage winter jackets and crates of 7.62mm ammunition, all paid for by the American taxpayer.

It was our first meeting with the Northern Alliance fighters, and they were of all ages and already dressed in fresh U.S. camouflage shirts and fatigue pants, with many wearing sneakers. Since turbans were the trademark of the oppressive Taliban, they were forbidden to wear them and instead had on a camouflage hat or a traditional Afghan wool hat. Each carried an AK-47 assault rifle and had three thirty-round magazines.

The overloaded trucks struggled to start and then eased into convoy formation and inched out of the parking lot, axles already screaming under the enormous weight of supplies. We wondered if they were mechanically fit enough to make the long trip over uneven rock-strewn riverbeds and torn asphalt.

Not to worry, called out Billy, who was going along on the ride. Just another character-building opportunity. He rode away waving, with a big wide smile on his face. The next time I ran into Sir Billy would be in January 2004, when he was strollin' and grinnin' in Baghdad.

Our own convoy loaded up, a couple of large trucks carrying a thousand AK-47s and hundreds of pounds of ammunition, all from the CIA. Our soon-to-be hosts, the Eastern Alliance, were also customers now and wanted their share of supplies. Well, I thought, the more, the merrier. At least our friends would be well armed.

In about an hour, as the midmorning sun ducked behind dark clouds, we drove through the guarded gate of the CIA house and slipped into eastbound traffic, heading for Jalalabad.

We passed through two Northern Alliance checkpoints without incident, reached the edge of Kabul, and got onto the main highway to Jalalabad. First would come twenty miles of deeply potholed and uneven road, and it was hard to imagine how the road could get any worse. Then it did. After the pavement gave out, the next seventy miles would be rocky and rutted, hardened, dusty ground that kept our pace to a tortuous average of only ten to fifteen miles per hour.

The route was what happens to a road in twenty years of thundering Communist tank treads, exploding land mines, and Soviet artillery shelling, the fighting of the Taliban, the muhj and our warplanes. Beyond the damaged hardball, the road was light brown dirt covered by three or four inches of dust as fine as talcum powder. In the wake of every passing vehicle, the dust rose up and then settled again over the latest tire tread marks.

Every mile demonstrated that Afghanistan was truly a war-torn country. We drove by old Taliban outposts, empty barracks, and onetime motor pools that were littered with dozens of banged-up tanks and vehicles. American airpower had ensured they never made it out of the starting blocks. Soviet War–era armored vehicles differed from more recently destroyed Taliban armored vehicles only in the amount of rust on the hulls and carriages, and all of them were now derelicts.

We had not slept well before leaving Bagram, and though Ironhead was still driving our Toyota truck, even he would need to be spelled out at some point on this hellish road. I popped two speed pills to help stay alert.

A few hours east of Kabul, we stopped before reaching the chokepoint village of Sorubi. Adam Khan said it was planned that we meet a second Afghan security force there, which would safeguard the convoy through what he termed "the lawless land from Sorubi to Jalalabad." Bands of thieves and bandits have raided that highway for centuries. We were not afraid of them, but staying in any one place too long while carrying valuable cargo invited unwanted trouble, and our mission was to go meet General Ali, not fight crooks along this sad stretch of road. The Afghan force didn't show, and we pressed on without them.

Sorubi was a small village straight out of the Wild West. Fighters loyal to Gulbuddin Hekmatyar, the former prime minister and mujahideen commander, had controlled passage through the village for the previous decade. Everywhere we looked stood an armed man of fighting age, deeply tanned and curious, with piercing eyes that warned all strangers. When we came upon a half-dozen armed men on the road who were carrying four or five RPGs and assorted rifles, they looked us square in the eyes. Our presence didn't bother them, and once we had passed, they began to climb a rocky outcrop, likely to one of the many ambush positions that had been successfully used by men just like them against the Soviets. After seeing this tough bunch, we not only wondered who they planned to ambush, but how in the world we would ever be able to distinguish friend from foe in this strange land.

We had just cleared the village when one of the large trucks in our convoy, which was hauling the heavy AK-47 crates, blew an axle. It was no surprise. Adam Khan took the initiative and directed an Afghan leader to commandeer an approaching large and brightly painted truck. An Eastern Alliance fighter yanked the driver from his seat and pulled him to the roadside, where Adam Khan stepped in and gave the man a wad of cash for his troubles.

With a dozen or so muhj, we went to work cross-loading the one hundred crates, each of which contained ten rifles, and several more large cardboard boxes holding load-bearing equipment, into the newly purchased vehicle. The Afghan convoy leader happened to finally notice that nobody was standing guard! He barked orders and waved his hands wildly until several young fighters obediently moved away and took up security positions by squatting down, placing the butts of their rifles on the ground between their legs, and staring out into the vast countryside.

The longer it took to cross-load the equipment, the more attention we drew from locals, who drifted out of the village to see what all the fuss was about. Some were allowed to approach and cautiously moved around, eyeballing us out of curiosity. Some were brave enough to shake hands. None accepted my offer of Redman chewing tobacco.

There was little danger, and no doubt existed about who was in charge. The Afghans in their new U.S. camouflage with their AK-47s had things well under control. After throwing the last few crates into the back of our Toyota and into Adam Khan's pickup truck, we were back on the road again, heading into the "lawless land."

For another seven hours or so, the convoy gained and lost thousands of feet in altitude. High in one mountain pass, a little boy with dirty feet and disheveled hair heard us coming before he saw us, and had already jumped into action. He scooped a small makeshift shovel's worth of dirt and poured it into one of the hundreds of small potholes that characterized every turn of the switchback road. I am sure he thought himself to be a road repairman, and waited for passing vehicles in hopes of securing a small reward for saving the occupants from the heavy jolt of another reverse speed bump.

Dark had fallen by the time the torturous dirt road gave way to the smooth and fast asphalt highway on the western edge of the historic city of Jalalabad. Our opportunity to enjoy the level asphalt did not last long, because the lead vehicle of our convoy abruptly stopped in the middle of the road.

It was a place called Darunta, which was known in terrorism circles as the former site of one of bin Laden's more sophisticated training camps. As we rolled to a stop, our rearview mirrors showed that some welcomers were banging on the driver's-side door of one of the transport trucks and barking orders. A moment later, several more men stepped from the darkness, a few gripping small handheld radios and most of them armed. A few of the more hardened ones peered into our windows and things were getting pretty tense. We reached down and checked our weapons.

We had no way of knowing whether this was a friendly encounter, but if these guys were not our scheduled link-up with General Ali's forces, we might be in trouble.

We were in the middle of fighters loyal to Ali's rival, the fairly notorious Pashtun warlord Haji Zaman Ghamshareek, who would become very familiar to us all.* They tried to intimidate and threaten our drivers by telling them that Zaman controlled the whole city of Jalalabad, so the trucks and that valuable cargo were intended for him. In other words, they intended to hijack the convoy.

We were outnumbered roughly four to one and did not want to get into a scrap with men who might be our allies, so the quick-thinking Adam

---

* Both warlords, Haji Zaman Ghamshareek and General Hazret Ali, were identified in Philip Smucker's book, *Al Qaeda's Great Escape*, and later inside USSOCOM's 20th Anniversary History edition on page 93.

Khan pulled an ace out of his sleeve. He agreed to follow Zaman's men into the city, because he had a good idea where General Ali's people were located and the new convoy route we had been ordered to take would drive us right by them.

We started up again and continued east for a mile or so to an intersection at a place called Du-Saraka, where two more pickup trucks loaded with a half-dozen armed men intercepted the convoy. Once again, we stopped.

This new force of gunmen approached Adam Khan, who filled them in on what was going on. The crew was led by Ali's nephew, just a teenager, who simply went over and started beating on the guy in charge of Zaman's group and yelling at him. The rest of Zaman's people, so brave a few minutes before with a few truck drivers, scurried back into their vehicles like whipped puppies and sped away. In this part of the world, direct and forceful action speaks loud.

That left us with the correct welcoming party and the nephew, who said he would now escort us directly to meet General Ali. If the kid was such a badass, I could hardly wait to meet his uncle.

After a few more checkpoints, we reached Ali's quarters in the middle of the city and pulled into a walled compound. An Afghan guard directed us specifically where to park, as if we were arriving at a crowded theme park. The two-story tan house was much more upscale than we had imagined. Guards were dutifully posted along the ten-foot-high walls and the building's rooftops to keep the general and his guests safe, perhaps not so much from the Taliban, which was no longer in power, as from rival tribes.

Inside the walls sprawled an uncanny contradiction to the rest of the town. The yard was well landscaped and manicured. Blooming pink and red flowers hung in large flowerpots from the window ledges, and nothing seemed out of place. Whoever was in charge of Ali's security was doing a fine job. So was his gardener.

Our bones, backs, and butts were happy to get out of the trucks after the long and grinding ride. One of Colonel Sutter's men, Manny, was waiting in the parking area and took us inside. He had been one of the first Delta operators in the country after 9/11, and now sported a thick black beard and long hair. He accompanied the CIA team that occupied Bagram Air Base during the Northern Alliance advance toward Kabul, and when the capital city fell, he moved in to scout the city and provided valuable information to our higher headquarters. Manny knew his stuff.

He took us inside and introduced us to a few of the CIA fellows before saying that we wouldn't be meeting the general as expected that evening, after all. Apparently, the general had been away all day at the front and was now a few kilometers from the battle line. With him was the forward CIA field commander, a veteran operative named George, who was Gary Berntsen's deputy.

Manny filled us in on current information. An American bomber had inadvertently struck a small town near the mountains called Pachier Agam, which just happened to be next door to the small village of Kolokhel, the general's current location, and a place where we were soon to go. The locals were not expected to be keen on foreign visitors for a while.

Part of an A Team of fourteen Green Berets from 5th Special Forces Group out of Fort Campbell, Kentucky, was also at General Ali's headquarters. They bore the code name Cobra 25, and had entered Afghanistan from Uzbekistan.

The previous day, six of them had attempted to infil to an observation post near the front lines but pulled back after running into a firefight between Ali's men and al Qaeda. They now were awaiting insertion to an OP several kilometers short of the front lines, and once established, they would become Observation Post Cobra 25-A. That was verbally shortened to OP25-A, and was a place that would loom large in the coming action.

The rest of the Green Berets were prepping to infil farther to the west, and would be called OP Cobra 25-B.

There was a serious internal struggle going on between the Americans. The Green Beret commander, Task Force Dagger's colonel Mulholland, who had been initially reluctant to commit any of his Green Berets to assist General Ali, apparently was still unconvinced.* He had been burned before by unreliable warlords.

A few weeks earlier, Colonel Mulholland had reviewed the CIA plan to go after bin Laden in the mountains and declared it was "flawed" and wanting on several counts. With no ability to evacuate casualties by air, winter growing worse by the day, no American quick-reaction force, and the prospects of a treacherous uphill slugfest—and working with a warlord who had not yet been vetted—the Task Force Dagger commander opted to pass until the CIA could present better intelligence. And who could blame a prudent commander for deciding not to risk his men against a well-prepared defense while supported only by an indigenous force of unknown reliability and quality?

Mulholland was also fully aware that the Soviets had failed to take Tora Bora. If the estimated enemy strength in the mountains today was valid, he could foresee a meat-grinder fight awaiting American forces.

Given his initial resistance, and with no other American troops available, Berntsen and Sutter adjusted their plans. The only choice remaining was to look internal, to pool their resources and retask the missions to their own people.

Both believed strongly that bin Laden was in Tora Bora and that to not act quickly would border on negligence, would be irresponsible and practically criminal. The experienced field commanders felt that not grasping the opportunity smacked too much of the slow-moving pre-9/11 culture that both the intelligence and special operations community had sucked down year after year.

They agreed with Mulholland that the risk was extremely high; they just were not going to take no for an answer.

After considering their options, which were not many, Berntsen and Sutter picked four of their best operators and sent them out to locate and kill as many al Qaeda forces as they could. And if they could develop the picture a little more, and maybe prove for sure that al Qaeda had in fact

* Gary Berntsen discusses the reluctance of Colonel Mulholland to commit Green Berets to Tora Bora in his book *Jawbreaker.* USSOCOM's 20th Anniversary History also discusses this on page 94.

taken up refuge in Tora Bora, then perhaps Mulholland or Central Command might be more willing to commit some muscle.

On December 4, Berntsen and Sutter's men took several donkeys and a half-dozen Afghan guides and reached their first observation post in the Spin Ghar Mountains. Brought together by the unpredictability of warfare, this small team consisted of a quiet and deadly Delta operator code-named Warf, an air force special tactics combat controller named Joe, a skilled CIA paramilitary operative, and a second CIA guy who was a former Army Ranger and Delta operator. Within hours, they confirmed a large presence of al Qaeda in the small village of Milawa, tucked deep in the mountains, and the killing began.

For the next several days, their "Victor Bravo Zero Two" call sign was summoning the pilots of inbound bombers and fighters looking to make their underbelly loads useful. The team went without sleep for fifty-six hours straight, and was the first to spot and direct ordnance on bin Laden's purported location.

I am certain they were thinking, *Where in the world is the rest of the army?*

They did their job in spectacular fashion, made believers out of CENTCOM, and generated enough pressure on Task Force Dagger for Mulholland to commit an A Team. However, Mulholland still was not ready to give the team outright authority to seek out and destroy the enemy face-to-face. Instead, the Green Berets of Cobra 25 went into Tora Bora with strict orders—"NO MANEUVER, TGO ONLY."

TGO meant "terminal guidance operations." They essentially were to establish a static observation post from which they could control aircraft and drop bombs. That constraint did not sit well with a bunch of warriors and specialists like the Green Berets.

Mulholland also required his men to follow a strict interpretation of the law of land warfare by wearing U.S. military uniforms, ostensibly to prevent friendly-fire incidents. As often happens when unrealistic demands are placed on independent-minded soldiers by a commander who is well removed from the skirmish lines, obedience becomes largely selective. The men from 5th Group determined that they could meet the intent of their commander's orders by wearing U.S. desert tan uniform pants, but everything else came straight out of an Afghan wardrobe. They had to blend in to have any hope of success.

Manny reported that intelligence was saying that bin Laden's second-in-command, the Egyptian doctor Ayman al-Zawahiri, had been killed in a bombing raid in the mountains. A similar report came from British intelligence sources, which added an interesting interpretation.

Mohammed Atef, bin Laden's military commander and number-three man, was killed in Kabul several weeks earlier. Now with the number two, Dr. Zawahiri, also reportedly eliminated, the Brits assessed that the weakness in leadership would make bin Laden remain in the mountains and slug it out to the finish.

However, the CIA followed that British report with sharply contrasting news that Pakistan forces had detained an unknown number of al Qaeda foot soldiers who had fled the mountains and attempted to cross the border.

Interesting. So which was it? Why were some of the bin Laden fighters running for Pakistan if bin Laden himself was planning to stay in Tora Bora? Was he planning to make a valiant stand and fight to the finish against the invading Westerners, something reminiscent of how Muhammad, the seventh-century messenger of Allah, would have acted? Or were the reported foot soldiers captured crossing the border just scouting a possible escape route for the boss, so bin Laden could also attempt to flee, and live and fight another day?

We had no answer, but it indicated that we needed to move, and fast. We were growing anxious to get to the battlefield . . . but first we needed some sleep.

Our new accommodations were reminiscent of a college frat house, sans the smell of alcohol, the pounding of loud music, and the sharp crack of colliding pool balls. Besides the Green Berets, the current guests ranged from local Afghan fighters to cooks and housekeepers to your standard mix of commando types. Before we bedded down for a few hours, Manny gave us a morning departure time of 0700 hours.

I powered up the mini laptop to check messages from the boss, Colonel Ashley. The in-box contained a lengthy message of great importance, and declared that General Ali must agree to three requirements before Dailey would commit additional Delta operators. Last-minute demands are always irritating, but it seems that it is never too late for additional guidance, especially if it serves to constrain or limit flexibility or freethinking on the battlefield.

These articles had to be articulated during our very first meeting with Ali.

First, we needed a promise that he would integrate our teams with his fighters as we moved into the mountains. Second, as we pushed our reconnaissance teams farther forward and higher to positions of greater tactical advantage, we needed local guides to help ensure that we didn't shoot the wrong folks. And third, because the closest American QRF was not even in Afghanistan yet, but several hours away by helicopter, we needed to borrow Ali's.

It was rather embarrassing to have to ask for any of these things. Moreover, as our education in the ambiguities of tribal warfare and the peculiarity of the Muslim culture improved, the more unrealistic and comical the "three requirements" became.

But very little specific advice was offered on what I should actually say to General Ali when we met. Most senior officials apparently were busy with other preparations, briefing higher headquarters, or still, amazingly to me, even going home. It was my responsibility to make it work, build rapport as fast as possible, and win Ali over from the start. Sure, we were told the CIA would make the introductions and put everybody at ease, but then all eyes would be on me.

As the old cliché goes, you never get a second chance to make a first impression, and this had to be my personal finest hour. The senior CIA folks that I needed to talk to before the meeting were not even in Jalalabad, for they were, after all, the busiest Westerners around. I would just have to wing it.

I decided to put out my own message first, a decision that only served to fill my head with a dozen concerns. Would Ali oblige me without interruptions, particularly since a Pashto interpreter was a must? Would he take to us, or shun us? What needed to be said? Whatever I said had to have the powerful backing of the USA, needed to be direct and to the point, and had to be recognized as genuine by the Afghan general. Most important, any fancy rhetoric had to be backed up with action. Talk is cheap on the battlefield, and Ali knew that better than most. One thing was for certain in my mind: *Screw this up, Dalton, and the Black Chinook will be coming in at nightfall.*

The fabled Black Chinook is a slang legend inside the special ops community. If an operator makes an extraordinarily egregious error in judgment or physical performance, then regardless of who he is or where he is at the time of the infraction, a mysterious black helicopter will arrive to sweep that person away. When the Black Chinook shows up, the Special Ops community no longer requires the individual's services. It was a nightmare every officer had worried about at some time or another. Tonight, I could almost hear those ominous blades whipping the air over my head.

I tried to catch some rack time, but the double dose of speed that I had popped during the long drive was still screwing with my system. Anticipating the meeting with Ali led to further restlessness, along with a bit of anxiety. As the others tossed and turned in a shallow slumber on the cold floor, I pulled out my small green notebook and a flashlight and scribbled a few more sentences. I wanted to get the words right, bottom line up front, get the point across, portray confidence, and have my act together. I didn't want to look like an idiot in front of the CIA and General Ali on our very first meeting.

Just another CAPEX, I told myself, and I had to be as comfortable in front of Ali as I would be in briefing some minor VIP making a routine visit to the Unit back home.

I wrote, rehearsed the words in my head, erased, crossed out, scribbled some more, and rehearsed again. I had to take care not to make "perfect" the enemy of "good enough." I committed the final version to memory, typed it up on the laptop, and e-mailed it back to the Bagram Air Base. The message read something like this.

Sir, this is the basic approach for my opening discussions with Ali this morning.

I'm Lieutenant Colonel Dalton Fury, commander of an American commando unit sent here by my country to help you fight al Qaeda forces and Usama bin Laden. We are here to fight next to you as a team with a common goal, to stand alongside you and share the same hardships, and face the same danger as your brave fighters. I was also sent here to help you and your people obtain a large amount of reward money from my country once the mission is accomplished. My mission is clear and simple, to kill or capture bin Laden. I cannot and will not accept any conditional surrender by bin Laden or surrender with special circumstances. One hundred percent nonnegotiable unconditional surrender. In the event bin Laden is killed, I must provide proof of his death to my country in the form of a photograph, fingerprints, or ensuring the remains are properly escorted to a higher authority. Failure to allow us access to the remains may delay any additional payment to you. Again, we are a team in this endeavor. My men and I do not seek glory, credit, or money—we just seek bin Laden. My men are ready now but before I can bring them forward to the front lines, I must have your complete assurances on three things. First, you must agree to embed my force within yours and provide mutual protection. Second, in order to ensure our forces do not inadvertently shoot each other, I need the assistance of five of your brave fighters to accompany us as we hunt down bin Laden in the Tora Bora Mountains. We will provide for their food and warm clothing while they are with us. I see these men as critical to our success and they will undoubtedly make you very proud. Finally, I must have your absolute word that if my men should come under attack while forward of your lines, you will do everything in your power to immediately dispatch a force to come to our aid.

END

FURY

Shortly after clicking the send button, I heard the local Afghans stirring in the kitchen area, preparing the morning meal. I had yet to fall asleep. *Not a good start.*

6

Green Eyes

You Americans cannot survive in these mountains against
al Qaeda, just like the Soviets could not survive against us.
—GENERAL HAZRET ALI, DECEMBER 7, 2001

On any battlefield the CIA visits, which is, arguably at least, as many fields as the U.S. military has walked, their operatives bring along large black duffel bags filled with freshly printed hundred-dollar bills, neatly wrapped in cellophane. One of the things the Agency does best is buy friends.

In late November 2001, a week or so before we first arrived at Tora Bora, the CIA had decided to become pals with Hazret Ali, the influential Afghan warlord in the area, and a self-proclaimed general. To secure the friendship, George, the forward director of the small CIA Jawbreaker Juliet team in Jalalabad, brought along millions of U.S. dollars, conveniently packaged in $250,000 bundles.

General Ali, a proud leader in the region, had told George that to muster enough fighters to pursue bin Laden into the Tora Bora Mountains it would cost, oh, say about $250,000.

George looked over at one of his deputies sitting in on the meeting at Ali's safe house and motioned for him to retrieve the duffel bag. Within a minute, the CIA operative was back and placed a brick of hundred-dollar bills about the size of a small microwave oven on the couch beside the general.

General Ali remained silent and stoic and never touched the money. He ended the meeting moments later and excused himself from his American guests. As soon as he moved out of sight, one of his subordinates entered and retrieved the cube-shaped package, cradling it like a newborn baby, and carried it downstairs to the first floor.

Another Afghan waited there, seated behind a single aged and wooden table with a notepad, a pencil, and a Dollar Store calculator. On his left was a large and faded stack of Pakistani rupees. The courier placed the quarter-million-dollar package on the right side of the table and delicately removed the plastic wrapping, and the moneychanger swapped the American dollars into local currency at a rate that was probably quite favorable to the general. The United States had just bought the services of another warlord.

On the morning of December 7, General Ali sent word over to the safe house to have our Delta party brought to his headquarters. We stood around on the green grass inside the walled compound for an hour or so as Ali's men prepared the route so the convoy would not have any unpleasant surprises, as had happened with our entry into Jalalabad last night.

As we waited, Manny filled us in on the complex muhj areas of control, both politically and militarily. Picking his brain was time well spent. Word came midmorning for us to head south for the meeting. Empty of the heavy AK-47 crates, our two pickups easily slid into the middle of a muhj escort convoy and the three-hour drive was uneventful. Any doubt that Ali and his men were the law in this town was dispelled.

The sun was high in the sky, with very few clouds, providing a comfortably warm day for the trip, although a chilly wind with a sharp edge blew out of the north. It was impossible not to notice the majestic mountains and the deep, long, and dark shadows of dozens of steep ridgelines and spurs. The breathtaking view of the legendary Hindu Kush seemed endless.

Dark brown contour lines on our U.S.-issued 1:100,000 scale maps showed the steep elevations of the long and wide mountain range that stretched east to west. The eastern end was marked by the Khyber Pass, which had seen an eternity of invading foreign soldiers, from Alexander's faithful legions and Genghis Khan's fanatic followers to the red-coated British and the camouflaged Soviets.

The Hindu Kush then extends west into the central part of Afghanistan, and provides natural protection for the frontier with Pakistan. A north-south-running boulder-laden dry streambed snakes to the east, and another deep valley runs north to south before it cuts hard off to the west, nearly clean through our area of interest.

These were centuries-old routes that provided relatively easy access for black marketers, drug smugglers, gun traders, Bedouins, refugees, and fighters wishing to cross back and forth into the Northwest Frontier Province in western Pakistan.

The area visible to my naked eye that day is formally known as the Spin Ghar Mountains, literally "white dust," most likely named because of the snow that blankets the high peaks throughout the year.

We would be more interested in the Towr Ghar Mountains, the "black dust" altitudes that were fortified and stockpiled in the 1980s and were now occupied by al Qaeda fighters.

Strategically, they sat along the forward military crest, roughly halfway between the Spin Ghar peaks and the light brown foothills to the north. From those positions, defenders had significant operational and tactical advantages, including a view all the way to the outskirts of Jalalabad.

Fir trees and sharp, jagged quartz boulders insulated the ridgelines down to the valley floors and connected draws that were filled with large masses of limestone and feldspar. Centuries of rainwater and melted snow had created large cracks and crags in the mountains' skin and provided numerous tuck-away areas for the fighters. Any student of military tactics would instantly recognize the stronghold's seemingly insurmountable and impregnable nature. It was becoming easier to understand Mulholland's meat-grinder analogy.

Should someone want to reach neighboring Pakistan, he would need to climb uphill to clear the 14,000-foot mountain peaks straddling the border. Should he choose to take one of the long, winding valleys, he still would have to negotiate the 9,000-foot passes. I looked at the puffy and snow-filled clouds hiding the highest peaks and had a foreboding feeling about things to come. Visitors beware.

Tora Bora and bin Laden have a long relationship. This place served as bin Laden's base of operations during the Soviet jihad, where he was on the defending end of numerous attacks. Legend has it the most massive attack involved an estimated two thousand Russians backed by another two thousand Afghan Communists, supported by fifty attack helicopters and MIG fighter jets. They attacked up the mountains for the better part of a week, and bin Laden, then considered only an average guerrilla leader, and his fellow mujahideen were never defeated in the mountains. They never ran.

The local Afghans knew Usama bin Laden well. Indeed, he enjoyed star status within the tribes and clans in the area, for since moving back in after leaving the Sudan in the late 1990s, bin Laden had distributed money to practically every family in Nangarhar Province. For years many an Afghan family named their sons Usama.

After the Soviet withdrawal and the establishment of al Qaeda as a living, breathing, and thinking terrorist organization, a meeting of epic proportions took place among the tall spires. The year was 1996, and Khalid Sheikh Mohammed visited the leader of al Qaeda inside one of the hundreds of caves that had been engineered into the ridgelines and mountains of Tora Bora. It was there that Khalid first laid out the ambitious plan to train terrorist pilots to hijack and crash planes into buildings inside the United States.

Now, in December 2001, the backlash of that meeting was becoming apparent. Only a blind man could miss the white parallel contrails of the engine exhausts of American bombers streaking across the blue sky like long fat chalk marks on a lesson board. They were so far up that the engine roar could not be heard, but only a deaf man could miss the thunder of bombs hitting bin Laden's positions.

The loud drum of war was again banging in Tora Bora.

At midafternoon, we reached General Ali's makeshift headquarters, located among rolling hills in the beige desert and inside the fork of two deep wadis that ran north and south. We could hear and see the bombs pounding around the peaks only a few miles away.

It once had been a school, and although it had seen better days, the building was modern in comparison to the ancient, mud-walled compounds that pimpled the surrounding area. The United Nations High Commissioner for Refugees had funded the construction years earlier, and the horseshoe-shaped tan, gray, and light blue slate single-story structure was built on a solid foundation, with nine rooms exiting to the middle of the horseshoe, with a small poured concrete porch that spanned the entire center. It had once been a beacon of learning, but any hope of education for local children was shattered when the Taliban came to power.

Windowpanes that had been carved by hand were splintered, and held little glass. The former classrooms were empty save for the trash and dirt the wind had blown into the corners. Some chalkboards still showed fragments of old lessons in Pashto and Arabic. Outside, the yard was quiet and deserted, like any Western schoolyard in the summertime, but there were no kids.

Oddly, there also were no signs of armed guards for General Ali.

Manny and Adam Khan returned with a large, tall man in an olive green multipocketed vest over a plum-colored, button-down shirt with long sleeves. It was George, the CIA counterpart for whom we had been looking, and we knew from the very first that everything would be okay. He stood roughly two inches over six feet, likely was in his late forties, and his long hair and beard were a combination of brown and gray hair. George carried a natural friendly demeanor, had a great sense of humor, and spoke with a slight Wild West cowboy accent.

Originally in Afghanistan as Gary Berntsen's deputy, it had tickled George to be named the team leader of Jawbreaker Juliet. He wasted little time in telling us that he was pressing General Ali to support our move into the mountains, but the general was proving to be stubborn.

"You ready to meet Ali and make your pitch?" he asked as we shook hands.

Ironhead, Bryan, and I looked at each other with relief. We had been worried that we would have to smooth out some friction or turn a cheek or two to ensure a positive relationship between Delta and the CIA. There had been dark days when the relationship was fragile at best. Half the time it seems that interoperability success depends more on personalities than on shared agendas. George had put us at ease from the start with his genuine welcome.

George had brought to Jalalabad with him four or five other agency professionals and one Special Forces lieutenant colonel who possibly had the most rewarding and intriguing job in the army for someone of that rank. They were a bunch of first-round draft picks, and all would prove equally talented and cool. But CIA guys pestered me all day about my rank of lieutenant colonel, wanting to know what year group I was in and if I knew any of their buddies. I had to guess at what year group a newly promoted fake lieutenant colonel like me should be. *Year group 85? Naw, hell, let's try year group 86. Am I so screwed up already that it's obvious I'm an imposter? I haven't done shit yet, so how could they even suspect already that I'm not a lieutenant colonel?* Not a good time to start second-guessing myself. But the spooks wouldn't let up. *Jesus Christ! How many of these CIA guys are gonna come in here and ask me about my rank?*

We walked a short distance from the old schoolhouse to where a large red carpet had been laid out neatly on the dirt. A few colorful blankets were folded to comfort some, but there were not enough for everyone. The outdoor meeting was to be held within sight of the majestic mountains to the south, our future battle zone.

The general and his young aide, Ghulbihar, slipped off their worn leather sandals and effortlessly flopped down and crossed their legs. Following the lead of both George and Adam Khan in this sudden introduction to still another point of the Afghan culture, I fumbled with my cold-weather boots, trying to remove them without showing discomfort. *Am I gonna have to take off these boots every time we talk? This is gonna get old fast!*

Ali was facing southeast, oblique to the White Mountains and the glare of the morning sun forced him to squint. George flanked me on the right, closest to Ali, and was trying to sit as comfortably as possible for a big Texan. I had the seat of honor, directly across from the general, and Adam Khan was to my left. Ghulbihar, the general's translator, was on the warlord's right.

General Ali did seem tired, but we didn't mention his press party the night before. He seemed shy and uncomfortable, almost as if the inevitability of the overall military situation had finally caught up with him. More Americans were coming into his land and he knew it. He leaned forward so that his oversized brown coat spread over most of his legs. A small notebook of dirty paper, a short stubby pencil, a handheld two-way radio, and two black cell phones were aligned neatly before him. One of the cell phones was standard CIA issue and the other was a foreign model.

Thirty feet away, just outside of hearing range, stood Ironhead and Bryan. Off to the side, Lieutenant Colonel Al of the CIA leaned comfortably against our red pickup, with an AK-47 slung crossways over his back, and several 7.62mm magazines bulging from his back pockets. I could feel their collective stares on the back of my head and knew they were pulling for me to not screw this up. They were itching to get up into al Qaeda territory but understood the first goal was to secure Ali's trust and support.

General Ali's wool muhj hat was propped back like a dog-tired Little League shortstop's cap after an extra innings game, and his coat had a large black fur collar. He nervously rolled a long strand of pearl prayer beads between his fingers, occasionally switching them from one hand to the other. Ali's mannerisms gave me every impression that he was a devout Muslim who was visibly uncomfortable with his new status as an American stooge.

George broke the ice and introduced Adam Khan and me. Ghulbihar translated Ali's opening comments in very rough English, and Ali looked at me through the sun-induced squint. With a slight tilt of the head, he asked Ghulbihar something in a low tone.

The aide turned and asked, "Commandos?"

I nodded, and George interjected. "Yes. Tell the general these are the commandos I have been promising. Many more will come." George looked over at me as if to ask, *"Right? Please tell me it's not just you five."* I nodded. "They will help us find bin Laden," George added.

It was my turn, and I glanced at Adam Khan to be certain he was ready to translate. I wanted what I had to say to seem natural, although I had spent much of the night rehearsing in the dark. If I had to repeat myself, I feared that I would lose my place.

I did a quick personal inventory of my heartbeat and started to talk,

and Adam Khan easily translated my words. Ali would softly mutter *"Wo"*—
"yes" in Pashto—and scribble on the white pad every so often. The general
rocked back and forth and his face betrayed him: He was very distraught
at having American fighting men here.

Just as I finished, Ali responded in his language, "Americans should
not be on the ridgelines."

He barely let Adam Khan finish translating before launching into a
lengthy lecture. Maybe he had been up last night, too, after hosting the
press, and was as worried about this meeting as I.

Having reached a fast speaking rhythm, he seemed to forget that
Adam Khan needed time to translate, but it was pretty clear that Ali was
putting me on the spot. He looked me dead in the eye for the first time and
said we were not up to the task, implying that Delta Force was not tough
enough to fight al Qaeda in the mountains.

Adam Khan caught the tempo. "Al Qaeda is dug in with many supplies
and weapons. Many fighters willing to die for martyrdom. You Americans
cannot survive in these mountains against al Qaeda, just like the Soviets
could not survive against us. What makes you think you Americans can do
what the Soviets couldn't do in ten years of fighting?"

*Ohhhh . . . Blindsided. I had not expected that response. Think fast, stay
cool!*

"Adam Khan, please tell the general that the men I bring are America's finest commandos," I said. "They are skilled in mountain warfare,
and they are hardened and deadly."

Ali allowed me to continue, just adding a few more *Wo's*. When it
was obvious that I had finished, he answered.

"I was an engineer when the Soviets were here. I helped build the
caves and know all of them. They occupied this same land where we
sit; they [the Soviets] never penetrated past the foothills and lost many
Russkies. It is too dangerous for you Americans. It will be very bad if one
of you is killed."

*So that was it. He was scared about what would happen if an American
got killed.* "I will be blamed," he confirmed, and looked at George.

I stayed on course. "Take me and the few men here that arrived with
me to the front lines today. Let us show you that we can hold our own. Tomorrow, I will have forty more commandos ready to fight, not drink tea."

Ali responded, "It is not good to attack right now." With a shrug, he added, "This place is different than Mazar-i-Sharif." That was the first Afghan city to fall to the Northern Alliance, with a lot of help from the United States, after 9/11. Ali was obviously among those who, despite the heavy fighting there, considered the victory to have been somewhat of a cakewalk.

The general pressed us hard for more bombing. "The Arabs are going to die in their caves. Many are living in the same trench lines on the mountainsides that were used when we defeated the Russians. My fighters are spread out in the mountains, near the caves. They cannot escape. We have all sides blocked."

George broke in. "We can't bomb forever. We have given you money, weapons, and equipment to attack, yet you refuse. Now we are giving you our best fighters. If you don't begin soon, thousands of American soldiers will be covering this entire area."

Whooaa. George had put his finger on a sore spot, but he meant business and was running this show.

"The Arabs will fight to the death," the general responded, trying to sound convincing, "I don't want to sacrifice all my men to get to them." Showing a slight frustration, he added, "Ten thousand fighters won't be enough to get them out of the trenches." Ali was agonizing over George's harsh words, which were almost accusing him of either corruption or cowardice.

I threw in a portion of understanding to help take the edge off things. "General, we can bring more bombs here to help, but we must get closer to the enemy to kill more, and to win this battle." High-level bombing cannot do everything by itself. Boots on the ground can pinpoint the payloads.

Almost conceding the argument, the general said, "My people must be first, in the end." Hometown pride. He wanted his forces to carry out the first wave of the final assault. That was fine with us.

I turned and pointed to the mountains behind me. "We must get on the back side of those ridgelines to see the caves and trench lines, to shoot al Qaeda where they eat, sleep, and hide," I said. "Give us what we ask for and you will be pleased." That was it. I ended my side of the conversation.

Ali looked down, shrugged his shoulders again and sighed, ending our meeting. *"Momkin,"* he said, a Pashto term of indecision, meaning "possible" but always used for "maybe." It was a frustrating word that we would become very familiar with over the next ten days.

After the little powwow, we learned that the CIA had already bankrolled the general to the tune of several million dollars, money that had been spent to rent his leadership, his men, and his courage. George was irritated that it was not spent to buy equipment.

Ali had feared that when we showed up at his headquarters, we would be accompanied by a massive amount of American tanks, jeeps, and troops. So our discreet arrival pleased him. Both Cobra 25 and the CIA folks wore traditional Afghan clothing and brought nonmilitary style vehicles, and we had followed that lead. Local clothing and vehicles, not American military issue, were the flavors of the day. He had been delighted with our stylish Afghan outfits.

And we had to consider the careful political balancing act he had to perform. If he lost face with the tribal leaders, the Shura, his supporters might think less of him and brand him as unfit and unable to handle the problem by himself. If rival tribes got wind that foreign commandos were being brought in to help *his* fight in *his* own backyard, it could prove the end of his reign, if not skillfully handled.

But on the other hand, he knew the muhj advance had stalled completely along the northern foothills, and like it or not, he needed help. Around-the-clock bombing, intermittent foothill skirmishes, and the monitoring of al Qaeda's unsecured radio calls for a week had convinced him of several things.

First, his enemy was organized and well equipped, having stocked hundreds of thousands of rounds of ammunition, crates of RPGs, a dozen or so SAMs, piles of foodstuffs, and even enough firewood to last the harsh winter.

Second, because the Russians never conquered these mountains during the Soviet War, Ali now faced a highly motivated foe that had already beaten a superpower. As far as the enemy was concerned, they were invincible soldiers of God, with Allah in their corner.

Finally, and something most troubling to Ali, al Qaeda possessed the ability to reinforce and counterattack any muhj advance. Skirmish after skirmish over the past week had only served to bloody the noses of the muhj and strengthen al Qaeda.

Ali had a lot on his plate, but was smart enough to reach out for help.

"How did it go?" Ironhead asked, as if he could feel that the little conference had not proceeded as we had hoped.

"I think he will come around by the time the boys arrive. He's skeptical. Doesn't think we can handle this."

"Well, Dalton, I guess we'll just have to show him," Bryan said with a smile.

"Yeah," added Ironhead, looking up at the mountains. "But we can't do it from down here."

Adam Khan came running over to our Toyota. "The general is going to the front. Do you want to go?"

After the tea party on the Afghan rug, our savvy translator had asked General Ali about his forward command. Where was it? Who was in command there? It turned out the man in charge was his brother-in-law, Haji Musa, who also was his cousin, not uncommon within the Afghan culture.

Adam Khan seized the opportunity and immediately pressed the general to get us involved sooner rather than later, reasoning that if his brother-in-law was up there, then it should be safe for us to visit him. Surely, Haji Musa should be able to provide adequate security.

Uncomfortable with such forwardness, the general didn't have anything to counter the argument, and since he was going to visit Musa in a few minutes anyway, he reluctantly agreed to take us along.

We grabbed our long guns, wrapped our scarves around our faces and blankets around our shoulders. Before the general reached the truck I asked Adam Khan, "Hey, what in the world was General Ali writing on that notepad when you were translating our message?"

"Nothing!" he said.

General Ali jumped in the passenger seat of our red pickup and I drove. A brown leather shoulder harness with a small ivory-handled revolver was half-hidden beneath his brown jacket. In the backseat sat one of Ali's subordinate commanders, complete with AK-47 and handheld radio. The only way to distinguish a foot soldier from a leader was the radio. And the danger of everyone, friend and foe, dressing alike is that it increases the possibilities of a blue-on-blue engagement, that is, *friendly* fire. We would really have to be careful once we got into combat.

Next to the commander sat the most valuable player of the tournament so far, Adam Khan. Ironhead and Bryan were perched like locals in the truck bed. Their guns were hidden but ready, and their eyes peered slightly above their colorful kaffiyehs. We headed for the front, and the general seemed to loosen up a bit. Obviously happy to be visiting his men, he commented, "What is mine is yours." It was an Afghan custom to do what he could for his guests and I liked the sound of it.

The drive to the front was an adventure in itself. Bone-jarring terrain with intermittent but well-placed boulders kept our speed down. We squeezed through mud walls that scraped the side mirrors, dodged donkeys, goats, children, and negotiated two precarious valley walls and a deep dry riverbed. The ride was worse than a roller coaster. Ali was constantly on his radio, and his hands-on command style was impressive. There seemed to be no end to his providing directions and guidance and receiving reports. His complete involvement and total command made me wonder just how fast this whole thing would unravel if he were to buy the farm. The chain of command had General Ali at the top, but was rooted by a flat lateral line of combat field commanders. We had a lot riding on this one man.

After thirty minutes, we rounded a turn and came upon the astonishing place called Press Pool Ridge. Round tents in bright red, green, and orange covered the rocky knoll to our front. The best spots for a long-range camera on a tripod facing the mountains had been staked out long ago. White vans and SUVs were scattered everywhere, and there was a tangled forest of satellite antennas and spotlights, all ready to carry the nightly story to the world.

I put on the brakes. "We can't go any farther," I said to Adam Khan, without taking my eyes off the mass of folks only a hundred yards down the road. I asked him to emphasize to the general how important it was that we not to be seen by anyone outside of his fighters—particularly the media.

Ali responded that news reporters were throughout the area toward which we were heading, but he agreed that he also wanted to keep us out of sight. The tinted windows helped. *We're starting to click,* I thought, and he said something else.

"General Ali says he needs to go up there to make an appearance," Adam Khan explained. "The reporters expect it, and he needs to be seen by his men."

"That's cool, but we aren't going with him. I'm not taking this truck up there with my guys in the back," I responded. "The place is way too crowded."

After a few seconds of discussion with Adam Khan, the general opened the door, stepped onto the rocky soil, and walked purposefully toward the mass of journalists. Sure enough, a heads-up reporter spotted the general and sounded the alarm. They all swarmed toward him.

We stayed put to watch, intending to wait for Ali's return to the truck, but one smart reporter had not been fooled. In less than a minute, a white van backed from the line of parked vehicles and turned our way.

Time for some emergency driving, but as I tried to turn the truck around to leave, the white van sped up close to our rear bumper and a small, blond, middle-aged woman dressed in a midlength dark coat with a gray scarf wrapped around her neck jumped out and approached Ironhead and Bryan, whose faces were covered.

"Have you all seen Usama bin Laden?" *Well, that isn't necessarily a surprise question,* they thought. *But does she realize that we are Americans?*

We took off, telling the subordinate commander with us to call General Ali and explain why we had ditched him. He would have to catch another ride.

In the mirror, I saw through our road dust that this reporter was not giving up easily. The van driver was in full pursuit, coming rapidly over the crest of the hill behind us. With Ironhead and Bryan holding on in the bed of the truck, I sped up. *This is ridiculous. How are we supposed to fight this war if we have to hide from the damned reporters?*

"Adam Khan, screw this. Have your buddy there jump out at the next turn, raise his AK-47 to get their attention, and stop that van! We'll keep going back to the schoolhouse."

"Sounds good!" After telling the muhj commander what we needed, Adam Khan gave me a nod and I hit the brakes. The commander dismounted even before the truck came to a halt and stepped into the middle of the road with his AK-47 over his head to bring the pesky press van to a stop. I could hear Ironhead and Bryan let out sighs of relief as we left the reporter, her crew, and the guard to figure things out among themselves.

Well, that trip sure went less than well: The press is closer to the front line than we are. We abandoned our general and got chased away by a blonde in a TV truck. Some warriors we are.

That night we gathered in the CIA's corner room of the schoolhouse. Sergeant Major Ironhead, Bryan, and I sat with a few CIA officers, while Adam Khan, Ali, and the aide-translator Ghulbihar were on a tightly woven green and white Afghan carpet. On any battlefield, you can bet the CIA has the best accommodations available. On another carpet, in the center of the group, were several small green-tinted teacups. A steaming kettle and basket of nuts followed moments later.

The carpet and place servings were in stark contradiction to the techno spreads of the CIA military and civilian gear hugging the walls. Black and silver radios and antennas, various equipment stored in black boxes, night vision goggles, satellite phones, and extra AK-47 magazines were carefully positioned for quick use.

After dispensing with the pleasantries, Ali reiterated his desire to end this battle as soon as possible and committed to doing whatever it took. But he also warned that some local tribes claiming loyalty to him could easily be bought off and change allegiances.

George immediately brought up the increasing crowd of journalists and asked what the general planned to do about them. Ali answered that he had assigned an individual escort to every journalist to take charge of them while they were here. "I also have ordered more checkpoints to control the reporters and keep them away from here," he said with confidence. My thoughts flashed back to the aggressive TV van that had been on our tail, and I believed the general might be overestimating his ability to control the ever-persistent press. The answer sounded rehearsed, too good to be true, and it was.

During the meeting, one of Ali's frontline commanders was ushered in. He rendered all the courtesies toward the general before sitting down. Ali introduced him as the commander of the fedayeen—men of sacrifice—who were Ali's best troops, some eighty of them. He had just returned from an hour-long skirmish with al Qaeda fighters just above the foothills.

He said the fedayeen attacked just before nightfall, and that they were successful in seizing three caves and killing several enemy fighters, but an unknown number escaped. Surprisingly, the commander's impromptu after-action review also highlighted what his men had done wrong.

He spoke of how al Qaeda counterattacked while his men were clearing the second of the three caves. His muhj were freezing in the hills, and always took plenty of time for freebooting and securing the spoils of war, particularly anything to keep them warm. After sustaining eight wounded and three men killed in action, the commander decided to give up the hard-earned caves and retreat for the evening.

Someone asked him to describe the al Qaeda fighters. "All black, from head to toe, with hoods masking their light-skinned faces," he responded enthusiastically, as if trying to convince us of his sincerity.

We were aware that the preferred Taliban dress was black on black, a semiuniform so distinctive that it was added to the rules of engagement early in the war: All black equaled Taliban or al Qaeda, which equaled threat, which equaled authorization of lethal force.

"Why did you retreat and give up the hard-earned caves and trenches?" I asked the fedayeen commander.

"It is too dark and dangerous at night," he stated, with a sheepish glance at General Ali. "We must rest at night and partake of food and drink."

The common daily itinerary for a Muslim fighter during the holy month of Ramadan required fasting from sunup to sundown for thirty consecutive days. Throughout this oncoming battle, that ancient Islamic tradition proved to serve as a consistent default for inaction by the muhj. Apparently the Muslim enemy also respected the same Quranic tradition.

In other words, everyone typically took a breather from the fighting at night in order to get some chow, grab some sleep, regroup, and maneuver forces into position for the next day's skirmishes. We thought that this particular fight that had been so carefully described by the fedayeen commander seemed to have been possibly staged for our benefit.

Ali and George began to bicker, with the big Texan pressing the general about supporting our move into the mountains with his fighters, and goading him about his lack of aggressiveness during the last couple of days.

Ali jabbed back at the CIA, arguing that Tora Bora was not his only area of concern. He had two thousand fighters at Tora Bora, but his other four thousand men were needed to run the everyday policing of Jalalabad and the outlying areas of the big and troublesome city. It might be possible to bring a few thousand more fighters, if only he had weapons to give them. That meant more money.

George didn't blink. He reiterated that he would provide everything Ali needed to accomplish the mission of killing bin Laden. I figured another black duffel bag of cash was about to be opened.

But the good news was that Ali had agreed, if only halfheartedly, to Dailey's three requirements, and that was the affirmation we needed before our boss would agree to do much more than sit around the schoolhouse waiting for a bin Laden sighting. Ali promised to provide us with guides to navigate the mountain trails, and also granted Bryan's request for pack mules to help move our equipment up the mountains. And he would position our forces with his.

He further pledged to do what he could to help if we ran into significant trouble in the mountains, essentially signing up to provide us with a

QRF, should we get into a mess. We doubted the "quick" part of any Afghan QRF. One simple look at the daunting mountains was enough to convey that we would have to hold on for a good while before any of Ali's men could reach us. It would take them hours, possibly days, to move up the mountains and flush out the al Qaeda fighters.

Throw in the complications that we like to fight at night, while the muhj prefer to sleep, and that we were in the middle of Ramadan, which had its own time limitations. Our chances of being able to depend on any of Ali's men coming to help us were slim to none, but beggars couldn't be too choosy. The nearest American QRF was two and a half hours away by helicopter. Those birds would have to land in the foothills to offload because of the SAM and RPG threats and the lack of suitable landing zones or fast-rope points in the mountains. So any Ranger QRF would have to start from the same spot as the muhj.

Nonetheless, Ali had taken the moral high ground and we left it at that. I took him at his word and believed he would send help.

After the meeting broke up, I went back into our room and disconnected my night vision goggles from my helmet, then walked the half-dozen yards over to General Ali's quarters. His trusty aide Ghulbihar was already dutifully stooped outside the door to await any of his general's wishes. I explained that I wanted to show Ali something important, how well we can see at night. To reach a boss, you first have to go through the receptionist, so I took time to demonstrate the NVGs for Ghulbihar. It helped persuade him.

Ali was tired but, ever the gracious host, acceded to my bothersome meddling. He was already in bed, but sat up. I knelt next to him.

First, I placed the goggles in front of my own eyes while Ghulbihar explained what I was doing. The slight flicker of a single gas lantern sitting in the far corner illuminated the general's all-white pajamas and made me wonder if I should have removed my boots before entering and stepping on the carpet. I turned the goggles around and carefully placed them in front of his eyes. Ali leaned toward them with both eyes wide open. The green glow from the NVGs greatly amplified the light of that gas lantern and highlighted his deep facial wrinkles.

I spoke to Ali directly, as if he understood English. "General, with these green eyes, we can hunt for bin Laden at night and see al Qaeda, but not be seen."

After Ghulbihar translated, the general sighed deeply, then tilted the goggles toward the window, which offered a view of the ongoing bombing of the distant mountains. I told him that the NVGs give a clear view in the dark at ranges in excess of three hundred meters on a starry night. He wasn't sold on the magic. "Maybe you can see at night, but al Qaeda does not sleep," he said. "They have brothers guarding every path and trail."

I couldn't resist a quick lesson on tactics, waiting patiently while Ghulbihar translated each sentence. "We need to get in and among al Qaeda to defeat them. We can kill those guards. You need to keep the terrain that your fighters capture, and not retreat at sundown. We will go with your men. You have my word," I told Ali. "Once my men get close enough to see the enemy, they will make the bombs much more effective, killing more enemy faster and ending the fight sooner."

Ali handed back the NVGs. He looked at me, rubbed his beads in his left hand, and mumbled something. "The general wishes to sleep. He asks you do the same," Ghulbihar politely translated.

Good enough. Let the guy sleep on it. I don't need an answer right now anyway. The boys are still two days away. I nodded to the general, smiled as if to say we are gonna have some fun here, then took my toy back to my own room.

7

Leaders' Recon

> So we believe that the defeat of America is something achievable—with the permission of God—and it is easier for us—with the permission of God—than the defeat of the Soviet Empire previously.
> —USAMA BIN LADEN, OCTOBER 21, 2001

Bernie's radio check back to Bagram awoke us on the morning of December 8, 2001. We had stayed up late taking stock of our situation and had managed only an hour or two of sleep during a night that had been chilly and restless. We dug in our rucks for some MRE packets that would be a cold breakfast meal and grabbed bottles of water from a box outside the flimsy wooden door.

As we slowly came to life, I could not help thinking how lucky and proud we were to have been handed this mission. Here we were, thousands of miles away from Ground Zero in New York City, at the most extreme and sharpest end of the spear in the hunt for Usama bin Laden. We were enormously thankful for the opportunity.

It was going to be "fly by the seat of your pants" war fighting, in which it would be impossible to predict what might happen within the next hour, much less a day in advance. My formal military schooling had ended as a young infantry captain at Fort Benning in 1995, where the approved course curriculum contained little on the art of ambiguous and unconventional fighting while connected at the hip to some third world warlord.

This type of work, however, was practiced at the Special Warfare Center at Fort Bragg, and few officers understood it better than the Task Force Dagger commander, Colonel Mulholland, who did not like it at all. He had voiced his strong objections to going after al Qaeda in a mountainous environment with an unknown army of indigenous fighters and without a solid support structure in place. If things fell apart from here on out, nobody could blame Mulholland. He had sent up the red flags of warning.

Our own task force commander was not without his own reservations. General Dailey certainly could not be described as impetuous or flippant when the lives of his men were on the line.* In fact, the general leaned slightly toward the cautious side, as most prudent commanders often do. But Dailey also knew the opportunities to nail bin Laden were going to be few and far between, and killing bin Laden was the premier mission of the war to date, no doubt about it. It required a commander willing to take a deep breath, grasp the moment, suppress the high-risk nature of the mission, and let loose the dogs of war. Whether or not Dailey was personally comfortable with the whole deal or not was irrelevant. He had pulled the trigger, and we respected him for that.

We had been warned by the CIA guys the day before that General Ali was a master of doublespeak, and often talked in circles. He would promise the world, but rarely deliver if he did not see the promise as being useful or helpful to his own agenda. The more time we spent in Afghanistan working with indigenous fighters and warlords, the more we realized Ali's behavior was far from unique. It was just common to the culture. You don't obtain warlord status without being able to play both sides, and the middle, and around the edges, too.

On the surface, Ali was physically small, quiet, and unassuming. His

---

* Retired Lieutenant General Dell Dailey's exploits as the JSOC commander are well recounted in numerous books by various authors. In *Jawbreaker,* Gary Berntsen shares his personal interaction with Dailey during the opening days of Operation Enduring Freedom in Afghanistan. In Sean Naylor's *Not a Good Day to Die,* and in *Cobra II,* by Michael Gordon and Bernard Trainor, the friction between Delta and Dailey is shared in detail.

formal schooling ended in the sixth grade, which meant little in this harsh environment. What did matter were the hard-knocks education, street experience, and the reputation he earned fighting the Soviets and rival tribes as a young mujahidee. These characteristics had produced a dangerous mix of politician, manager, and warlord who, when stirred sufficiently, became as cocky as a cornered rooster in a henhouse.

General Ali was in good spirits that morning, and was quick to praise his own efforts. His men "generally" had bin Laden surrounded and cut off from any support by the locals, and Ali strongly implied that escaping from Tora Bora was not an option for the al Qaeda leader. This was welcome news to us, for we did not have the manpower, or the permission, to surround the massive battlefield, and we didn't expect a sizable infusion of reinforcements anytime soon.

We crossed our fingers and took the general's declaration at face value, since it meshed with the fact that few other people believed the al Qaeda leader would cut and run. Indeed, early radio intercepts told us bin Laden wanted a fight in the mountains, which had been prepared so well in advance. Al Qaeda was confident it could stem the fighting spirit of their fellow Muslim adversaries so as to better focus attention on the American forces that were assumed to be coming.

So we had no reason to doubt that bin Laden wouldn't fight to the death.

The Prophet Muhammad faced worse odds at the Battle of Badr in the seventh century, an event well known in Islamic circles. Muhammad's army believed their victory against an overwhelming force of unbelievers was possible only by placing their fate in the hands of Allah.

Certainly, bin Laden, who repeatedly invoked the life, times, and sayings of Muhammad in his war against Crusaders and Jews, knew that a retreat in the face of onrushing *kufars* would expose him as a superficial follower of Allah's will and an apostate himself.

After the aborted attempt to get a look at the front lines before running from the press, General Ali offered to take us to the front again this morning. The general said he had taken care of the media problem, so Bryan, Adam Khan, and I agreed to go. We *had* to go.

George went along as well, a good move, since Ali seemed to respect him. General Ali was not stupid. He knew that George held the large sums of money he so eagerly desired and he seemed to be figuring out that the newly arrived commandos represented his best chance of eliminating bin Laden. The body of Usama bin Laden, dead or alive, equaled a cool $25 million bonus.

This time, we jumped in Ali's lime green SUV and departed the schoolhouse headed for the southern foothills along the western flank of the battlefield. A few minutes after crossing the dry streambed, Ali's radio came alive. One of his forward commanders was begging him to stop the bombs from pounding their positions. A U.S. Air Force B-52 was overhead and supposedly their bombs were hitting the friendly muhj, having mistaken them for al Qaeda. *Easy to do from 30,000 feet when everybody is dressed the same down here.*

Ali pleaded for George to stop the bombing, and George looked at Bryan and me sitting in the backseat. "Can you guys get them to stop?"

"Uh, well, er, okay. Pull over," I said. I jumped from the SUV, grabbed the handheld GlobalStar satellite phone from my belt and dialed up the guys back at Bagram, who quickly relayed the message.

Whether or not the word would make it all the way to the aircraft high above the clouds was anyone's guess, but I jumped back in the vehicle and gave George a thumbs-up. Ali smiled and thanked us graciously, then radioed his forward commander, likely telling him the problem had been fixed. Bryan and I looked at each other with poker faces, savoring the moment as we rolled along, knowing that a B-52 could only carry so many bombs.

Sure enough, the bomber went Winchester—empty on ammo—and curled out of the area to return to its base. In a real sense, this unforeseen event likely raised our stock with Ali. Having some Americans who could order up or cancel falling bombs whenever they wanted might not be a bad idea after all.

We passed through the press with no problem that day, but not necessarily because of Ali's promise the night before. More likely, most reporters were napping inside their tents after having stayed up all night awaiting a much anticipated drop of a giant BLU-82 bomb. The drop had been postponed several times already.

Developed in the 1960s to cut helicopter landing zones in the triple-canopy jungle of Vietnam, the fifteen-thousand-pound BLU-82 was tested during Desert Storm to clear minefields. Now receiving renewed attention in the new global war on terror, it had been yanked out of mothballs as a potential cave buster. If the $28,000 bomb, which was about the size of a Volkswagen Beetle, could nail bin Laden, or even scare the shit out of him, it came at a bargain price.

As we crept along a north-south narrow dirt road that skirted the edge of a major streambed, we passed small pockets of Ali's fighters. We noticed among them a couple of light-skinned Afghans who wore lighter colored beards than the traditional dark-skinned locals. We learned they were from Nuristan Province, and their appearance gave us a little more confidence that we gringos might be able to fit into the surroundings.

The road ended a couple of kilometers farther south, where we dismounted and moved into the foothills. The air seemed thinner, even at this relatively low altitude, and we outlanders were forced to breathe more heavily while trying to hide the pounding of our hearts. Ali appeared to be immune to the physical strain.

After several hundred meters of tough ground, we reached two aging T-55 battle tanks and a T-62, all formerly Soviet property and now controlled by the muhj. They were ominously positioned, with a commanding view of the entire mountain range, their main gun tubes raised skyward as if they were ready to shoot rounds over the tall peaks and hit Pakistan. A couple of muhj crewmen were still asleep on the ground behind one of the tanks, wrapped in thin blankets. Two alert fighters had seen the general's vehicle approaching and were on their feet, waving and smiling, certainly wondering who the hell the new light-skinned fellas accompanying Ali were.

Somewhere up in those beautiful White Mountains waited a thousand or more al Qaeda fighters, hunkered down and largely invisible to the American bombers circling overhead and invisible to us on the ground as well.

Bryan and I made a few notes, checked our maps a dozen times, and marked our location on our Garmin GPSs. Ali pointed to the bombers far above and said that if the bombers were not overhead, then al Qaeda mortars would be in full swing and certainly would have welcomed us by now.

He also mentioned that enemy snipers had been harassing his tank crews the last few days, which kept his men down behind the tanks or buttoned up inside. Ali seemed to be testing us, always alert to our reactions.

About twenty minutes later, we loaded into the vehicle and drove back through the journalists' base camp again before turning south to head for the eastern front. The drive was quiet until we turned the last corner, where we came face-to-face with dozens of reporters mingling with muhj fighters.

As Adam Khan maneuvered to turn the vehicle around, we noticed two more tanks and a couple of armored personnel carriers. Whether or not they worked was anyone's guess, but they apparently made excellent backdrops for the international picture-taking media. The news of a sweet photo spot must have spread quickly that morning. As we made our way back to the schoolhouse, we counted four more press vehicles crammed with reporters and photographers zooming past us, heading to the choice real estate and the collection of old armor before their next deadline.

As much as Ali's inability to control the roaming scores of journalists and their paid local *chogi* boys had become a problem, the real issue was the questionable constraint placed on us by our higher headquarters. The requirement to not be seen or photographed by the press actually limited our freedom of movement more than the enemy did.

Both comical and frustrating at the same time, the snag prompted George to berate Ali a little. He reminded him again of the importance of keeping the presence of American commandos secret, for his own good and ours. Ali nodded in slight shame, and again shrugged his shoulders as if to say that he was unsure whether his men had carried out his order for media control. This is when we started to wonder if Ali's orders were ever disseminated at all, much less enforced, or if such orders were more like advice to be taken or left at one's whim.

For the second time in as many days, our attempts to conduct a solid reconnaissance of the battlefield had met with limited results, but that was about to change.

As we arrived at the schoolhouse, a notorious special guest was waiting for General Ali, the distinguished-looking rival warlord Haji Zaman Ghamshareek, the defense minister of the Eastern Shura and leader of a second opposition group of muhj. About a dozen of his fighters were with him. We vividly remembered that it had been Zaman's boys who had tried to swipe our trucks just a few nights earlier.

In his fifties, Zaman was of average size, and his jet-black hair so noticeably contrasted with his close-cropped gray beard that I wondered whether he colored it. He wore a tan traditional Afghan wool hat and had a habit of talking with his hands, which exposed surprisingly well-manicured fingernails. He was well educated, and had at least an elementary command of the English language.

Zaman had been one of the more infamous mujahideen junior commanders during the Soviet-Afghan War. When the Taliban took over, Zaman departed Afghanistan for France. He had visited Alexandria, Virginia, numerous times over the years and was known to favor the bite of fine Johnny Walker Red scotch.

When the Taliban fell from grace after 9/11, the articulate and cunning warlord returned to his homeland to reclaim his former VIP status. He was said to have influential friends within neighboring Pakistan, including members of the Pakistani intelligence service.

Fundamentally, his rivalry with Ali stemmed from the desire of both men to be the sole ruler of Nangarhar Province in general, and the city of Jalalabad specifically.

Zaman was an ethnic Pashtun, whereas General Ali claimed allegiance to the minority Pashai tribe, which meant that he had to augment his small following of loyal fighters with men from other tribes. The recruitment effort could secure loyalty only as long as the daily CIA paycheck continued, highlighting the importance of keeping George happy. For the present, Zaman's rival group of muhj was allied with, but subordinate to, Ali's command for this particular battle. Keeping all of the players straight was going to be difficult.

It did not take a master of observation to notice the high tension between the two warlords and their men as Ali and Zaman met on the front porch and shared some tea. After a few minutes of the usual meaningless pleasant welcoming, they were arguing on a subject unknown to us, so George and Adam Khan joined them.

Zaman was disagreeing with Ali's tactics. He felt that relying solely on heavy bombing without threatening al Qaeda with maneuver forces was a mistake. Zaman even pressed Ali to employ the new American commandos immediately. All of that was good news to us. *Should we be dealing with this guy instead?*

Zaman then offered to take us right up to the front, all the way up, to get a better look. He confidently said there would be no problems with the press.

Ali balked. Making the same trip again unnerved him, but after some squabbling between the two, Zaman seemed to have shamed Ali into it. *Were they playing chicken?*

Ali agreed to go, but he was adamant that the number of vehicles be limited to reduce the attention we would surely receive from both al Qaeda and the press.

As the bickering came to an end, I put in a fresh wad of Redman leaf chew and hopped in the general's SUV to head to the front. Zaman ignored Ali's desire to limit the number of vehicles, so our lime green SUV was just one of eight vehicles making the trip, and every pickup truck was jam-packed with gun-toting muhj.

Officially, all of them were Ali's fighters, but some were more loyal to Zaman. The other warlord seemed more aggressive, but Adam Khan told us after the meeting that Ali had accused Zaman of allowing forty Arabs to pass through his lines and escape into Pakistan last night. Zaman vehemently denied it. Keeping score of who was doing what to whom was difficult.

Enemy spotters high in the mountains must have laughed at the massive dust trail created by our line of slow-moving vehicles. Forget a stealthy approach. They saw us coming. The general was noticeably flustered, and bitched and moaned about Haji Zaman during the entire trip, calling Zaman a "politician" who was only interested in personal fame and fortune.

We took a slightly different route this time in hopes of bypassing the press, but no luck. The media seemed to have every road into Tora

Delta operators Jamie, left, and the author, right, during a low-visibility urban reconnaissance mission in the Balkans circa 2000. *(U.S. Govt)*

In late November 2001 Secretary of Defense Donald Rumsfeld visited Delta. Here the author takes time out from the posted itinerary to introduce the secretary to longtime Delta operator Cos. Cos was wounded during the initial raid into Afghanistan and was home recovering from his wounds. *(U.S. Govt)*

During the drive from Kabul to Jalalabad in early December 2001, one of the local trucks broke an axle. Adam Khan flagged down and commandeered a passing truck. Sergeant Major Ironhead,

Sergeant Major Bryan, Shag, and the author help cross-load 1,000 brand-new AK-47s earmarked for the Eastern Alliance Opposition Group. *(U.S. Govt)*

Sergeant Major Ironhead shown after a harrowing resupply mission to the boys in Mission Support Sites (MSS) Grinch. With helicopters not available everything was carried on their backs. Ironhead made the resupply trip twice, covering over twenty kilometers and gaining 3,000 feet in altitude each trip. *(U.S. Govt)*

Members of India Team and MSS Monkey near hilltop 2685—close to 9,000 feet high. *(US Govt)*

How are we going to be successful?

- End state - Kill/Capture UBL

- OG supported operation

- Unilateral Recce for immediate vetted ground truth of cave sanctuary
  - Recce conduct CAS on area to pressure Bin Laden to relocate
  - Provide EW to Aslt Force

- Assault Force - lower altitude concentration focusing on likely resupply and UBL exfil routes ε valley floor
  - At day - higher up to act as additional OP to EW Recce
  - At night - conduct road interdiction/ambush of elements moving toward or away from cave
    - PSYOP effect
    - BDA capability
    - pressures UBL to move
    - Night fighting capability
    - effects UBL supply and advance elements

- OG/ODA - Seal LOC's for resupply or UBL fleeing
  - Resupply Recce/Aslt as needed
  - Provide mobility to reposition force
  - OG presence might draw Al Qaeda fires out of cave

Handwritten notes composed by the author in late November 2001 that served as the baseline concept of the operation to hunt Usama bin Laden at Tora Bora.

Under a bright late morning sun on December 7, 2001, and within view of al Qaeda's mountain sanctuary at Tora Bora, left to right, Adam Khan, the author, and CIA chief George persuade General Hazret Ali, wearing hat, to accept several dozen American commandos and attack up the mountains. *(U.S. Govt)*

The first Americans to enter Tora Bora were sent by CIA chief Gary Berntsen and Lt. Col. Mark Sutter, commander of the Northern Advance Force Operations element. At enormous risk these men were sent to the mountains to do two things—confirm the presence of al Qaeda fighters and kill as many as they could. Within a few hours of reaching a high peak, these extraordinarily brave men accomplished both tasks—which served as the impetus to send our task force to the battle. *(U.S. Govt)*

A group of 2002 Toyota pickup trucks carefully parked to remain out of sight from long-range lenses across the valley at Press Pool Ridge. Prior to deploying to Afghanistan, the Delta mechanics made a dozen modifications to the vehicles to meet various mission requirements. Here Delta snipers Ski and Dallas pull guard in the early morning hours of December 10, 2001. This home sat just forty yards from the schoolhouse. *(U.S. Govt)*

Delta Force operators waiting in the foothills for the "cease-fire" to play out before ascending the mountains into al Qaeda's sanctuary. Left to right, Crapshoot, Blinky, Brandon, and Lowblow. Kneeling, Pope and Juice. *(U.S. Govt)*

Leader of one of two Mission Support Sites, assault troop Sergeant Major Jim, code-named Grinch, waits during the "cease-fire." His patience was running out rapidly. *(U.S. Govt)*

Jackal team snipers, left to right, Lowblow, Murph, Hopper, and air force combat controller the Admiral, second from left, sitting, wait for the order to proceed up the mountain during the "cease-fire." Two days earlier, Hopper and the Admiral participated in a mujahideen frontal attack on al Qaeda's dug-in strong point. During the fighting both of them, along with fellow American Adam Khan, were abandoned by the muhj and forced to escape and evade capture. *(US Govt)*

The "head shed" of MSS Monkey high in the Tora Bora Mountains. MSS Monkey penetrated the western side of al Qaeda's sanctuary, giving us true 24/7 capability to punish enemy fighters. Left to right, Dirty, Shen Dog, Bryan, and a young mujahideen scout. *(US Govt)*

During a lull in the battle the CIA chief of Team Jawbreaker Juliet does what he can to hold the fragile alliance of two Afghan warlords together. George spent a significant amount of time refereeing long-held differences and animosity between the two. Left to right, Haji Zaman Ghamshareek, Gen. Hazret Ali, George, and Ali's trusty aide, Ghulbihar, who translated for the group. *(U.S. Govt)*

Delta snipers Ski, kneeling, and Dallas comb over the remains of an al Qaeda 14.5mm antiaircraft piece positioned high in the Tora Bora Mountains. Al Qaeda gunners hid inside the cave until the bombers passed over and moved to the AAA piece in anticipation of shooting down an American helicopter. *(U.S. Govt)*

12/14/2001

American controllers had to penetrate deep into the mountains to positions close enough to identify moving al Qaeda fighters and cave and bunker entrances with the naked eye. Once in position the controllers relayed the correct coordinates to the aircraft or designated the targets using infrared lasers. *(U.S. Govt)*

Delta assaulters, left to right, the Kid and Grumpy, moving with the muhj deeper into al Qaeda's sanctuary. Notice the large rucksacks carried by the Americans and the knapsack and bedroll carried by the muhj. It took a few days of leadership by example by the Americans to convince the muhj to remain in the mountains at night to retain hard-won terrain and not retreat at nightfall. Eventually the muhj came around. *(U.S. Govt)*

Delta operator Noodle shares a smoke with an allied muhj during a lull in the fighting. The Afghan, who preferred smoking hashish while Noodle favored Marlboro, is seen rolling up his pants leg to expose a vicious battle scar. When asked by Noodle how he came to have the scar, he simply replied, "Al Qaeda!" *(U.S. Govt)*

Assaulter Grumpy reads the fine print on the bottled water al Qaeda fighters left behind in their caves as they made their hasty retreat. *(U.S. Govt)*

Snipers Hopper and Shrek return to the MSS after scouting out a new forward observation post. *(U.S. Govt)*

Charlie team, part of MSS Monkey, pauses for a quick snapshot with a muhj subordinate commander. The operators at Tora Bora went into the mountains without Kevlar helmets or body armor. (L to R) Nitro, Bullets, muhj commander, Catfish, Hobbit, Stalker, and Shamus. *(U.S. Govt)*

A special intelligence collector attached to Delta questions al Qaeda prisoners before they descend the mountain. The muhj were very nervous about this and feared the Americans would kill any fighters on sight and in cold blood. *(U.S. Govt)*

Tons of ammunition, mostly Chinese-made 7.62mm and 14.5mm, filled numerous caves in the mountains. Well camouflaged from the air, most of the caves remained hidden from view until the observer was upon them. *(U.S. Govt)*

On a cold winter morning Delta assaulter Hobbit returns from an early scout for al Qaeda fighters high in the Tora Bora Mountains. *(U.S. Govt)*

Early on the morning of 16 December 2001, members of MSS Monkey, both American and British commandos, linked up with Kilo team from MSS Grinch in the forwardmost location on the western edge of the battlefield. Here they pause before continuing the push on al Qaeda positions deeper in the Tora Bora Mountains. *(U.S. Govt)*

An operator snaps a photo from inside one of al Qaeda's caves with his back to the far wall as an allied muhj enters. The enemy fighters made such a quick retreat from this cave that they left the water boiling and the fire smoldering. This was typical of the carved-out positions that potholed the Tora Bora complex. *(U.S. Govt)*

Three members of the British Special Boat Service brew up a spot of tea while waiting for the word to move out. A dozen British commandos participated in the Battle of Tora Bora and played a significant role in routing al Qaeda from their previously believed impenetrable mountain redoubt. *(U.S. Govt)*

Delta Force snipers Dugan—the brawn—and Jester—the brain—two weeks after the battle. These were the first two operators of our task force to deploy into the foothills and link up with a half-dozen Green Berets to direct bombs and bullets on al Qaeda fighters and positions. *(U.S. Govt)*

Jackal team a week after the battle, now redeployed to a warmer part of Afghanistan. On the ends are team leader Hopper and air force combat controller the Admiral—both of them heroes of the early days at Tora Bora and Silver Star winners. In the center, left to right, Shrek, Murph, and Scrawny. *(U.S. Govt)*

Delta operators crammed inside the back of a 2½-ton Afghan cargo truck for another trip to Tora Bora in November 2002. After a bone-jarring ride of seven hours the operators scaled a mountain wall and successfully captured a known al Qaeda facilitator suspected of harboring a wounded Bin Laden during the last few days of the battle eleven months earlier. *(U.S. Govt)*

Eleven months after the battle, most of the men who participated in the fight gathered atop the Speer Medical Clinic—named in honor of Delta Force medic Chris Speer, killed in action in July 2002—to receive their awards. This was the same building we occupied and slept in on December 5 before moving to Tora Bora. Here the author pins the Bronze Star and Combat Infantryman's Badge, 2nd Award, on the chest of team leader Stormin', a.k.a. the Bod. Seen on the right are Skeeter and the Kid. *(U.S. Govt)*

Bora covered. Nonetheless, we pressed on through and continued to the front.

Well past the press, the convoy stopped along the right edge of the narrow dirt road, and General Ali, George of the CIA, Adam Khan, and I moved up the high ground to get a look over the hill toward the front lines. I looked skyward in hopes of seeing reassuring signs of aircraft contrails. None!

Haji Zaman arrived with several of his men and started to point out the enemy positions. His English was not much better than a first-grader's, but it was good enough for me to understand as he briefed us on the lay of the battlefield.

While we stood there, a single enemy mortar round dropped in about a hundred meters to our front right and exploded. Zaman said it was a 120mm, but to me it seemed more like an 82mm. It had landed too far away to hit us and I thought that we were just out of range, that the gunners had given it everything they had, but didn't make it.

The incident spurred Zaman to complain of how he had been unable to find and destroy the enemy mortars that had plagued them for a week. That assessment jived with Ali's.

Not long afterward, six or seven more mortar rounds landed and detonated simultaneously to our front, this time only about fifty meters away. The smoke signature revealed a linear sheaf of impacts spread across roughly five hundred meters. This was textbook work—a single tube firing a spotter first round, then multiple tubes using that one to adjust range and fire for effect. This signaled three things to me.

First, al Qaeda certainly had us under observation from somewhere up in the mountains. Second, there definitely was more than one mortar tube at work. Third, and most important, was that these were not being operated by just some bums hastily dropping rounds down the tubes: The crews obviously were well versed in the finer points of indirect fire and trained in bipod and bubble manipulation.

Zaman and Ali were standing by their vehicles, kind of yelling at each other, a useless sort of bickering that would prove to be routine every time they got together. The only words I recognized in their rapidfire conversation were "al Qaeda, al Qaeda."

With wild arm gestures, Zaman was daring General Ali to venture closer to the front lines and see for himself why they had not been able to get past the dug-in defenses and al Qaeda trenches. Ali clearly was uncomfortable and didn't want to continue.

"Ask the American commando what he thinks," Zaman barked.

I told them both that the current observation posts did not offer enough views to support an advance deeper into the mountains. I still needed a firsthand look at the battlefield to refine our plan of action.

As soon as Zaman understood that I still wanted to go forward, he told his men to get into their pickups. The cautious Ali once again said he did not think it wise to go farther, now adding the reason that darkness was near.

Zaman, as a further insult to Ali, invited me to ride with him, an offer that I declined. Our convoy crawled south another three hundred meters before Ali decided caution was the better part of valor and stopped his vehicle again. When Zaman saw that in his rearview mirror, he also stopped and came back on foot. Another heated discussion erupted between the two muhj warlords, with Adam Khan refereeing and translating. Ali tried in vain to raise one of his subordinate commanders up ahead over the radio.

"What do you want to do, Dalton?" Adam Khan asked.

Nothing had changed for me. "Tell them I absolutely must get a look at the enemy positions. It's critical to see what lies ahead. If it will get things going, then I'll get in with Zaman and link up with you guys later."

Zaman liked that idea and smiled broadly, which made Ali even more nervous. "The general is deeply worried about getting George and you hurt," Adam Khan offered. "He believes he will be blamed."

"Do you *really* need to go any farther?" asked George, who was frustrated with the whole show and its accompanying histrionics. He already knew the answer.

That left Ali as the sole vote against moving up. He didn't like it, but gave in, and the little convoy headed deeper into the base of the mountains.

Another three hundred meters. Another stop. It was time to ditch those mortar magnets, the vehicles, and continue forward on foot, which neither warlord was keen to do. They finally agreed on something—that it was getting dangerous.

The muhj dismounted and the vehicles were taken around the hill to a position out of the enemy's view, while we headed for the southern hilltop that overlooked the al Qaeda positions. Zaman and George were to our right and a little below us as Ali, Adam Khan and I climbed on the east side of the approach.

Finally, however, we had reached a worthwhile spot. From a military tactician's point of view, the terrain to our front was ugly for an attacking force. We had been told that al Qaeda held the advantage of the high ground and assumed they were well positioned to thwart any advance on foot. After seeing it firsthand, all doubts were gone. Numerous positions provided al Qaeda interlocking fields of fire and excellent observation of anyone approaching. For the attackers, plenty of defilade offered respite from direct fire but not from the high angle of mortar rounds. We were about to get proof of that.

As we talked about the enemy dispositions, several of Zaman's fighters took cover behind some large rocks and others hurried down the hill a bit and went prone. I had heard nothing to warrant such an action, but they had picked up the telltale muffled *thump, thump, thump* of mortar rounds leaving their launch tubes. Our short advance had brought us within range.

Within a few seconds, the mortar rounds came raining down and impacted between our vehicles and where we were standing. The barrage lasted at least two minutes and flung rock, shrapnel, and soil in all directions at blistering speeds. The sound was deafening, and all too personal.

When I looked back, the smack-talking Zaman and all his men had taken cover, but General Ali had not moved. My first inclination was to get my rear end down, but Ali was showing no fear, and stood steady only a few feet from me, which meant I was going to stand firm, too.

A slight smirk was on the general's face as he stared directly into my eyes. He was at ease, almost as if he had been in this situation many times before. OK, I got it, he was brave, but it seemed crazy not to take cover. We had too much riding on this guy to risk having him shredded by some random mortar round just to show up his rival warlord and the visiting Americans.

Ali heatedly resumed discussing the mortars with Zaman, who was cowering on his knees behind a large rock formation. Several more rounds dropped in and exploded so close by that we were both momentarily knocked off balance, but still remained upright. I couldn't tell if Ali was still testing me, or if he was simply placing his life in Allah's hands—a customary gesture expected of a mujahideen commander in battle.

Ali screamed at Zaman, waving his free hand in the air while clutching his radio tightly in the other hand. It was obvious that Ali wanted to leave immediately and probably was telling Zaman that it had been foolish to come this far. Made sense to me.

In beween the impacting of more mortar rounds, the irate general called out, "Look at the vehicles. Who is going to retrieve them?"

Apparently he decided the answer to that question was Adam Khan, who suddenly asked me to hold his AK-47.

"What the hell are you doing?" I demanded. This was getting silly. Adam Khan, in my mind, was just as important to the mission as General Ali.

"The general asks that I get the vehicle," he calmly said.

"Whoaaa! Adam Khan, you are way too important to this gig," I said. "I recommend that you part with a thousand dollars and have one of the muhj go get it."

Adam Khan shook his head and gave a little smile, knowing better than to take my recommendation. The money was no big deal to me, a Westerner, but offering money to some common soldier to act in a dangerous situation would be regarded as an egregious slight on his courage. Another matter of cultural pride.

General Ali changed his mind and ordered one of his bodyguards to retrieve the vehicle. Deciding to build a little bit on the image that had just been explained, I told the general that I, not Adam Khan, would go along with the young fighter.

We ran around the hilltop toward the vehicles, and two more rounds impacted nearby. I crossed the road and took up an overwatch position with my weapon as the fighter broke for the general's vehicle. Another round exploded near the trucks, and this blast threw him down like he was sliding into second base to beat the catcher's throw. Shrapnel had given him a slight wound in the thigh, but he popped back up and hopped forward until he reached the general's SUV. The explosion had blown out the rear window.

I went back to Adam Khan and Ali and tried to explain the obvious—that it was time to stop arguing and start moving. We were definitely under enemy observation, and they had a bead on our location.

It was crazy. I was talking fast, Adam Khan was translating, mortar rounds were bursting all around, Zaman appeared to be frozen in fear, crouched behind his rock, and General Ali just stood there doing whatever it was that he was doing. The sparring warlords seemed quite content just to yap at each other while the enemy was trying to kill us all. Neither was giving any commands, which left everything at a standstill, not a good move on any active battlefield.

If they would not issue orders, then I would. I told them to move their fighters to the back side of the hill, to our rear, and have them spread out. This would get them out of sight of the al Qaeda OPs. I also said not to worry about the vehicles until it got dark, but as Adam Khan translated this, it was immediately obvious that my suggestion was going to be ignored. Mortars or no mortars, these people wanted their vehicles. They were not walking home.

Having come this far, I decided to get a still better look while the mortars were searching for other targets. As the muhj took off running for safety, General Ali, Adam Khan, and I went the other way, crouched over and moving farther up the hill. We crested it just enough to observe the enemy trenches, and were actually eyeballing the enemy's forwardmost lines.

We hoped for some signature of a mortar tube firing or to spot any movement of al Qaeda fighters. No luck! Al Qaeda was smart. They didn't expose themselves. No need to, really, as they knew we were not there to conduct an attack.

Some more mortar rounds looped overhead and impacted behind us and wounded two of Zaman's fighters, prompting the warlord to shake off his paralysis before pleading with us to leave the battlefield. The idiotic game to see who was the braver of the two was definitely over.

Earlier, Zaman had questioned Ali's bravery. Now, the shoe was on the other foot. Ali appeared almost comfortable under fire. As Adam Khan translated, I tried to share with the general the concept of creeping mortar fire, but now that Zaman had blinked first, Ali was also ready to leave. We all took off down the hill.

But we were still in range. As soon as we reached the others, another mortar round landed only fifteen meters away with a tremendous roar. This provided good motivation for us to continue another hundred meters or so, when we saw the lime green SUV and the other vehicles, waiting with the engines humming. We jumped into whatever vehicle had room in a classic Keystone Kops free-for-all and the convoy sped north along the narrow dirt road.

In days to come, this area became known as Mortar Hill, because it was a vital piece of terrain that any attacking force had to transit before attacking the dug-in al Qaeda positions. The trip to the front had been more than worth the risk. Now I knew what we were facing.

As we approached Press Pool Ridge, we found Ali's gutsy young nephew waiting in the middle of the road. He walked over to the general's window and handed him a small shiny video camera taken from one of the photographers. The general was having trouble trying to figure the thing out, so I offered to help.

I flipped open the side screen and rewound the saved footage. As the tape began to play I turned the volume to max so all could listen.

A horrific scene unfolded, gruesome and personally saddening for Ali. The camera zoomed in on a few of Ali's men who had been killed or captured and executed somewhere in the mountains. All were dead and half naked.

The screen went blue for a moment before showing a couple of older men placing two large brown burlap bags on the ground. The camera zoomed in closer as their hands unrolled the outer edges of the bag to expose the contents. Body parts!

Ali sat motionless as the screen blued out again. He bowed his head, and softly said, "We have had no word of these brothers for days. I thought they had changed loyalties." The mystery was solved.

George of the CIA secured the tape for intelligence reasons and handed the camera back to Ali, who leaned out his window and gave it back to his nephew. Warn that Western reporter, he said, but take no action. Should he be caught a second time with this sort of material, the general would be less understanding.

8

We Must Attack

When the hour of crisis comes, remember that forty selected men can shake the world.
—YASOTAY, COLONEL, GENGHIS KHAN'S ARMY

While we were at the front, Sergeant Major Ironhead and Bryan searched the area for a suitable location to hide some forty more Delta operators and ten vehicles. Just north of the schoolhouse, they found a small U-shaped compound with a mud floor that provided enough space for an adequate sleeping area, equipment storage, and vehicle parking.

We bargained to have the muhj who were already living there vacate, but a dozen or so either never got the word or simply chose to bunk with us. We made a couple of attempts to clear them out, but they basically ignored us and went about their business. After a while, we let them be because their presence provided some indigenous cover from roving Big Eye journalist lenses that were positioned over on the next ridgeline.

Even though Ironhead and Bryan negotiated to have the rooms cleaned of all the garbage and human waste, the place was still filthy when our boys moved in. It did not matter much, since we didn't plan to spend too much time inside anyway.

Ironhead and Bryan also managed to designate two areas for helicopters to land, big enough to handle a large supply helicopter and to evacuate any wounded. Landing Zone Condor was just south of the schoolhouse, and the second LZ, Sparrow, was two thousand meters to the east.

We had left our staging base with a fairly solid plan, a course of action that would gain the necessary approvals from the various levels of brass. It was not binding, of course, and once we were able to get a good look at the playing field and the enemy formations, we could easily audible off of it. Now that the game had begun, I didn't expect much pushback from our commander, or from any level above him, for that matter. Things had to remain flexible.

Indeed, the guys back at Bagram, Colonel Ashley and the rest of the staff, were working hard to collect and analyze every piece of intelligence they could get their hands on. Everything from sensitive CIA cables to fixed-wing reconnaissance photos that identified "hot spot" signatures—telltale locations of inhabited caves with warming fires—from 30,000 feet, to signals intelligence (SIGINT) that might help find bin Laden's location. They were what-ifing themselves to death to ensure our success on the battlefield. The Delta Intelligence and Fire Support officers, Brian and Will, worked up a targeting plan to buttress our coming push into the mountains.

Inside our spartan headquarters, we also were dissecting and analyzing what we had learned after the few looks we had gotten at al Qaeda's front lines. We wanted to modify and refine our original battle plan so that it would best fit the reality on the ground.

Bryan worked on the initial reconnaissance plan, while Shag, our Pashto-speaking signals interceptor, was already set up in the room next door, picking up sporadic al Qaeda radio calls, friendly muhj radio traffic, and the transmissions from the international media over on Press Pool Ridge. Shag's talents, and those of his signals teammates who would arrive shortly, gave us a discreet secret weapon that let us keep tabs on everybody in the game.

Bryan recommended that we marry up our reconnaissance guys with the two observation posts set up by the 5th Group Green Berets. Half of Cobra 25 was already in position, roughly a mile from al Qaeda's front lines over on the eastern flank. The other team inserted that day was to relieve the joint CIA and JSOC team that had been in position since December 5. Augmenting those OPs would give us some eyes forward to help develop our attack plan. And once the attack began, we would have our own folks in overwatch positions, men who understood our task, purpose, and intent as we maneuvered on the battlefield. They would be invaluable.

Then we met with General Ali to go over progress, tactics, and battle plans in between sipping on hot tea, grabbing handfuls of nuts, and trying to remain comfortable sitting Indian style on the hard floor. I jotted down the key points in my small green notebook. What I could not get down on paper, I tried to commit to memory and would add it after a meeting.

Ali was adamant about picking the small groups of muhj fighters that would best augment our recon guys and assaulters. We had to be careful who we picked, for Ali claimed that while he had several thousand loyal fighters, not all were controlled by family members, and thus not deemed loyal. Others were under the command of friends, who might or might not be faithful when the going got tough, and still others were handled by longtime rivals and even enemies. Ali was very specific about the latter group, and insisted that we not marry up with those units.

The general offered up some fantastic descriptions in our discussions, no doubt to ensure that he remained the CIA's chosen son and also to create an atmosphere and feeling that bin Laden could not be taken without his personal leadership, as well as his fighters.

Ali described a Balkanized organization among the jihadists, who were grouped by nationality and ethnic lines and separated tactically by mountain passes, valley floors, and ridgelines. Any man who makes a conscious decision to have more enemies than friends, as bin Laden certainly had, does not survive long without surrounding himself with people he can trust, and placing them wisely.

As we sketched a sort of enemy pecking order, the lower and outer defense ring comprised Afghans, Algerians, Jordanians, Chechens, and Pakistanis. Bin Laden's more trusted fighters, the Saudis, Yemenis, and Egyptians, occupied higher terrain and protected the queen bee. Hell, rumor even had it that Chinese advisors were on bin Laden's team. The technique is similar in some ways to how the U.S. Army operates, just not as personal and much less politically sensitive.

One of the most telling bits of information Ali shared was about al Qaeda's indirect fire and armored capability, mainly mortar tubes and tanks. Firmly entrenched in the towering defensive position, bin Laden's people held superb observation posts. The well-camouflaged spots on the northern ridges offered long-range visibility of any activity in the foothills and valleys and were a tactician's dream come true for any battle.

Those observation posts served as the eyes for the hidden mortar sections—which we estimated at two or three Soviet-made 82mm tubes—that were laid in on the reverse slope, out of sight of any opposing ground force. When the bombers overhead didn't force the crews to retreat into nearby caves for safety, the positions doubled as even more early warning posts to guard against unwanted visitors.

For over a week, Ali's mujahideen had made their approaches over well-known dirt roads, and the telltale clouds of dust telegraphed their every move. Since night fighting was not yet in Ali's repertoire, al Qaeda could stop those daylight probes with mortar fire alone.

Ali said that of the twenty-seven men who had been lost since the fighting began, all but thirteen of them died by mortar fire. He claimed the enemy mortars were extremely accurate because they were "computerized." For us, it was obvious that one of the first major steps had to be to stop those costly daylight attacks and remove the enemy mortars from the equation.

We were skeptical when Ali praised his fighters for locating three former Soviet tanks that were now used by bin Laden's people. His men had come upon a series of caves just past the foothills and heard the rumbling of metal tank treads rolling over uneven rock beds. We knew how difficult it was just to walk over that terrain and considered that it was probably too difficult to maneuver with heavy armor. Ali insisted that several of the caves carved out during the Soviet jihad could easily hold several tanks. We just didn't buy it. We were unaware that just a few days earlier, the combined CIA and JSOC team had photographed several armored vehicles from a distance before eliminating them with powerful smart bombs called JDAMs, joint direct attack munitions.

Within seventy-two hours of doubting Ali's claim about the tanks, those same tanks moved from fiction to fact. Our own snipers spotted them even deeper and higher in the mountains. Hard to believe, but it was true. The tanks must have been part mountain goat.

The result of all the discussions, picture taking, and planning led to a pretty elementary conclusion. The Tora Bora Mountains were to our front, and bin Laden was reportedly garrisoned up there with as many as three thousand loyal fighters. The solution was to launch a full attack. *I love the way these men think.*

Some great mind once said that there are two kinds of original thinkers. There are those who, upon viewing disorder, try to create order. And the second group does just the reverse. It is made up of those who, on encountering order, try to create disorder. That's us. Delta operators thrive on chaos like no other group of humans alive. It's intoxicating. It's intense. And it is extraordinarily addictive.

The fundamental Delta principle has long been "Surprise, Speed, and Violence of Action." It applies to commando tactics. If during an assault you lose one element, the implied response is to increase it in the next. For example, if we lost surprise during a stealthy approach to a target before reaching the breach point, we would increase the pace from a deliberate move to a stepped-up jog or sprint. At the breach, if it became obvious to the team leader that whatever or whoever waited on the opposite side of the door or window was alert and expecting visitors, we escalated to an even more violent explosive entry.

Regardless of how Delta enters the crisis point, the expression "slow is smooth, smooth is fast" still applies when conducting close-quarter combat, or CQB. Watching Delta operators conduct "free flow" CQB on targets with unknown floor plans is one of the most awesome sights of controlled chaos one can imagine. The sequence is anything but choreographed, but the operators effortlessly sweep through a structure like red ants going through familiar, twisting corridors. Delta's method and skill in CQB is unmatched by any other force in existence.

We absorbed an enormous amount of information by studying the muhj style of warfare during the first couple of days.

Afghans are afternoon fighters by nature, and their methods are straight out of Barbarian Tactics 101. Sometime after midday prayers, they would muster with AK-47 rifles, PKM machine guns and RPGs as far forward in the foothills as they safely could. After clustering around, seemingly as if nobody knew who was in charge on that particular day, they would plough straight uphill, firing wildly. It was a good show that apparently was played out to convince the watching reporters that General Ali's forces were on the offensive. But it was also grossly ineffective.

This was centuries-old tribal warfare, more symbolic than savage, more duty than deadly, more for spoils than scalps. It was not intended for anyone to really get hurt. The skirmishes would last a few hours, then the fighters would do some looting and call it a day and retreat back down the ridgelines, giving back to al Qaeda any of the day's hard-earned terrain.

This style of fighting was nothing new to these people. Since the days of the Prophet Muhammad's assault on Mecca in 622 A.D., fighters have halted to loot captured enemy stores and sift through overrun fighting positions, cave dwellings, and linear dugouts. War booty and cave treasures provided the same financial incentive to fight al Qaeda in Tora Bora that Saladin provided to his Muslim soldiers many centuries ago. Booty or martyrdom, one or the other, is a promise from Allah. The cost of living in eastern Afghanistan was probably less than a dollar a day, so a little looting could go a long way.

We wanted Ali to switch gears, throw bin Laden some curveballs, and add a few night games to a schedule of day games only. But he wanted us to just sit tight in relative safety while his muhj did the fighting. Let him worry about locating bin Laden. The general wanted more bombs, but no American casualties, and he would let us know when it was safe to come out and play. Not unexpectedly, some American commanders in the upper echelons shared Ali's concern about American casualties and preached the same wait-and-see attitude. More than once, I heard them say, "Let things develop." It was vexing.

Ali's desire was to maximize the bombing to save as many of his troops' lives as possible, and Colonel Ashley had a similar wariness. Ashley's caution was meant to stave off our natural impetuousness and was hard to dispute, for he still carried with him his experiences in the deadly streets of Mogadishu in 1993.

Ashley's point was well taken, but it made us wonder how America would react to hearing a commander state, "Let them [the Afghans] finish the job. This is about using surrogate forces; it's their war."

As much as I respected both of their positions, I also disagreed with them, and so did my men. We did not like hearing such statements while the rubble was being cleaned up from the attack on the World Trade Center.

Ali's track record so far was analogous to throwing firecrackers into a fishing hole. Sure, you get a few dead fish to float to the top, but if you want the kingfish, you had better be prepared to do some serious trolling in dangerous and deeper waters.

Fortunately, our CIA partners also were in no mood to sit around, and George consistently hounded Ali to attack. Our immediate deployment into the mountains could motivate, or even shame, Ali's fighters into action, and the idea slowly gained traction.

What Ali really needed, even if he didn't know or even desire it yet, was example. Combining the best of modern Marine Corps recruiting mottos, what was needed here was "A Few Good Men" to enter the mountains and prove that "Superior Minds Have Always Overwhelmed Superior Force."

We American commandos had to prove to the general that we could operate inside the mountains, surrounded by al Qaeda day and night, and not stamp our time cards at the end of the day. We certainly planned to give Ali his wish by throwing more fireballs into bin Laden's mountain castle: lethal fireballs in the form of bombs from the bellies of B-52 and B-1 bombers, bombs that came complete with nasty attitudes and pinpoint accuracy to collapse the hidden cave openings that protected the elusive terrorists. But we also needed to see where the projectiles landed in relation to the pockets of enemy and the well-camouflaged cave entrances.

And we were growing very impatient. We wanted to do it soon! As the Greek writer Euripides stated back in 425 B.C., the God of War hates those who hesitate.

After the ten-hour drive from Bagram, through Kabul, and then east to Jalalabad, the boys finally linked up with Manny on the outskirts of the city. A short time later, Jim rested the boys safely in a large two-story safe house in Jalalabad that had been provided by the good General Ali.

The snipers led the way, with an hour's head start, to break up the convoy. When their lead truck blew a tire just on the other side of the volatile town of Sorubi, the convoy pulled over to wait for it to be repaired, a move that left the rearmost vehicles still in the heart of the town. Within a few heartbeats, hundreds of locals, many armed with AK-47s, spilled out of the shops and market area. It looked like a giant ant hill had been stepped on.

Some school-age children curiously reached under the tarps covering the equipment in the truck bed, and one daring young thief reached through an open window and grabbed a Garmin GPS off the dashboard, then dashed into the crowd. Delta sniper Dugan dismounted from the backseat with only his concealed Glock pistol for protection, and began playing with the children to draw their minds away from messing with the truck.

A bunch of armed locals started rocking the Land Rover of the British SBS commandos because they refused to get out. As Dugan tried to keep the crowd back, a rock came flying out of nowhere and smacked him in the back of the head. Dugan was now seething with rage. He jumped back in the truck and told the driver to just gas it and get them out of there before things got a whole lot worse.

Now they were at the safe house after the long jaw-jarring drive, and the boys spent some time doing minor maintenance on the trucks before getting a welcome hour of rack. Four tall walls surrounded the house for protection, but just in case some uninvited guests decided to make an appearance, Jim put the boys on the second floor and left the muhj guides down on the ground floor.

We were anxious to get the snipers and assaulters down to the school-house so we could get some things rolling. One thing was for certain: come morning, the boys would be in no mood to sit around the schoolyard with coloring books and marbles. They would be arriving hungry and chomping at the bit.

And unlike Allah, the Merciful and Compassionate, Delta planned to show no quarter, no mercy, and no compassion for al Qaeda.

General Ali had some visitors waiting that afternoon, the council of elders—the Shura—from the surrounding area. We noticed them as soon as they stepped out of their vehicles, and we made it a point to get out of sight. They were a lively bunch, roughly a dozen older men with long gray beards and dark skin with deep wrinkles from the decades of unrelenting sun. All were dressed in pseudo-formal attire—large, bright yellow turbans with matching shawls. There had been a rumor of American soldiers coming to Tora Bora to help the general fight al Qaeda, and they were concerned about them and reminded Ali that this was not the true Muslim way.

The general assured them that he had a handle on things. Americans were not welcome as long as he was in command. That was not quite the same as saying we weren't already there. But convinced of his sincerity, likely with a wink and a nod, the village elders pledged their support to Ali in eliminating bin Laden.

With everyone having done what was required in the strange political dance, the elders promised to activate their version of the neighborhood watch program for any sign of bin Laden. Then they left.

George, Adam Khan, and I met with Ali for a final time, inside his sleeping quarters, as the day came to an end. Boots off at the door and teacups in the middle of the rug.

The major topic of interest to the general was the status of the BLU-82 drop that had been postponed several times and was now expected early the next morning. I assumed the changing of the drop times had been the harebrained idea of someone far removed from the battlefield realities. It was likely some staff officer just doing his job by trying to provide his best operational advice to his commander. But the big bomb had kept us all waiting.

George brought Ali up to date, with Adam Khan meticulously translating and Ali nodding in the affirmative. Ali said that he planned to exploit the bomb drop, as soon as it was safe to do so, by attacking with about two hundred fighters. A reserve of another two hundred fighters would be held nearby to provide him some flexibility.

His tanks would roll out in full force as well, and one would move farther up the foothills to throw some direct fire straight down the valley. Several mortars to the east would also support the attack. Ever the gracious host, Ali insisted we be his guests for this special trip to the front lines, so as to observe his fighters' skill. It all sounded good, but terrifically unrealistic.

The reported danger radius for the BLU-82 was four thousand meters, which meant that all friendly forces had to be that substantial distance from the intended point of impact. If anyone realistically expected the muhj to exploit the attack in a timely manner in the rugged mountains of Tora Bora, the distance should have been reduced to about four hundred meters, not four thousand! Even a professionally trained army would have their hands full if they expected to maneuver four thousand meters uphill under mortar, rocket, and small-arms fire in the middle of the day.

Even so, we resisted the urge to rain on our host's parade. At least he was showing some initiative and finally displaying an offensive mind-set.

I politely asked the general to keep us informed as much as possible about how far his troops had advanced to the south so we could adjust the bombing and ensure that the weapons were killing the correct folks. Just as Adam Khan began to translate the request, the general's bedroom lit up with a flash and we turned in time to see a spectacular strike up in the mountains through the bedroom window. It shook the ground under the schoolhouse. General Ali's smile grew wide!

George praised him for his actions to date. After that compliment, as if on cue, the radio sputtered to life with the excited sound of hardcore Pashto being spoken. Some of his men had spotted enemy fighters descending the hills, heading for a small village, and Ali's force was lying in ambush. The general beamed with the pride of a first-time father and motioned to us as if to say, "See, we are doing good things here."

Our meeting turned back to operational matters. George asked Ali where he planned to command the battle from once things got rolling. The response was typically noncommittal, and he palmed the ball right back to the CIA man. "Wherever you go, I will go," he said, gesturing to both George and me.

The general was fairly upbeat about finding bin Laden. He said his men were motivated and thankful of America's help and the willingness to commit her "special commandos." His men were committed to the end and wouldn't fail. With that, we pushed our teacups into the center of the rug, lumbered to our feet, put our boots back on, and slipped out into the frigid night air.

I was ready to bag out on the dirty cement floor of our own building for a couple of hours after the meeting with Ali, but it was not to be.

"Sir, there is a message you might want to read from the commander." Bernie, our communicator, hit me with the news as soon as I came through the door of our corner classroom. It was dark in the room except for the bright green LED readout displays on the state-of-the-art communication suite, the weak flickering glow of a kerosene lamp that had been purchased locally for about fifty cents, and the screen of the small Toughbook laptop computer.

Colonel Ashley was asking for the grid locations of where we planned to put in our sniper teams and what area they planned to lase for the bombers. In his words, he had to "feed the beast."

I commented to Bernie, "Can you imagine the pressure that must have rolled downhill through four or five levels of command to get this request to us?" And it was not only several layers of general officers breathing down Ashley's neck for the information, for he explained, "Everybody from POTUS on down is asking for details." It went all the way up to the White House, for POTUS is the acronym for the president of the United States.

"Bernie, this is exactly why we will never be as good as the Israelis at killing terrorists," I said. "We have too many bureaucratic layers and decision makers who stifle initiative and waste precious time."

Before replying to the anxious brass up the chain of command, I briefed Ironhead and Bryan on the particulars of the meeting as an evening lullaby of thundering bombs impacting on al Qaeda positions rolled from the mountains.

After that, I thumbed open my notebook, turned back to the small laptop and wrote a subject line for the message: NIGHTLY FIRESIDE CHAT WITH THE GENERAL.

"What the hell," I wisecracked to the boys. "If George W. cares enough to ask, who are we to hold up the show?" I started writing.

9

The Daisy Cutter

Tora Bora

The name is so familiar
Sounding so close, so ancient, so complex
As the cave complexes witnessing the conflict
Between the latest, highest, most lethal modern technology
And the most primitive, backward, pointless theology
—KURDISH POET KAMAL MIRAWDELI

The much-anticipated drop time for the BLU-82 had finally been set for the early morning hours of December 9. There was no point in dropping the big bomb at night, when the al Qaeda fighters were warming themselves inside their caves and the muhj had done their evening retreat because they did not play in the dark and the press couldn't witness the explosion.

Almost everybody in our compound got up early that morning to watch the show. The CIA operatives mustered in a close group in front of a short rock wall just behind the schoolhouse, each wearing an outfit that was part Afghan, part stylish North Face gear. Some stood proudly with their arms around each other, some held on to their AK-47s. For a memory photo, one held a small piece of cardboard with the inscription "Tora Bora, AF, BLU-82, 9 Dec 2001" scratched in thick black letters. The CIA was gleeful, confident, and hopeful of a turning point in the battle.

General Ali also made an early appearance, dressed in his white pajama-looking garb, his trademark dark brown leather jacket, and a tan *pakool* hat to ward off the morning cold. Although the CIA had promised great results from the bomb, and certainly seemed pleased with themselves, the general remained apprehensive. He gripped his two-way radio and spoke to his forward commanders to confirm that all his fighters had moved back the minimum safe distance from the planned target area deep in the mountains.

The huge bomb was called a Daisy Cutter, and one had not been dropped in anger since the Vietnam War, when it was employed as an easy way to clear away the jungle to create an instant landing zone for helicopters. Naturally, the CIA hyped its capabilities, and after hearing the celebrated buildup, I was also anticipating a spectacular show.

Above us a small dark spec came into view against the clear blue sky, far above the 14,000-foot peaks. The MC-130 Combat Talon entered the area from northwest to southeast at such a high altitude that it appeared to barely be moving. Any al Qaeda fighters up at dawn must have looked up with curiosity. They had become accustomed to the four white contrails of B-52 bombers flying at 30,000 feet or fighter-bombers streaking down lower, but this was different. The lumbering MC-130 might have the look of a cargo plane, but its belly was full of something the enemy fighters had never experienced.

Fittingly, after their extraordinary work over the past five days, the busy observation post with the call sign Victor Bravo Zero Two cleared the aircraft hot to drop its load. The Combat Talon turned it loose and banked sharply away from the target area to the west, as if the blast might reach up and snatch it from the sky.

"There she is, and here it comes," one CIA operative called. "Look out, al Qaeda."

"I'd hate to be the bad guys with OP duty this morning," commented another.

At this point, I would like to write about shock and awe and fireballs and mountain-shaking thunder to describe the explosion that took place at 0611 hours local time. We expected a huge blast that would rattle the buildings and momentarily lift us off our feet.

In reality, there was barely a tremor beneath our boots at the schoolhouse. *Poof.* The big bomb was a bust. *We got up early for this?* The first reports trickling back from the pilots observing the impact from far above told of a possible "low order detonation." In other words, the bomb didn't strike as advertised with maximum destructive force, but it certainly did not fizzle either.

It didn't matter; General Ali had clearly expected a better performance. He had no idea whether it exploded properly, but it did not take long for him to find out exactly where it landed.

Frantic reports squawked over the radio from his men, reporting that the bomb had hit close to them. We all listened intently as the distress calls poured in nonstop for several minutes. The general looked at the CIA guys and waved his hands about, pointing toward the mountains while still transmitting commands to his men.

Ali was saying the Daisy Cutter had hit one ridgeline too far to the east, was roughly five hundred meters off its mark, and exploded near one of his groups' positions. I didn't need any translation to understand the general's obvious disappointment.

Adam Khan pulled out his own portable satellite phone and punched in the speed-dial code to reach Gary Berntsen of the CIA back in Kabul. Gary answered so fast that it almost appeared that he was expecting the call.

"It does not seem as if the BLU-82 exploded," Adam Khan said calmly. "The general is frantic and pissed about it. He says it hit the wrong place."

Gary was not buying it, and barked back, "You tell that son of a bitch the bomb hit the right target and it exploded properly!"

Adam Khan didn't argue with the CIA chief. "Well, it was not much of one," he said, and cut the connection.

Fortunately, the BLU-82 show was followed a couple of minutes later by a pair of B-52 bombers that laid down three separate strings of multiple JDAMs. The first load of smart bombs looked like a linear strike along the crest of a ridgeline, and General Ali, in utter dismay, began waving his hands again and calling out loudly to us that those bombs also had struck a location where his men were holed up. Apparently, the muhj had ignored the warnings to pull back to a minimum safe distance of 4,000 meters.

The second load appeared to be more of a pinpoint strike and went in at the exact spot where Ali said the BLU-82 should have landed. Finally, there was something to cheer about. The general and the few fighters with him jumped up and down with joy, jigging around like children as they watched the flashes of massive red and orange explosions that gave way to thick, rising dark gray plume of smoke.

"Yes, yes, yes," Ali said, "That's where al Qaeda [*sic*]!"

The third B-52 strike was much less impressive than the previous two, hitting farther to the west, although closer to us. Ali's temporary euphoria evaporated and he let us know, once again, that the air force had hit the wrong spot. Some quick math gave us one out of four, or only a 25 percent success rate. Not good. The B-52s put on a great show and were fairly accurate, but the main item on the menu was to have been the showy BLU-82 provided by the American taxpayer, and it did not live up to expectations.

In defense of the U.S. Air Force we can say, dud or no dud, that bomb landed where the flyboys were told to put it. All the pilots had to do was get their plane to the correct release point and let her rip, and that they did. Any blame for the off-mark strike had to lie elsewhere.

No Afghan on the battlefield could look at one of our maps, or even one of the Russian maps from the Soviet-Afghan War, and tell us where the pockets of enemy fighters were. In fact, they couldn't tell us even where friendly fighters were. The best you could hope for was a good guess, depending on where the muhj pointed from a distance.

That was the totally unsophisticated technique used to designate the target for the BLU-82. A signal intercept of bin Laden communicating with his fighters in the mountains provided the baseline location, and that had been corroborated by locals as being bin Laden's current location.

A day or so before we arrived, General Ali himself had provided the target refinement. He stood outside the schoolhouse and pointed to the spot where the chief terrorist was located. When that discussion ended and it was time to send the targeting location to the air force, the coordinates were transmitted.

Either the terrain was read incorrectly or there was a typo in the co-ordinates that were sent; the bomb hit right where it was supposed to, but was off by almost a thousand meters. Whatever the cause, it was an egregious error.

It underlined the absolute need for putting the Delta boys up in those mountains to set up observation posts that could provide the needed high-tech target guidance, not just an "over there" estimate based on finger-pointing.

Bin Laden once said that it was the duty of all Muslims to kill not just American military personnel but any American who pays taxes. If the few dozen Tomahawk cruise missiles launched in 1988 at Zawir Khili, near Khost, in retaliation for the U.S. Embassy bombings in Africa didn't impress him, we would soon be introducing him to tons of bombs, courtesy of those same American taxpayers. Although the hype outshone the performance, I'm certain the sheer power of the Daisy Cutter got bin Laden's attention that morning.

I never saw the photo op cardboard sign of the CIA again.

Thirty minutes after the BLU-82 drop, ten Toyota pickup trucks rolled up to the schoolhouse carrying the Delta snipers and assaulters. They had managed only an hour or so of sleep in Jalalabad before beginning the final leg of their journey. The three-hour trip was uneventful except for a few stops to pick up additional muhj fighters and grab some chow at roadside stands. They even managed to watch the BLU-82 drop and subsequent JDAMs light up the early morning mountainside.

The boys were all smiles, and it was a relief to see them: Caveman, Stalker, Stormin', Grumpy, Murph, and Crapshoot, to name but a few. Most were full bearded, with long hair dangling out of the back and the sides of their traditional Afghan wool *pakool* caps. They were embarking on a journey they would remember for the rest of their lives.

I caught a glimpse of General Ali stealing a peek at these guys from his doorway. Even Ali couldn't resist wanting a glimpse of such an awesome set of American commandos.

While bombs grumbled along the ridgelines and valleys every twenty minutes or so, we gave the boys a quick info dump to orient them to the area. After the highlights, they stowed their gear inside their temporary new home and hid the vehicles inside the compound walls.

Ironhead and Bryan coordinated a reconnaissance of al Qaeda's positions for Jim, another seasoned Delta troop sergeant major who had just arrived, and they left within the hour. It was critical that these leaders got a good look at what I had seen the day before in order to give a quality check to my information and plans. With just a single vehicle and several muhj piled in the back, they slipped by the press and made it up to Mortar Hill without incident.

A bomber was in the sky, so al Qaeda stayed still and let them take in the view and orient their maps, but when the bomber cleared the airspace twenty minutes later, the mortars cranked up and several rounds impacted fifty meters away. They had seen enough, and with no need to push their luck, the three most experienced commandos on the battlefield returned to the schoolhouse.

I gathered the team leaders to update them on the changes in our concept of operation since we had departed the ISB a few days earlier. We had little patience for sitting around or hoping to get lucky with a golden nugget of intelligence. Instead, with the full support of our CIA friends, we were determined to make our own Delta luck by forcing the issue, by making things happen, and by pressuring General Ali to crank up the pressure on Usama bin Laden. Did the American people expect anything less?

Our first call was to split Kilo Team in half to augment the pair of observation posts already in place. OP25-A, occupied by Green Berets of Cobra 25 for the past two days, was located in the eastern foothills several kilometers short of the front lines and abreast of the Agam Valley. The other Green Berets had just joined the second one, OP25-B, which covered the western portion of the battlefield, near the Wazir Valley.

These two observation posts were either unknown to bin Laden and his fighters, or at least al Qaeda had chosen to do nothing about them. Both had done incredible work before we arrived, but were located four miles from the front lines and could not see over the distant ridgelines where the muhj were attacking. We were planning to move beyond both of the current OPs and establish new and flexible forward positions to take over those duties.

Although the Green Berets were in those OPs first, we needed to put Delta men in there, too, because our guys were familiar with the current game plan, our techniques and tactics, carried compatible radios, and understood the commander's intent. To maintain unity of command, we needed tactical control of the positions in order to synchronize the fight. The last thing we wanted or needed was another friendly-fire incident like a recent tragedy in Kandahar on December 5, when a bombing strike was called in to block the Taliban from crossing a bridge. The errant JDAM struck the wrong spot, killed three Green Berets, and wounded a half-dozen other Americans with flying shrapnel and rocks.

As expected, the requirement for us to take control became a source of significant friction with Green Beret commanders at higher headquarters, but as often happens when two elite units find themselves occupying the same piece of the battlefield, the guys on the ground eventually worked things out for the common good.

We tapped Kilo Team snipers Jester and Dugan to enter the battlefield first and prepare for insertion to OP25-A that afternoon, December 9. Once they linked with the 5th Group Green Berets and had a chance to acquaint themselves with the terrain, they were to move farther forward and scout for deeper spots where we could establish future OPs and would cut the angles to let us see past the high ridgelines.

We desperately needed human eyes on the back sides of those ridgelines to conduct what the military calls terminal guidance operations—TGO—a fancy way of saying directing bombs to intended targets, either by a laser designator or by providing GPS coordinates.

The other half of Kilo Team would get ready to move the following morning to augment the other post, OP25-B.

The rest of the reconnaissance troop would be preparing for an intended insertion within twenty-four hours, with the assaulters on standby as both an emergency assault force, should we receive actionable intelligence about bin Laden's location, and as a quick-reaction force should observation posts 25-A or 25-B get into trouble.

The reconnaissance troop was pumped. Seeing the look in the

assaulters' eyes, I knew it would be hard to hold these guys back. I prayed for a bin Laden sighting.

After returning from his recon of the front lines, Troop Sergeant Major Jim took one of the CIA guys around the schoolhouse to examine the mountains. He looked up at the highest point he could make out with the naked eye, referred to his map, looked up again, and set his finger on that peak on the map. The map legend confirmed he was looking at Hilltop 3212, which was nestled in the middle of several other slightly lower peaks. Jim raised his compass and made a mental note of the 172-degree magnetic azimuth.

The CIA guy thumbed the edges of his own map and began to explain what they were looking at. He pointed left.

"Half of ODA 572 is over there, up on that piece of high ground. That's OP25-A," the CIA man stated.

Jim nodded. "Okay, now point out the other OP."

"Ummm, over there. That's OP25-B," said the CIA guy, pointing to the southwest. "See those three hilltops that are fairly even? Well, that tallest one is Hilltop 3212, the tallest one in the area, and it lies directly on the border with Pakistan."

Jim paused for a moment, and then turned to look at the CIA operative. *You must be kidding.* He wasn't. The CIA man had misidentified the highest peak within view from the schoolhouse.

"Give me your map, pal," Jim calmly told him. "That is definitely not Hilltop 3212, it's Hilltop 2685. Hilltop 3212 is about two thousand meters farther southeast." He traced his finger across the map before handing it back.

"Huh? You sure?" the Agency operative said sheepishly, studying his map closely. "Damn, maybe it is."

Jim raised an eyebrow and walked away. No wonder bombs were sometimes being delivered to the wrong address.

He had a low tolerance for bullshit, and I had received that silent arched eyebrow reprimand many times myself during the more than three years that Jim and I spent together as troop commander and sergeant major.

He was six feet tall, usually wore a ball cap, and sported a dark thick goatee that he only shaved off once a year, for his required annual Department of the Army photo. I considered him to be one of the best operators in Delta, and a twenty-first-century warrior who was the equal of the seventeenth-century French commander Jean Martinet, whose name has gone down in history as meaning strict and stubborn. Jim could be almost a despotic taskmaster at times, but the difference was that he was respected by every person in the building.

He had grown up in the 3rd Ranger Battalion and moved to the elite 75th Ranger Regimental Reconnaissance Detachment before heeding the call of Delta. Shortly after returning from the invasion of Panama, he found himself in the mountains of the northeastern United States in the Delta tryouts, which were almost a formality since Jim was destined for Delta. The physical portion of the testing was almost ridiculously easy for the thick-muscled but remarkably limber and quick Ranger. He was not as fast as some of the others, but nobody could really outrun him. Jim would stay right next to you until you quit or one of you passed out.

He was a gifted shooter with his own unique style of drawing his .45-caliber pistol that was indiscernible to the naked eye, but if he slowed his draw stroke down a bit and allowed a good view of his technique, you wouldn't believe it. It was shocking how much faster he could lift the pistol from the holster and place two hardball rounds inside the space of a dime of a target forehead by using his patented unorthodox draw. We slung a boatload of brass downrange together, and I was usually still looking for my front sight post when Jim was already policing up his spent brass.

However efficient I became as an operator was a direct reflection of Jim's extraordinary training skills, his patience, and his genuine friendship. I consider myself darn lucky.

Around noon, our friend Colonel Al stopped in to our humble corner room for a visit. He brought news that the initial reports received about the BLU-82 being a dud had been untrue. I guess with all the hard sell, almost everyone had expected an explosion of earthshattering intensity. Even better, Al said that back at the Pentagon and in Langley, Virginia, the home of the CIA, the Daisy Cutter was being hailed as a spectacular success.

All of us who had watched its impact agreed, however, that even if the bomb had not been a mechanical dud, it had been a psychological dud among our allies. The CIA folks out here who had been charged with selling the bomb's capabilities to General Ali knew the fireworks had been so lame that it had shaken the general's confidence in American technology. I'm not sure what exactly Ali had hoped to witness, but the BLU-82 obviously was not what he expected.

In fact, that morning he had summoned his subordinate commanders for an impromptu war council. Originally, he had planned to exploit the expected devastation of the Daisy Cutter with a ground attack up the mountain as soon as the debris stopped falling. That ambitious plan was now off the table.

Further, Ali told his men they could no longer rely on giant American bombs to get the job done, and that they needed to make do with the situation at hand and find ways to salvage something of today's planned attack. He ordered several tanks to move forward and promised them 82mm mortars in support.

An Afghan fighter burst through the doorway, holding his little radio in the air. He told the general that their fighters at the front were once again pleading for him to stop the bombs from landing on them. Another of Ali's commanders fidgeted nervously, his body language clearly signaling his desire to get out of the meeting. *They must be his men under fire.*

It was hardly a surprise. Ali's men dressed like the enemy. Hell, we dressed like the enemy! No one could tell us on a map where anyone was located, and everyone looked alike, so how could the bomber and fighter pilots be blamed for any confusion? They were doing their best with the information they had. So, this blue on blue, or friendly-fire, engagement was simply the fog of war. It wouldn't be the last incident. Unfortunately, America lost face with our allies every time it happened.

Precision was needed in the dangerous business of calling in those air strikes, so the sooner we got our guys going, the better.

Still, General Ali remained surprisingly upbeat and appeared highly motivated in the presence of his lieutenants at the meeting. George, the senior CIA man on the scene, had been noticeably frustrated by the BLU-82 debacle and then was further chagrined by the new blue-on-blue incident, but Ali told him to lose the long face and promised that his army would win the day.

For two days, George and his Agency operatives had been promoting this bomb drop as the singular event of the young campaign, maybe even the decisive point that would clear the way for Ali to advance en masse and roll over al Qaeda. Now, despite what Washington was hailing as a success, the CIA chief here was quite logically concerned about the Agency's credibility with Ali. From my point of view, George still held all the cards. The BLU-82 was one minor event in one minor battle, and there would be many more ups and downs before the fighting was done in Tora Bora. I sensed that Ali knew that as well.

Our special intelligence interceptors, set up inside the room that separated Ali's bedroom from our room, eavesdropped around the clock on all al Qaeda's transmissions, so bit by bit we learned that the BLU-82 had been much more effective than originally thought. The enemy was overheard repeatedly calling out in anguish, crying, obviously hurting bad and requesting help from others located a valley or two away. Frantic calls from one fighter outside the blast area to his brother, and then to a third brother, went unanswered. Even if it was off the intended mark, the big bomb had put a big hurting on al Qaeda. It had left them bloodied, weakened, and introduced them to the rare feeling of being vulnerable. It was definitely time to reinforce success with a full-scale attack.

Jester, Dugan, and four muhj started their journey for OP25-A at 1500 hours. The two Delta operators were close friends, in many respects cut from the same cloth, but were exact opposites in just as many ways.

Jester was famous for pushing even the relaxed grooming standards enjoyed by the Unit and consistently received flak from some less flexible superiors. He proudly grew a thick blond Fu Manchu mustache, a facial hair style that gave him the look of a 1970s porn star. But he had an extraordinary intellect that forced a person to really have his act together before entering a debate with him on almost any subject. Best of all, Jester's sniper skills were second to none. He could tell you the ballistic characteristics of every cartridge in the book, read the winds blindfolded, and manipulate a laptop computer with the knowing touch of a repair geek.

Dugan, a former Georgia high school state wrestling champion, was the brawn of this unlikely pair. I think he was born with a scoped bolt-action rifle in one hand, a turkey call in the other, and wearing a jujitsu gi. Often during hunting season back home, he skipped breakfast with us in favor of prowling outside the compound in one of the training areas, calling turkeys and tracking deer. He never missed a day in the gym, with the result being a perfectly shaped body, biceps the size of cannonballs and a chest that was like a power plant.

Their trip started out with a half-hour pickup truck ride to a rendezvous point where they met up with two teenage boys and a couple of shabby donkeys to provide porter duties for the long uphill move. The snipers strapped their heavy rucksacks to one of the animals and loaded the other with a couple of cases of MREs and water cans to resupply the Green Berets already in the OP.

Our snipers followed the donkeys and young guides and watched with disgust as one of the boys constantly smacked the trail donkey's backside with a big switch. With every whack, the donkey was building a grudge. About halfway to the OP, they stopped for a short break.

The teenager with the switch was about five feet behind the same donkey he had been whipping when the animal suddenly raised her tail high and her rear end exploded with a gush of the most awful green diarrhea imaginable. The stinking, liquid crap bathed the boy from the waist to the top of his bare feet. The two Delta snipers tried to hold back their laughter so as not to embarrass the switcher, but that was impossible, and the totally humiliated kid started beating the donkey hard before Jester and Dugan stepped in to calm him down. The Delta boys needed that poor donkey. Anyway, they thought the animal had done the right thing.

An hour later the snipers arrived at OP25-A and met up with the current team which was in place there, a Special Forces A Team augmented by an air controller, about a half-dozen men led by Warrant Officer Dave. The group had been handling a majority of the close air support missions for the past two days,

There is no doubt that the Green Berets wanted to slug it out with the al Qaeda fighters, too, but had been prohibited from taking one step closer to the battlefield beyond their position four miles away. That emphatic order had come straight down the pipe from their commanding officer, Colonel Mulholland. They were restricted from moving forward, but somebody had to.

With Delta now in town, the Green Berets knew the handwriting was on the wall: They would no longer be running the show, although official word to turn over control had not yet reached them. It was understandably not an easy pill for those professionals to swallow, although it was just the wheel of war, rolling along.

The two Delta snipers immediately recognized the effect of their arrival at that desolate little place, but there was a war to fight, and the elite Green Berets were having to take a major hit to their pride. Some handled it well, such as the air force combat controller who had worked with Delta in some previous assignments. He didn't really care who was in charge. The team leader at the observation post, Dave, and one other Green Beret would prove to be enormous assets. Others were ready to simply call it a war, and remained well to the rear of the OP, goofing off and bitching like all good GIs, and just waiting to exfil. Hobbled by headquarters and unable to take the fight to the enemy, they had good reason to grumble, and I could not really blame them.

By the end of the day Jester and Dugan had taken charge.

To the south, the majestic mountains rose to the clouds, and deep valleys divided by steep ridgelines snaked generally south before merging together at the mountaintops. Shades of green, tan, and brown slowly gave way to various tints of gray as the sun began to set.

For the next thirteen hours, the snipers, the combat controller, and the willing hands among the Green Berets directed several AC-130s, B-52s, B-1s and an unmanned Predator that slammed al Qaeda positions.

At the schoolhouse, we heard the radio calls as they orchestrated the warplanes, and we could see the flashes of bright orange-and-red fireballs that lit up the dark mountainside. Meanwhile, we continued preparing a rescue force of Delta assaulters. Should an OP need emergency help, we wanted Americans to be ready to go. The assaulters prepped their gear and vehicles, and Jim implemented needed sleep rotation.

Delta was finally in the game, and things would start changing rapidly.

spots, but after about a thousand meters of stalking, Jester realized that they were not going to find anything in the area with a better angle than the original OP provided, so they returned, frustrated but with no good options.

The Delta snipers were uncomfortable with the terrain association the Green Berets used to direct the bombs; the map terms did not match actual features on the ground. The disparity convinced the Delta team that naming the prominent terrain features in the target area would make it easier for the pilots to recognize the correct spot on the ground. The Green Berets had named one hilltop already, but there were dozens. Once it was agreed to expand the recognition template, everybody chipped in and named the remaining significant terrain features. The most prominent three hilltops on the primary ridgeline became Knuckles One, Two, and Three . . . and then became even easier to remember as Larry, Curly, and Moe, of the old *Three Stooges* comedies.

After hours of "glassing" the area, looking through high-powered binoculars and spotting scopes, Jester and Dugan discovered three tunnel entrances in the side of a ridgeline, targets that had so far gone unnoticed. They worked up a modified nine-line solution with the combat controller. At this point, the Green Beret chain of command had caught up with the situation and finally radioed the official order to their men that Delta was to direct the fight. It caused another round of muttering, but the Green Berets realized that they worked for the people sending down the orders, so there wasn't much they could do in the way of protesting. Anyway, they knew this was a specialty of Delta snipers, who had been calling in bombing runs for years.

Jester wanted to pack up and move closer to the battlefield to gain a better position, but none of the Green Berets could or would budge an inch. Colonel Mulholland, the Task Force Dagger commander, had remained rooted in cement with his orders that his elite teams not get involved in any direct action situations.

That left Jester and Dugan with no choice but to try and move forward without them. A local guide would be needed to get through the terraced farmland in the valley that separated their position from al

10

The Decisive Point

Gunfight at the Afghan Corral

How are things in Tora Bora? Do the bombs rain every night?
Al Qaeda fortunes turning, do they shrink away in fright?
How are things in Tora Bora? U.S. made, now terror run.
Does Osama feel the pressure as he reaches for his gun?
How are things in Tora Bora? Frozen caves in mountain tops.
His supporters' numbers falling, U.S. pulls out all the stops.
How are things in Tora Bora?
Long ago and far away, 'twas the land of tribal warfare.
Where it ends, no one can say.

—AUTHOR UNKNOWN

On the morning of December 10, Jester and one of the Green Berets headed southwest, out toward the al Qaeda lines. The primary intent was to locate a route that the incoming India Team could use in leapfrogging past OP25-A later that evening. Jester also hoped to identify a spot that might provide a better angle to look into the mountains and at suspected tunnel entrances. Beams of bright and glowing sunshine seen from a different angle might reveal a cave entrance or bunker that had so far escaped detection.

Moving a few hundred meters, they found a couple of promising

Qaeda's, and also to weave through the friendly muhj positions so they would not be met by a hail of 7.62mm bullets before any handshake of friendship. Unfortunately, the Green Berets owned the guide and refused to give him up. That lack of cooperation stopped the Delta snipers in their tracks.

India Team, the second Delta group to enter the mountains, was led by Ski, our most senior reconnaissance troop team leader. I had watched him work in the Balkans and knew that this unassuming guy who loved being at the center of the action was once again in his element. Many of his exploits remain classified, and when he finally left the unit two years later, he held more decorations for valor than any other operator in the building. Rounding out India Team were Caveman, Sling Blade, Dallas, and their air combat controller Spike.

They were to carry supplies up to Jester and Dugan at OP25-A, then continue farther south and set up a new observation post about a thousand meters deeper into the mountains. The truck ride to the donkey rendezvous took thirty minutes, and with a quick payoff of American cash, a young Afghan guide and his animals were hired. When the beasts were loaded, Ski slapped the lead donkey on its ass and the animal trudged off to the south, as if it had done the task a thousand times before.

Ski and his team arrived at OP25-A before nightfall on December 10, ready to stop only long enough to drop off the supplies and get a quick brief, and then move on past them. Although Jester had already given the bad news about the lack of suitable OPs in the area back to the schoolhouse, India Team had not gotten the word. Ski decided to keep his operators at the OP overnight and return to the schoolhouse the next morning to get a new mission. That decision would have far-reaching consequences.

I remember that day, December 10, like it was yesterday, for while things seemed stalled for our boys who were up at OP25-A, things started to hop around the schoolhouse.

One of General Ali's frontline commanders radioed back that he had information that the enemy positions in his area were vulnerable. The commander wanted to attack and asked that the general to come forward to take a look.

The request came at exactly the right time, because Ali had lost some confidence in the bombing campaign, but remained under continued pressure by George to attack. The general had also spent some time during the day pandering to the press pool and likely decided that an attack would have the added benefit of being a good media show. It does not take much to brew up an Afghan attack, because like everything in the Afghan culture, there would be little precoordination or advance notification of anyone else. Just decide and then do it. Such impromptu attacks also had a habit of ending just as fast as they began.

Adam Khan had been translating for George as he listened to Ali's half of the conversation with the commander, and the Americans saw an opportunity to get us off the bench. They pressed the general to take us along. The general balked, still uncertain of just how we could help, and still squeamish about getting an American killed. George compromised and convinced Ali to at least take along someone who could support the attack by talking to the bombers. Without an American controlling the planes, the general's men would be susceptible to the same bombs, particularly after nightfall.

Ali consented and gave us no more than five minutes to get ready. Adam Khan dashed over to our room with the news, and we understood how incredibly important it was to support this rare advance by Ali. We couldn't afford to miss a single opportunity to show the general and the muhj that we were indeed there to share the same dangers.

Because we had been planning to insert several teams into the same part of the mountains later that evening, the group that jumped out at us was Jackal Team. If nothing else, at least a couple of them could steal a look at the cover and concealment available at the contemplated location.

Without a moment of hesitation, team leader Hopper volunteered, and one of our air force combat controllers, a young kid code-named the Admiral, was told to go with him. Adam Khan would go along to translate. Together, they became the Jackal Team, because that was Hopper's team. They had only five minutes to pack, and as they hurriedly prepared, we gave them simple orders: Go wherever the general goes, provide close air support, and kill as many al Qaeda as you can.

We took a stab at the location to give them the six-digit grid of a spot located near the base of the mountain. That was a waste of time. The muhj were never able to provide even a guess as to the exact location of their men, or the enemy fighters either. We could have just as well fat-fingered the map to give Hopper and the Admiral their intended location.

Off they went. Hopper and the Admiral looked like any other muhj on their way to a gunfight. Dirty, unkempt, *pakool* hats tilted, scarves around their necks ready to hide their gringo facial structures, and wrapped in light brown blankets threaded with thin lines of bright green, red, and orange.

Adam Khan drove and a couple of muhj fighters climbed into the truck, confidently sporting aged Kalashnikovs that they had adorned with feathers, colorful string, and shiny stickers of many colors. Each would make do with three thirty-round magazines of 7.62mm ammunition until more could be stripped from the vest of a dead Muslim brother.

In sharp contrast, the two Special Ops boys brimmed over with the sort of arsenal expected from a superpower: two 5.56mm M-4 assault rifles with AN-PEQ2 laser designators and Bushnell reflex HOLOsights. One rifle was outfitted with an M-203 launcher under its barrel to fire 40mm high-explosive or smoke rounds. Their custom-made load-bearing vests had special pockets for hand grenades, first aid equipment, water, ammunition, flashlights, and handheld secure radios. They had an MK-7 laser range finder that could be seen by pilots miles above them and a powerful 117 satellite radio that would allow them to talk to those pilots, or anyone in the world for that matter. Another special toy was a Special Operations

Force Laser Marker, or SOFLAM for short, a twelve-pound black box that was worth its weight in gold because it provided accurate ranges and designations for laser-guided munitions out to five thousand feet.

It took about a half hour of driving to reach Mortar Hill, where they found the road was jammed by a faded green and rusted T-55 tank that was struggling to remove a stuck muhj antiaircraft artillery vehicle. Hopper, the Admiral, and Adam Khan knew enemy OPs would spot the multivehicle convoy within minutes and call down the mortars.

Adam Khan maneuvered the truck to a masked location, and they jumped out only moments before the fun began. The initial mortar rounds arrived like clockwork but were off the mark. The three Americans moved away from the vehicles because the mortars were clearly targeting the stalled convoy. Nearby, a group of muhj squatted together, immobile, as if waiting for someone to tell them to do something different. Seconds later, a round struck them center mass.

Adam Khan was warned by another muhj that things would only get hotter further up the road as the route went into the enemy's mountain lair. The hair on Adam Khan's back stood up and he lost that warm and fuzzy feeling so important in combat. Although it clearly was not his job, his concern was for the safety of Hopper and the Admiral, and he was well aware of General Ali's concern about getting an American killed. Adam Khan wondered if it was worthwhile to proceed. Why press the issue in daylight when they were already compromised and under mortar attack? Tomorrow would be another day, and they could try again. The former marine was unafraid, but felt it was too dangerous to continue.

He told Hopper to radio the schoolhouse that they were returning, and that they should not go any farther without an okay from the commandos' commander, me. Hopper didn't think the situation was all that dangerous, just a couple of mortar blasts, and anyway, he knew what our response would be. He already had his orders.

With the rounds still landing intermittently and the three of them squeezed behind a jagged rock face bordering the road, Hopper now repeated those instructions: Go where the general goes. Hopper reasoned that it was no surprise that they would take some rounds once they were forced to stop at this particular place. After all, that was why it was called Mortar Hill. The debate ended when the cheers of the muhj signaled that the tank had gotten the stuck artillery vehicle out of the way and the road was again clear. The three Americans scrambled to their vehicle and continued the mission.

The warning Adam Khan had been given about the increasing intensity of the enemy activity ahead had been correct. He pressed the gas pedal and sped through the curves, dodging the impact of several mortar rounds. The bed of the truck was peppered with shrapnel twanging into the thin metal as he roared deeper into the foothills until a group of muhj on the road forced them to stop.

They had driven as far as they could go. The rest of the way would be on foot. Another muhj fighter emerged to warn the group that the mortars were much more accurate at this close range. As Hopper and the Admiral took up security positions and manipulated a GPS to pinpoint their location, Adam Khan rapped with the muhj for whatever information he could muster. The distinct rattle of machine-gun fire could be heard to their front.

As anticipated, al Qaeda would not be causing all of the problems. Word that a few American commandos were coming forward with the permission of General Ali to support the late-afternoon attack never made it to the frontline folks who most needed to know about it. For the next half hour, several muhj acted like they were in charge and corralled our guys, shuttling them aimlessly from one group of fighters to the next.

At one point, a muhj leader motioned toward the sky and made some flickering hand signals to mimic bombs dropping. They wanted the Americans to make it rain death. The Admiral was happy to grant their request, and radioed some aircraft to work up a fire mission.

Then another set of muhj that they had been with earlier came and interrupted the Admiral's call for fire to ask why the Americans had stopped moving with them and had taken up with this new group. It was a bizarre scene that was to be repeated several times. Hopper, the Admiral, and Adam Khan were mixed up with a bunch of foot soldiers who had no clue why the Americans were there, who had sent them, or where they were supposed to be going.

The one thing that kept Hopper and the Admiral happy was that, despite the headaches, at least they were heading in the right direction—south toward al Qaeda.

After moving several hundred more meters, their latest muhj escort took a break along the military crest of a steep ridgeline. Hopper and Adam Khan moved to a nearby hilltop in hope of getting "eyes on" a suitable target so they could start the aerial fireworks. In the meantime, Adam Khan found a forward command post where small-arms fire, machine guns, and sporadic rocket rounds were clattering about. The three of them made themselves at home in the position, deeper into the Tora Bora mountain range than any other Americans probably had ever gone.

The Admiral asked for all aircraft call signs in the area to check in, since he would be orchestrating the fight that night, and everyone was ready to demonstrate the art of the possible to General Ali. But General Ali was not there.

The Admiral is one smooth talker on the radio. Most important in this business was his willingness to risk everything for his fellow man, an unhealthy but common trait among air force combat controllers.

Darkness was falling fast, and Hopper attempted to reach OP25-A on his handheld FM radio and pass along their current location, in case things took a major turn for the worse. No luck. The FM was not working in that jagged landscape.

The boys of Jackal knew that India Team had arrived at OP25-A, but the reverse was not true. Things had developed so quickly back at the schoolhouse to move Hopper, the Admiral, and Adam Khan out in just five minutes that word of their departure had not yet made it to OP25-A. So the boys in the observation post remained unaware that their teammates were under fire on the other side of the valley.

But OP25-A had received an astonishing report from a muhj commander that the prime target of this entire mission, Usama bin Laden, had been seen on a hilltop and was surrounded. The commander was positive it was the al Qaeda leader and was adamant that "Bouyahs! Bouyahs!" should smash the hilltop now. "Bombs! Bombs!"

Once again the map problem complicated matters. The Delta snipers and the Green Berets worked with the excited muhj to make sense of what he was trying to say. *Where is bin Laden? Show us!* They actually resorted to drawing in the dirt and holding up fingers to represent the various crests and peaks and finally agreed that the target was Hilltop 2685—the First Knuckle, better known as Hilltop Larry.

The Delta snipers, Jester and Dugan, passed the data to a nearby warplane and set about developing another modified nine-line fire mission solution. Just as the combat controller at OP25-A began to call for the aircraft to make its run, they saw several bombs slam onto what they thought was their target, just below the peak of Hilltop 2685.

The perplexed combat controller now asked if the pilot had dropped the bombs early. The pilot told him the attack had been guided by someone down there using a different call sign, and passed the frequency they were using. It had been the Admiral doing his thing.

The men at OP25-A were stunned. They had been handling the majority of the calls all day long, and now someone else had taken over, someone they knew nothing about. The OP25-A combat controller switched to the new frequency and heard the Admiral passing a correction for the next bomb run. The boys in the observation post quickly figured out that somehow the rest of us back at the schoolhouse must have launched an attack and perhaps as many as a couple of dozen operators were down there with the Admiral. Chances were ripe for a friendly-fire, blue-on-blue incident if too many people started talking to the pilots, so the crew in OP25-A quickly relinquished control of the air space. They would watch the fight unfold from a distance, silently hoping that the Admiral also had the reported location of bin Laden.

Frustrated, the Green Beret A Team's attached air controller at OP25-A flung his hand microphone to the ground, let out a few choice cuss words, and stalked away.

I can't say I blame him. Keeping them informed was my job, and I had failed to promptly update everyone because I had lost sight of the big picture at a critical time. I was focusing more on the location of bin Laden being reported by the muhj than on the boys currently at the tip of the spear; and I was not aware that the two groups could not communicate with each other. Nevertheless, it was a colossal screwup with the potential of catastrophic results. That's what I got for assuming something.

Our boys in OP25-A wasted no time pouting that someone else was now on the playground, for they knew that was exactly what was supposed to be happening. The communications snafu was solved, the emergency was over, and so they dreamed up another mission on their own.

For the past two days they had a front-row view of the sporadic attacks and retreats of General Ali's troops and had watched the muhj reeling under heavy mortar fire time and time again. The boys decided to confine their search to anything that would help them destroy the al Qaeda mortar position that had been such a thorn in everyone's sides.

They finally established a sketchy FM radio contact with Hopper, the Admiral, and Adam Khan that would allow OP25-A to serve as a hasty radio relay back to us at the schoolhouse. As the temperature on the mountain dropped, everyone listened to the Admiral steadily bringing in the bombers while the distinct sound of gunfire muffled some of his calls. Just listening raised goose bumps on Jester's arms.

The Jackal bunch had taken cover behind a stone building about the size of a Volkswagen, and most of the muhj also were snuggling up behind it as an al Qaeda PKM heavy machine gun laid fire around the area, severing tree branches above the heads of Hopper and Adam Khan.

Even more deafening was the outgoing racket of the AK-47s. Two or three of the muhj would jam fresh thirty-round magazines into their rifles, lean around the corner, and open up, holding down the triggers for four to five seconds. While they ducked back to reload, another couple of muhj would do the same thing. One fighter with a shouldered RPG stepped away from the group only slightly and frantically jerked the weapon's grip trigger without pausing to aim.

The stone structure offered only an illusion of safety. Hopper tried to get the muhj to spread out and press the attack and use the nearby tree line to maneuver to better locations, which at least would make the enemy have to worry about more than one or two targets. Although the muhj were more vulnerable when they clustered in large groups, they were also much more comfortable doing so. At present, although they were pinned down, the muhj seemed willing to leave well enough alone and would be ready to call it a day after a few more impressive bursts of unaimed automatic rifle fire. Besides, it had worked this way all week, so why change anything just because a few Americans had shown up?

Hopper had no intention of remaining a sitting duck behind the small building. They needed to move, and fast. I was on the horn with the Admiral from the schoolhouse as he updated us on their situation, and we all heard the chaos, the rocket explosions, and the stuttering machine-gun fire in the background as the Admiral coolly relayed their plan to reposition.

He then directed the first available F-18 fighter to drop his payload on the enemy machine-gun position that was pinning them down. The first drop was impressive but did not silence the position, so a second F-18 repeated the engagement and put his bombs right on the money.

The three Americans then absolutely astonished the muhj by using the lull in firing to dash from safety behind the structure to some trees roughly forty meters to their front—heading even closer to the enemy! This was not the way the game was supposed to be played, but our guys were aggressively moving up to deliver the coup de grace with B-52s.

At the schoolhouse, we looked at each other with strain on every face. We didn't need to discuss it; Jim and Bryan had already ensured that the rest of the boys were ready to head out to assist the Jackal unit should it become necessary. The courageous actions of our forwardmost people, worming their way steadily into enemy territory while under fire, made me proud to be not only their teammate, but an American as well.

Adam Khan managed to coax, or threaten, five muhj into coming along to supply more protection. They moved, shooting as they went, although at what no one was sure. Hopper's attempts to get them to preserve their ammunition fell on deaf ears. It was as if the muhj figured if they didn't shoot all of their ammo, they would just have to hump it back down the hill.

About the same time, we received word of a signal intelligence hit that had been intercepted, stating that "Father [meaning bin Laden] is trying to break through the siege line."

Had Hopper, the Admiral, and Adam Khan truly struck gold? Could they be flushing out al Qaeda's command group?

The al Qaeda mortars got back into the game with a first volley that landed right in a group of muhj. Remaining active, the mortars opened a tremendous window of opportunity, and Jester, Dugan, and India Team over at OP25-A were hard at work trying to spot the elusive mortars' firing signature. Just some sign, and they would take out al Qaeda's favorite indirect fire asset. They hunkered down on the cold mountainside, waiting for the mortars to reveal their position.

For the next two hours, the Admiral called in relays of bombing runs while contending with enemy machine-gun fire and mortar rounds that sent rock shards and huge splinters from trees whizzing through the air. The friendly muhj continued firing their AK-47s from behind him, often directly over his head. The Admiral had one ear to the radio and the other one pinned to the ground. The muhj began to retreat slowly back down the ridgeline. They had had enough for one day with these crazy Americans who wanted to always get closer to the enemy. Eventually, the majority of them snuck away without saying a word, abandoning Hopper, the Admiral, and Adam Khan.

Back at the schoolhouse, some thirty minutes before the sun set behind the mountains, George received another special intelligence spotting of bin Laden. Reportedly, feeling pressure from General Ali's hasty attack and the sustained and increasing bombing, bin Laden had spent too long on his radio conversing with his subordinate commanders, and his general location had been determined. This new information, combined with the earlier intercept of bin Laden "trying to break through the siege line" strongly suggested that not only was bin Laden's location pinpointed but that the muhj had him surrounded!

Inside our corner room, George handed me the eight-digit grid location scribbled on a small piece of paper. Wow! An eight-digit grid is accurate down to ten meters. As far as we knew, this was the first time since the late 1990s that our country had such an accurate location on bin Laden.

Ironhead and I looked at each other, and then over at George. The seasoned CIA operative said he had no further information, but his eyes were screaming: *Run with it!* His unspoken expectation was that Delta would launch. He got that right.

Ironhead took off to notify the troop sergeant majors and I grabbed the laptop to send a data message to Ashley. Within minutes, our headquarters sent us a six-digit grid, acquired through military channels. I hoped it would be similar to the one George had gotten, but it was only accurate down to one hundred meters. Either bin Laden was on the move or the data was several hours old. The second grid was almost two kilometers from the first one, a very long way to travel in a relative short time given the rugged terrain and while under duress. No matter. We would go and see.

It suddenly hit me that Adam Khan, our trusted liaison, was already in a gunfight and therefore unavailable to be our Pashto interpreter. So I grabbed Shag, our special intelligence collector, who had been busy intercepting al Qaeda transmissions, then I reached for my kit and rifle and headed out the door to the waiting trucks and the boys.

General Ali apparently had undergone a change of heart after having watched Hopper and the Admiral in action from a safe distance. After being so stubborn earlier in the day, he was now radioing back to inquire if the other American commandos were coming. The general was getting excited about the possibilities, but we first had to convince our two Afghan guides that their general was indeed asking us to come to the front. At least we assumed he was at the front. Assuming, once again.

This might be it, Ali must have thought. *Bin Laden might actually be killed or captured on this very night.*

Thirty-three of us loaded onto nine vehicles and we took off, receiving word that Ali would meet us along the main road near Mortar Hill. That was strange. Had the general mentioned in one of his radio calls that he would lead us to within striking distance of bin Laden, say a ridgeline away, or had we simply thought that he would? It's hard to recall now. In any event, we kept going, thinking that we would link up with the general and probably do some hasty planning on the spot. There was a lot at stake now, and fast decisions and action were called for. Our guys were under fire and we had a hot location for bin Laden.

Things had turned from bad to worse for the Jackal boys: Hopper, the Admiral, and Adam Khan. An enemy machine gun opened up from the north, which was behind them! Evil green tracer rounds tore the tree trunks apart and forced the boys onto their bellies.

Hopper's first thought was that it was friendly fire, since it was coming from their rear, likely from a few muhj who were as uncertain as they were about where the lines began, ended, or overlapped and had already proven they didn't mind shooting over the heads of the Americans. Adam Khan looked back in time to see some muhj skedaddling down the ridgeline while machine-gun bullets literally drilled holes in their footsteps. In a matter of minutes, these supporting fighters were back in their Toyota pickup trucks and disappearing into the darkness.

That left only five muhj with the Americans, and none had bargained for this sort of predicament. Too scared to attempt a run through the machine-gun fire, they had little choice but to stay put. Adam Khan could not calm these frightened men, for darkness was falling, and in their minds, the enemy owned the night and a black-clad al Qaeda fighter or two would be behind every rock and tree. They also were convinced that the enemy was maneuvering and searching for the Americans who had delivered so much death and destruction during the past two hours.

One of the nervous fighters aimlessly let rip his recoilless rifle with its concussive roar and another fired his RPG. A third curled up behind his bipod-mounted PKM machine gun and squeezed the trigger so long that his belt of ammunition ran out. He yelled for more ammunition, but his ammo bearer was long gone.

Adam Khan chewed their asses for revealing their position to the enemy. Then Hopper tried to settle their nerves and dispel the idea that the enemy owned the dark by letting the muhj look through his NVGs. A green-tinted look at the valley might reassure them that al Qaeda was not counterattacking. Truth be told, however, now that the bad guys had a machine gun in place behind them, neither Hopper nor Adam Khan could be certain that more al Qaeda fighters were not heading their way.

The faces of the muhj lit up like kids at a carnival as they looked through the goggles and passed them around. Suddenly, they all were curious as to how the NVGs worked and asked Adam Khan to explain. The machine gun kept firing but they were more interested in this amazing new gadget than the weapon that was slashing away in the dark. They resembled a bunch of beer-bellied men sitting in the nosebleed seats at the World Series, sharing a single pair of binoculars.

The Admiral had emptied the payloads on nine F-18 fighters and a B-1 bomber, an incredible amount of ordnance concentrated on a small area. He had no idea that he was likely the primary reason that bin Laden, the most wanted man in the world, was on the run.

With the arrival of night, the fighters and bombers were replaced by an AC-130H Spectre gunship, the side-firing prince of darkness. As the Admiral talked to the aircraft to pass his requirements, Hopper retrieved his NVGs, then thumbed his handheld laser to mark enemy positions. If they could get the gunship to rip into the enemy positions with the deadly 40mm and 25mm cannons, or a couple of 105mm Howitzer rounds, it might take care of the enemy machine gun and also might draw out the enemy mortars.

While most men would be moving in the direction of safety, Hopper, the Admiral, and Adam Khan moved still another thirty meters toward the enemy machine gun in front of them. The muhj decided to stay put. Green tracers passed by the left side of the Americans and tore up the ground around the muhj they left behind. The Admiral keyed his hand mike to contact the AC-130, and Hopper gave Adam Khan the SOFLAM to help laser the machine-gun nest. Thick cloud cover hampered the gunship, which would have had to break the minimum safe altitude to drop low enough to engage the targets. It was something they were not authorized to do and not smart business for slow-flying aircraft in the mountains.

Adam Khan had taken inventory of what remained to fight with. All of Ali's fighters, save five, had abandoned them on the ridge, the gunship couldn't help until the clouds moved on, and the enemy had a pretty good idea of their location. He told Hopper it was time to go.

Hopper asked if Adam Khan could convince the remaining few muhj to circle the wagons, hold their fire, and just quietly sit things out until the clouds parted. Once the gunship engaged, its protection could last for hours. Adam Khan chuckled at the suggestion. *You're kidding, right?* He recommended that they move back to a safer area.

Hopper understood the situation was beyond salvage. They had done a mighty amount of damage, but the lowering clouds meant there would be no air cover, and the only people he could rely on were the Admiral and Adam Khan. The muhj were scared and low on ammo and might disappear at any moment. Reluctantly, he gave the order to initiate escape and evasion.

The admiral keyed his handset and, as calm as ever, passed the code word: "Warpath. Warpath. Warpath."

Now all they had to do was make it out of there alive.

11

Men and Mission

Attacking is the only secret. Dare and the world yields, or if it
beats you sometimes, dare it again and you will succeed.
—WILLIAM MAKEPEACE THACKERAY

It took us about twenty minutes to get loaded after George
gave us the bin Laden sighting report. Shag and I jumped in
the backseat of the lead vehicle. We basically had to threaten
a pair of locals to motivate them enough to take us up the road for the
linkup with General Ali. Neither man spoke a word of English, nor was
either a fighter, so they were pinging off the walls, nervously rocking back
and forth in the front seat as we rolled out.

Shag did his best to get my questions answered, but the two locals
knew little more than we did about what awaited us. Halfway into the
trip to the front, word came from back at the schoolhouse that Hopper,
the Admiral, and Adam Khan had been pinned down by enemy fire, had
been abandoned by the muhj, and had made a "Warpath" call. Our boys
were in deep shit, escaping and evading, which made our mission even
more urgent.

Not only were we on our way to take care of bin Laden once and for
all, but we also had to weigh the significance of three of our men being in
trouble and needing our help. This same classic dilemma is presented in
military schools around the free world. What is more important: accom-
plishing the mission or taking care of your men? Sergeant Major Ironhead,

Bryan, and Jim were wrestling with the situation as well, but they would look for me to make the call. I probably had about fifteen more minutes to ponder our response.

We had initially felt that the news of bin Laden being found was too good to be true, and as we proceeded slowly along the bumpy and narrow dirt road, that doubt bubbled to the surface again. This just didn't have the feel of being the ultimate battle that would capture the most wanted man in the world, and the twilight time of day weighed heavily in our thoughts. The muhj had already abandoned three of our guys, so it was no sure bet that they would stick around after dark with us.

When we rounded a tight corner, we came face-to-face with a long convoy of vehicles that was blocking the road, with the good general himself in the lead vehicle. They were heading away from the fight!

Ali ceremoniously exited his SUV and approached us, illuminated by the headlights of our two vehicles crisscrossing each other. Ali ignored the jumpy Afghan guys in the front seat and approached Shag's window, leaned inside and extended his right hand toward me, gave a victory smile, and said, "Commander Dalton!"

Then came a torrent of Pashto, and Shag and I had no idea what the general said, although it was obvious he was welcoming us and was happy about our arrival.

After only a minute or two of geniality, Ali was back in his SUV and once again was on the move, heading north, away from the fight. But he left us with the impression that he was merely looking for a place where he could turn his convoy around, so we could all move to the sound of the guns. That was not going to be the case. Not even close.

I didn't want to believe what was really happening, but Shag pieced together enough of what our guides were saying to determine that Ali's fighters were finished for the evening. They were all headed home to break their Ramadan fast.

The muhj force that we thought had bin Laden surrounded and trapped apparently had packed it in for the day and was hightailing it off the mountain in full retreat. It didn't matter. *We are pressing on and will figure it out when we get there.* We proceeded south, hoping that we were wrong and that Ali and his boys were turning around and coming right behind us. Wishful thinking.

For the next few hundred meters, we wormed through a giant traffic jam as if swimming against a riptide. Dozens of muhj fighters were crammed inside the beds of pickup trucks or perched on the sides, most of them wrapped in blankets. Some strained their necks to get a look at our newer pickup trucks with mounted M-249 squad automatic weapons or M-240G machine guns, and loaded with Delta commandos who were strangely heading toward the fighting after dark.

Hope was fading that one of the general's vehicles would eventually zip in front of our convoy, take the lead, and guide us to where we needed to be so that, together, we could all assault bin Laden's location. The harsh truth was that we would not be seeing General Ali again for the next fifteen hours.

Something good was happening back at the schoolhouse. Reinforcements were coming in, trained professionals who could be an instant quick-reaction force if we needed help.

We had scooped up every task force member except Bernie, who was left at the base to monitor the radio and brief our squadron commander, Colonel Ashley, who was bringing in the new force—seven more Deltas and a couple of dozen Royal Marine commandos.

Lieutenant Colonel Al and another CIA man marked the landing zone for the inbound helicopters. They dropped five infrared light sticks on the sandy ground in the shape of a Y, to direct the pilot of the lead MH-47 helicopter to approach from the north, fly directly over the schoolhouse, and land facing the mountains. Instead, the bird ended up with the tail facing an adjacent building, with its big rotor whipping up an instant sandstorm.

Once the ramp hit the ground, the troops exited the helicopter carrying their heavy rucksacks and immediately headed into the nearest, but wrong, structure. The second helicopter mirrored the lead of the first and landed next to it and the rest of the troops hustled into the same building where their buddies had gone. A CIA operative hurried over to retrieve them.

The rotors of the two helicopters had created a blinding, massive brown ball of dust that roiled and churned over itself, darkening it to the point that only the static electricity of the rotor blades was visible. Within that dark and swirling cloud, one of the helicopters began to roll . . . directly toward the schoolhouse.

After moving roughly thirty yards, the helicopter's front refuel probe smacked a three-foot-high stone wall and pierced it like a temperature gauge going into Mom's roast. Colonel Al ran up the back ramp, grabbed the crew chief, and hauled him off to show him the damage.

"It was a brownout!" the crew chief calmly yelled over the engine noise, apparently not upset in the least. "Pilot must have taken his foot off the brake!"

By now the giant rotor blades were spinning violently, with the tips just a few feet above the roof of the schoolhouse in which Bernie was huddled. The helicopter had rolled itself into a mess. The pilot couldn't back up, because any attempt to change the rotor blade pitch would have sheared off the roof of the schoolhouse and been catastrophic for both the aircraft and anyone inside or nearby.

So, he just gave the helicopter all the power it had and slowly lifted from the ground right there, the fuel probe simply forcing its way up through the loose stones of the fence. Fortunately, the United Nations had only built a single-story schoolhouse.

The British Royal Commandos were not too happy about having carried their heavy rucksacks into the wrong building, and that they were not welcomed by anyone. The CIA man rounded them up, when the helicopters were gone, and pointed them in the right direction. They ran across the yard to the schoolhouse and took a knee inside the yard.

One of the Brits remarked to Lieutenant Colonel Al, "Well, mate, that was quite the faf [sic], right?" Al didn't need a translation. Apparently, the British slang term is synonymous with the American term "fubar" (fouled up beyond all recognition), and Al, who knew a potential disaster had narrowly been averted, was in total agreement.

Up the road, our convoy continued through the night, driving in blackout mode, with headlights off on all but the lead vehicle to prevent al Qaeda from seeing that an entire convoy was approaching. In retrospect, I probably should have jumped into the driver's seat, killed the lights and driven on by using my NVGs. But I didn't know where we were going, and giving the NVGs to the driver would have been of little use, for I doubted any Afghan local's ability to drive with only 10 percent illumination and no headlights. We just had to rough it out. Perhaps General Ali had radioed ahead for his remaining troops to pick us up.

The boys up in OP25-A spotted the headlights probing through the darkness and Dugan commented with his Georgia drawl, "Those guys are gonna get hit if they don't turn off those white lights. There's still a mortar tube out there." Sure enough, a couple of rounds soon impacted near the rear of the convoy.

Our guides became nervous, whispering, "Al Qaeda, al Qaeda." When our driver came to a stop, I expected to see some muhj force that could guide us to within striking distance of bin Laden's "surrounded" cave. Short of leading us to such a point, perhaps they would navigate us through the front lines and get us halfway there, or join us to make sure that we didn't shoot the wrong folks.

There were no friendly muhj waiting, and our hired guides frantically pointed toward the dark peaks and warned us al Qaeda was only fifty meters down the road. They were nervous wrecks and had gone as far as they planned to. Beyond this point, they would not budge.

Jim sorted things out up and down the convoy, and the boys took up security positions. I walked up the road to see if I could make out any sign of friendly or enemy activity. Nothing! I radioed Ironhead, who was bringing up the rear of the convoy, to ask about Ali's column.

Ironhead said that there was nothing behind us but pitch-black darkness all the way back down the road we had just traveled. No sign of the general or his muhj army in back, and no linkup party in front. Not good.

We tried to radio the schoolhouse for updates on bin Laden's grid location, but again the jagged landscape played havoc with the transmissions. We could not talk to the schoolhouse, only half a dozen miles away, but the radio frequencies somehow bounced all the way back to our task force headquarters at the ISB, clear across the Arabian Ocean.

Much closer, we were also able to talk to Jester, Dugan, and India

Team up in OP25-A. They filled us in on the status of Hopper, the Admiral, and Adam Khan. Then machine-gun and small-arms fire interrupted what had been until then a confusing but peaceful night for us.

With the Admiral on the run, the bombing and air cover had come to a halt because there was no combat controller to direct the planes. OP25-A could not take control until the condition of the evading Jackal could be determined, or risk hitting them.

So al Qaeda and the muhj took advantage of the absence of airpower. They occupied the tops of the ridgelines directly to our front and rear and opened fire. Caught in the middle, we all took cover behind rocks and vehicles as bright green and red zipped through the night sky. Several rockets screamed overhead.

The only thing preventing us from being engaged in the firefight was the low elevation of the road we were on. Unless al Qaeda maneuvered forward, we were safe, and we doubted that they would leave their prepared defense positions to take their chances in the open. Our biggest concern was that the enemy mortars would attempt to engage us with indirect fire, but we believed that we were too close to the enemy's own front line for the mortars to fire without hitting their own men.

Out of nowhere, a muhj fighter appeared from the darkness and told the guides that all of Ali's forces had withdrawn, and then he also continued on down the road. Our guides were in a panic, for they were responsible for the vehicle in which we rode and couldn't abandon it. But if it had not been for the string of vehicles blocking the road behind them, I'm sure they would have turned around and floored the gas pedal.

It was like a bucket of cold water over our heads to realize that there was no friendly muhj force coming forward, not General Ali, not even a lowly private. We were now the first string, and behind al Qaeda lines. Delta never minds being behind enemy lines, since we do a lot of that sort of thing, but the whole mission was unraveling.

Ironhead, Jim, Bryan, and I gathered at the fourth vehicle to sort out our next move. After the mass exodus we had seen on the road, it was pretty obvious that bin Laden was no longer surrounded, and perhaps never actually was. We had received no update on the grid position for more than an hour. Usama bin Laden, who had seemed so close, was now fading like a ghost.

Jim pulled our current location off his GPS and made a quick map check under a red-lens flashlight. We were roughly 2,500 meters in straight-line distance from the last sighting spot given to us by George before we left the schoolhouse. Out here, though, it was impossible to walk anywhere in a straight line.

The friendly situation was as uncertain as the enemy situation, not an abnormal condition for anyone who has ever suited up to stand in harm's way in the fog of war. Our guts told us that General Ali was finished for the night, but we did not want to stumble upon some muhj outpost we didn't know about that wouldn't be expecting us.

We still had no word from Hopper, the Admiral, and Adam Khan. Neither had the boys at OP25-A, nor those back at the schoolhouse.

We could not change any of those adverse developments, but we could certainly try to reach our missing men. They were still alive, still evading, and needed help. Finally, we managed to establish some basic radio contact with them, but the rugged country kept the transmissions spotty and inter-mittent.

It was time for a decision. Ironhead looked at me and said, "Your call, sir, but whatever we do, I don't think we should leave here until we have our boys back." Jim and Bryan withheld their comments, for this was a decision only the commander could make.

I certainly wasn't going to leave without our guys, but I had to factor in that we still just might be within striking distance of bin Laden, the ob-jective of our mission. The overall order had been to "kill bin Laden, and bring back proof," and the idea of giving up this chance of taking the top terrorist off the board was abhorrent to me.

I let the whole mess churn in my brain for a few seconds. It was my call because that's the kind of complicated decision a commander must face on a battlefield. Nobody said it was going to be easy.

I looked at all three of my veteran sergeants and said, "Okay, we'll have another shot at bin Laden. I absolutely agree with you all. We need to concentrate on recovering our boys first. If things change between now and then, we'll go for bin Laden, too. If not, we'll return to the school-house and prep for insertion of the teams."

Jim and Bryan replied, "Roger that," and went to ready the force to locate our evading teammates.

We couldn't reach Ashley back at the schoolhouse to fill him in, but I was again able, through the bouncing radio signal, to contact the Delta deputy commander back at the ISB. After explaining the situation with as much brevity as possible, he agreed with the decision.

I was not surprised to hear no second-guessing or armchair quarterbacking from the colonel. They had been monitoring the activities of the evening and had been only cautiously optimistic about the possibility of finding bin Laden anyway. But they also believed that other opportunities would come later, because we were so sure that he was trapped in Tora Bora.

It was both the hardest call I ever had to make and the easiest.

We left the guides behind and moved forward to the last known location of our evading teammates. Al Qaeda opened up, but although the heavy firing seemed all around, it actually was going over our heads since we were in a low position.

The mortars finally debuted with their whumping launches and wild explosions. It was a totally scrambled scene, and impossible to define. Was al Qaeda at our front, back, or sides? Or were there some friendly muhj out there actually engaging al Qaeda, with us caught in the middle? Then, it also could have been al Qaeda fighters firing at each other in the confusion of darkness, or friendly muhj shooting at other friendly muhj.

The one good fact was that al Qaeda obviously didn't know that a whole bunch of Delta boys was in their midst, which gave us the edge. But we didn't want to get into a shooting war with al Qaeda at this point, because the last thing you need when trying to recover friendly forces is to get bogged down in a direct firefight with the same folks your boys are trying to evade.

Alpha Team, led by Crapshoot, was given the nod to take four assaulters and scout the area forward. Getting some eyes up on the high ground might let us sort out the enemy positions so we could bring the AC-130 gunship into the game if the cloud conditions were safe.

Additionally, by gaining altitude, Alpha Team hoped to get Hopper, the Admiral, and Adam Khan up on the FM radio. Crapshoot led his group into the night without hesitation, and I watched with pride through my NVGs as their dark green silhouettes moved into the unknown.

Crapshoot soon split his team and sent Juice and Brandon to the very top of the hill to settle into an overwatch position, prepare to call in close air support, and try to reach the missing guys on the radio. Meanwhile, he took Blinky and Mango, and the three of them curled beyond the hill to take a position from which they could assist the evading guys if one or more of them should be wounded and need to be carried.

From the schoolhouse, the special intelligence interceptors gave us a running commentary on al Qaeda's shortwave radio calls that were being monitored in Arabic, Urdu, and Farsi.* It was clear the enemy knew that someone was still in the neighborhood and not everyone had left the field for the night. Fortunately, Skoot, the top interceptor himself, was along on our mission and listened to the various enemy groups attempting to find us. None of this was too alarming, until Skoot picked up a transmission that they were readying the RPGs.

Was that newly arrived QRF attempting to infiltrate the mountains in their helicopters? This was unlikely, but certainly possible, particularly since radio communications with the schoolhouse was sporadic and we wouldn't have known that such an assault was in the works. But it would have been a suicide mission. There was no place to land among the tight crags, and to hang up there long enough for the boys to fast-rope down would make the noisy helicopters sitting ducks for al Qaeda shooters.

The more likely scenario was that the nervous al Qaeda gunners were planning to waste their precious RPG rounds by firing at the relatively high-flying AC-130 gunship that was still droning above, waiting for the clouds to clear. This was something we observed on numerous occasions during daylight hours, when the enemy tried to reach a bomber at 30,000 feet with a shoulder-fired grenade with a range of only several hundred meters.

We had more to worry about than the enemy's RPG stockpile. Like whether al Qaeda was readying to assault us, or if Alpha Team was walking

---

* Michael Smith, in his book *Killer Elite,* discusses in detail the history of these special signal collectors.

into an ambush, or if things were going to hell for the three Americans still on their Warpath escape-and-evasion trek through bad-guy territory.

On their way down the ridge, Hopper, the Admiral, and Adam Khan came upon a small group of muhj hiding behind an old, burned-out tank, hoping that their fighting was done for the night. Our boys were not keen about approaching the muhj at night after a major engagement, particularly since the muhj had shown nothing but fear of al Qaeda's reputation for night fighting. There was a definite possibility that the muhj might mistake them for al Qaeda and open fire.

Hopper and the Admiral took the lead, since they were wearing the best NVGs money could buy. Adam Khan and the few muhj fighters still with them fell in to the rear. Hopper then realized the line was out of order. If he happened upon a local with a nervous trigger finger who barked out any command in a language other than English or Russian, then Hopper would be woefully unprepared to calm the challenger. That could spark an unintended firefight. So he shuffled the line and moved the muhj to the front while he, the Admiral, and Adam Khan stayed within earshot.

It turned out that the retreating muhj had positioned small groups of fighters to control passage along the ridgeline trails, and General Ali issued a new password to his fighters every day. When they challenged the approaching group, it took only a few seconds to realize the password the escorts were trying to use was wrong. As AK-47 bolts slammed forward and the rifles were being raised, it was Adam Khan's turn at bat. He had to try to talk their way through before anyone started pulling the trigger.

Accusations of being al Qaeda were thrown around, but once the muhj at the checkpoint finally recognized that they were all on the same side, they immediately changed their tune and began to demand money. Adam Khan bargained a toll of one hundred American dollars, to be paid later by General Ali. Adam Khan was biting his lip in fury, but it would have been a waste of time to admonish the checkpoint personnel over a bit of bribery, which was a common custom in tribal warfare.

They were allowed to pass, but within the next thousand meters the team had to get by two more checkpoints, and each time Adam Khan was forced to negotiate through the extortion. When it was finally over, he "forgot" to remind Ali that the general owed those guys some money.

We later learned they were not even Ali's men, nor were they all particularly loyal to the other Jalalabad area warlord, the slippery Haji Zaman Ghamshareek. Some were not on either side, but were just armed fence-sitters who would play for the highest bidder and demand bribes of passersby.

While Adam Khan made deals and Hopper watched everything that was happening, the Admiral tried the radio again, manipulating his satellite antenna to increase the range, and was finally able to reach the schoolhouse and update their situation.

Crapshoot's team also picked them up on the transmission, determined that they were close by, had not been detected, and were unhurt. Within about fifteen minutes, they all linked up south of Mortar Hill. Only two muhj were still with them. Hopper, the Admiral, and Adam Khan had spent more than two hours covering some two thousand meters over incredibly unforgiving terrain, under fire much of the time and at constant risk. When we finally reached the little group, I'm not sure who was happier to see whom, because I honestly had thought we wouldn't find them alive.

I'm not sure how many pounds of bombs the Admiral called in during his excursion, but the local field commander was amazed the following morning at how accurate the bombs had been and how the Admiral could get them so close to the friendly positions without causing casualties among the wrong people. It would have been nice if that local commander had stuck around the battlefield a little longer the previous night.

Then there was the sterling performance of Adam Khan. Sure, he was a former marine and understood normal military tactics and procedures, but he also was a former civilian. How would he react when left behind enemy lines with two American commandos? He could not have performed any better.

With the successful recovery of our teammates, we refocused on whether to continue on after bin Laden. It was tempting, but the more Ironhead, Jim, Bryan, and I discussed the situation, the less prudent the idea seemed.

To push forward unilaterally meant that we would be going it alone, without any muhj guides or security. Without a local guide's help in identifying friend from foe, we would have to treat anyone with a weapon as hostile, even a possible friendly muhj. Otherwise, we would risk being stitched with machine-gun fire, because we knew al Qaeda was roaming about. Dropping one of the general's fighters by mistake would sour our developing relationship with Ali and compromise much of the careful work done by George and his team.

Then there was the problem of the checkpoints. We did not have the luxury of prior coordination to pass through them, and how many might be out there was anyone's guess. In addition, we were unsure of their loyalties. While on their E&E, Hopper, the Admiral, and Adam Khan had no choice but to negotiate their passage, but a full assault force of more than thirty Delta operators would not bargain passage through makeshift Afghan tollbooths.

One final variable was that our higher headquarters had repeatedly directed us *not* to spearhead any assault on bin Laden's cave sanctuary. Our job was to facilitate the muhj advance, follow closely behind, and be in a position to exploit their progress. That was bullshit. Even if it was not in the approved script, should the battlefield dynamics dictate that Americans move to the front and lead the attack, well, Delta was more than willing to oblige.

Only days earlier, I had looked General Ali in the eye and given him my word that we would share the danger but not the glory. I promised that we would move into the mountains to drop bombs and assist his advance. It just was not that clean. Were we only to occupy the schoolhouse grounds and not really fight unless we all happened to be in bin Laden's cave at the same time? All things being equal, this concern had little weight.

Jim, Bryan, and Ironhead spoke their pieces and offered suggestions and options. They remained noncommittal whether to press on or to withdraw to the schoolhouse to coordinate an assault with Ali's forces and dedicated bomber support the next day. I could feel their eyes on me.

Again, it was my decision. I stood there for a moment before reaching for the handset and calling Ashley, who was now at the schoolhouse. I passed him our intentions. We were coming back.

I was uncertain if Sergeant Major Ironhead agreed until he simply said, "Good call, sir."

I'm still not so convinced that it was. My decision to abort that effort to kill or capture bin Laden when we might have been within two thousand meters of him still bothers me. In some ways I can't suppress the feeling of somehow letting down our nation at a critical time.

On our way back to the schoolhouse the boys up at OP25-A tracked our movement through their long-range spotting scopes. They weren't the only ones watching. Skoot intercepted an al Qaeda transmission: "Don't wait for the lights, just fire." They didn't even come close.

I laid my M-4 assault rifle against my ruck next to the gray wall. I removed my black Kevlar helmet and the attached NVGs and gently laid them on my cardboard sleeping mat. The flimsy door creaked open as I bent over to take off my black assault vest and I saw Lieutenant Colonel Al silhouetted by the yellow flickering light of the kerosene lamp. He was shaking his head slowly, and I could faintly make out his slight grin.

"Man, you guys are some brave-ass mothers," he said. "I've never seen anything like that before." Coming from a Special Forces officer and long-time member of the CIA's Special Activities Division, it was quite a compliment.

"Just another day at the office, Al. It's what we are here for," I offered.

"Yeah, I know all that shit. But your guys just got here, someone yells 'bin Laden,' and y'all haul ass into the fire. Any other unit would have thought about it for a day or two, developed a risk assessment, called for permission, or figured out a way not to go."

"Well, Al, that was the pre-nine-eleven military. I'd like to think all that conventional bureaucracy crap and risk aversion went out the window when the Towers fell." I dug into my pouch of Redman tobacco. "Want some?" I mumbled with my mouth full.

I slept the sleep of the righteous that night, curled up next to Adam Khan.

While we were dead to the world, one of the CIA 'terps reported that the journalists over on Press Pool Ridge had heard the helicopters' arrival at the schoolhouse and were stirring for a story.

Ali's subordinates reasoned it would be bad publicity for the general if the QRF was still around when the sun came up and the reporters and photographers spotted American and British faces. That just would not do!

So the MH-47 Dark Horses, pride of the 160th SOAR, returned, landed only meters from the schoolhouse and took away all of the new arrivals, including Ashley, to resolve the delicate situation.

I slept through it all.

The boys in OP25-A were magnificent that night. While we rested, they didn't sleep a wink, and that yielded the payoff moment for Ski's decision to have his India Team spend the night at the observation post. One of his boys was Dallas, who was using a MilCAM Recon thermal sight that we affectionately called the Darth Vader, and Dallas finally saw what everyone had been hoping for—the signature flash of an outgoing mortar round as it left the tube.

Fellow sniper Dugan slipped his wool hat back and grabbed his Izlid infrared marking laser. Dallas talked Dugan onto the mortar location by using the horizon lines of Larry, Curly, and Moe, and the OP25-B opposing ridgeline as reference points.

That may sound simple, but writing about it and executing it are two entirely different things. Words can't do justice to how difficult this was because the difference between the view through a hot thermal system and a set of night vision goggles is literally night and day. As Dugan and Dallas worked their side of the magic, Ski and Jester came up with a target grid, which they handed to Spike, the team's air force combat controller. Spike rang up the gunship. The clouds that had shielded the enemy had moved away, and the Spectre was eager to pounce.

As the AC-130 bored circular counterclockwise holes in the sky, the boys labored to tag the mortar tube for the gunship, and Dugan managed to get the Izlid's infrared laser exactly on the spot that Dallas had found, although they were working with entirely different tools. Dallas's thermal imager picked up heat sources, not infrared sources—so he couldn't actually *see* the laser that Dugan was using to sparkle the mortar.

The gunship aimed at the tip of the laser and fired a single round from its 105mm howitzer and scored a first-round direct hit. Spike followed up with the order to fire for effect and the gunship lit up the target area with more 105mm rounds and a great many pickle-size bullets from the ripping 25mm Vulcan cannon.

The boys didn't need to see warm bodies flying through the air to know they'd hit the mark. After taking a moment to pass high fives around the OP and to slap Dugan and Dallas hard on their backs, they all got back to work. Knocking out that pesky mortar was just another piece of business.

Signals intelligence would confirm there were no further enemy transmissions from that location. The elusive and persistent enemy mortars that had nagged us for several days were finally out of the game. It had taken less than ten minutes from the moment they were spotted.

Spike continued to control close air support missions throughout the night while India Team worked the thermals and Kilo Team worked the NVGs and radios. Spike orchestrated the dropping of payload after payload on known and suspected enemy locations, sending the clear message that darkness no longer would protect the al Qaeda mountainous sanctuary.

12

Press the Attack

So let me be a martyr, dwelling high in a mountain pass among a band of knights who, united in devotion to God, descend to face armies.

—USAMA BIN LADEN

After only a few hours of rack, we awoke to a gorgeous and peaceful view of the majestic mountains on December 11. We sipped freshly brewed green tea or coffee to cut the morning chill, picked through a cold MRE, and hoped that bin Laden was still around up there, that he had stuck around for another day's fight.

During the night, our signal interceptors monitored numerous radio calls between al Qaeda fighters, many of which went unanswered. The descriptive but choppy intercepts indicated that mass confusion, uncertainty, and a sense of vulnerability pervaded their camps.

Trying not to underestimate the man's physical courage, we all assumed bin Laden would be true to his word and would fight to the death—to martyr himself in those mountains if necessary, and not duck out that open back door into Pakistan. He could probably travel overland and crest the 14,000-foot peaks within a few days, or he could descend to the major north-south valley and cross into Pakistan at only a 9,000-foot elevation.

He had definitely been on the run that night, but all indications were that bin Laden would man up and stay put. I liked that choice.

His personal magnetism remained strong among Muslims and would be a factor in his decision on whether to stay, for he had a lot of local support. Our signals intelligence interceptors regularly picked up radio calls when bin Laden attempted to motivate and recruit fighters. He played on the Muslim faith of General Ali's men by offering them an opportunity to live and redeem their Muslim honor. All they had to do was drop their weapons, stop supporting the infidels, and return to their homes. Let the Americans, the "Far Enemy," enter the field and fight us, he said. He reminded them that Muslims fighting Muslims at the urging of Americans was clearly counter to Allah's will.

His words always found an audience. Numerous times throughout the battle, whenever a muhj subordinate commander believed he was listening to bin Laden himself, we would hear that officer call out excitedly to his men. They would gather around, and the commander would hold the radio high overhead so all could hear the words of the man they considered to be larger than life. As they listened, the mesmerized muhj would turn to the south and stare off into the forbidden mountains, as if they knew exactly which group of fir trees bin Laden was behind, or which cave he might be using, and that he was speaking personally to them.

But after the aerial beating that had been laid on his nest the evening before, first at the hands of the Admiral and then through the long night from the boys perched up in OP25-A, it wouldn't have surprised any of us to find out that the Lion of Islam had been killed.

Alive or dead, the most obvious thing to do today was deliver an encore presentation—press the attack!

Another six hours passed before we learned the details about General Ali's sudden disappearance from the battlefield. After leaving us along the side of the road, the general had continued north for another two hours to his comfortable home in Jalalabad. When he finally showed the next morning, he explained that had rushed away in order to mass two hundred more fighters and had planned to return. *Oh, well, in that case, we forgive you.* We didn't buy it for a second.

The general's trusty sidekick, Ghulbihar, later unwittingly revealed that his general was tired this morning because he had been up most of the night entertaining selected journalists and providing colorful commentary about bin Laden's fate.

Jim and I caught up with Hopper and the Admiral to hear details of their drama, and when they were finished, I asked them to put their experiences in writing. We used those personal accounts, and Adam Khan's description of events over the next few days, to write Silver Star recommendations for both of them. A few years later, Hopper earned a second Silver Star during the first days of Operation Iraqi Freedom. As of this writing, Hopper and the Admiral are both still in the SOF community.

Adam Khan later told me that Hopper and the Admiral were the "two bravest sons of bitches" he had ever seen, and had he known that we were sending him out with two guys who had no fear of dying, he wouldn't have gone along. Right. His humility was evident. We couldn't pin a medal on Adam Khan's chest, but the Delta commander signed a personal letter for his boss back in Washington, D.C., commending the man's extraordinary bravery and other qualities.

The majority of Delta operators are products of the Ranger or Special Forces community. The solid foundation of skills necessary for success in those elite organizations—shooting, moving, and communicating—provide a base mold that, with some advanced tooling, can be forged into an idiomatic counterterrorist icon. But every now and then a candidate with less of a warriorlike background defies the odds and surfaces during the Delta tryouts. By design, the *right guy* for the unit might have been the barracks computer whiz kid, the barracks lawyer, or even the barracks rat in some other unit.

Hopper was one such person, coming to Delta without Ranger or Green Beret experience. His previous military specialty had been as a Russian linguist, and he had been standing near the Berlin Wall when the East and West Germans started knocking it down! The unexpected selection of such noncombat types speaks volumes about Delta's secret recruitment and

assessment process, which is as well guarded as the Coca-Cola recipe.*
They can teach the new selectees how to fight our way, but the new ones
also have to bring intellect and individuality to the table.

One day, teammate Shrek described Hopper by saying, "Whatever
he touches, he can do it better than a pro." When not on the rifle range
working the bugs out of custom-made assault rifle concealment holsters
or removing the ten-ring of paper targets at twenty-five meters with his
MP5K submachine gun, he was probably out on his hog or jammin' with
his hot guitar. A talented musician with a liking for electric guitars and
loud drums, Hopper rocked alone in his private band room at home.

During our morning review, or hot wash, of the previous night's work,
we all recognized the obvious: Nobody, short of al Qaeda maybe, actually knew where the front lines were. Ground that was contested during
the day would serve as the front line only until nightfall, when the muhj
would retreat and al Qaeda would reoccupy the ground, light their warming fires, and bed down.

Delta was not going to play by those rules.

Our original concept had been to send small teams of a few snipers
and air force combat controllers out with Ali's forces to conduct terminal
guidance operations, but since the muhj did not stick around at night,
that plan had to be modified. After watching the latest tedious performance of the muhj–al Qaeda minuet, reality dictated that if we wanted to
rapidly respond on an ambiguous battlefield then we had better be able to
commit immediately. It was as much a force protection matter as a tactical requirement.

So on the night of December 11, without asking permission, we re-
configured our mission. Instead of holding most of our assaulters back at
the schoolhouse to comprise an emergency strike force, we decided that the
forward observation posts and the assaulters needed to occupy roughly the

---

* Author Derek Leebaert in his book *to Dare and to Conquer* discusses this unique characteristic of Delta's selection process.

same terrain. Nobody was coming to the rescue, so we had to depend on ourselves and would later inform our bosses, "This is what we are doing." In Delta, you are expected to make decisions when faced with something that doesn't work.

Basically, we were creating mobile security forces that could also double as forward observers. For lack of a better term, such a unit was called a mission support site, and known by the acronym MSS. Perhaps the name was awkward, but we all knew what it meant, so what the heck. The packages would be known by the nicknames of the leaders, so one would be MSS Grinch, and the other would be MSS Monkey.

While Jester, Dugan, and the Green Berets from 5th Special Forces Group occupying OP25-A on the eastern flank stood down for a rest, the other Green Berets now occupying OP25-B, on the western flank, took over managing the bombers for the day on December 11. The original four guys who had established that outpost as Victor Bravo Zero Two went home once the Green Berets arrived, and we never saw them again. Things were starting to move fast.

Back at the schoolhouse we spent the rest of the day preparing for the afternoon infil of MSS Grinch. Troop sergeant major Jim would be in charge, and he was backed up by half of our troop headquarters—combat medic Durango, communicator Gadget, combat controller the Admiral, and an attached Arabic tactical signal intelligence collector.

Jim also would field a half-dozen snipers, with Hopper leading them, which meant his nickname of Jackal would remain in place for that unit. The other shooters were Murph, Shrek, and Scrawny. Pope and Lowblow, who had been split off of Kilo Team earlier with original assignment of going to OP25-B, would now instead go along with Grinch. The augmentation of the Green Berets at OP25-B would be tasked to others.

Two teams of assaulters rounded out the package. Crapshoot's Alpha Team members would be Blinky, Brandon Floyd, Juice, and Mango. The Bravo Team was to be led by Stormin', and contain Grumpy, Precious, Noodle, and The Kid.

To fatten the package even more, we attached the first four-man contingent of British SBS commandos.

This tough and deadly bunch of professionals was about to take the fight to al Qaeda, and would not be coming back when the sun went down.

For the record, we had no choice about accepting the Brits. When Ashley asked if we wanted any additional commandos from the SBS, our response had been, "No, thank you."

It was not because we questioned the skill of these professionals in any way, because we certainly did not. We would have felt the same about anybody. We had never worked with them before. After having acquired a good look at the battlefield, we knew that just resupplying ourselves would be a major challenge, and adding more bodies would increase the difficulty. Their presence also would exacerbate the problem of trying to hide from prying eyes.

Besides, Adam Khan reminded us of the long trail of bad blood between the British and the Afghans. At the end of the First Anglo-Afghan War in 1842, an embattled garrison of about 4,500 British troops and perhaps up to 10,000 camp followers was promised safe passage through Afghanistan's snow-covered passes to return to India. They were repeatedly ambushed, and, according to legend, all were slain but Dr. William Brydon. The lone survivor was instructed to tell everyone he saw that the same slaughter awaited anyone else who considered occupying Afghan soil in the future.

Now the Brits were back.

Within another twenty-four hours, Ashley asked us to figure out how to use still another eight SBS commandos. Again, I responded negatively, at which time I was told in no uncertain terms that Rumsfeld had said this would be a coalition effort with our most trusted allies and friends and we would just have to figure it out.

So, another eight British commandos and an intelligence operative from the United Kingdom would be added to our party at various intervals throughout the coming fight.

Now, this is as good a time as any for me to eat crow. I was wrong.

Our British friends fit in smoothly as soon as they arrived and could not possibly have performed better. They were brave, talented, professional, and passionate, and all of us in Delta were extremely impressed with their skill and courage, and proud to call them teammates during that cold December. The relationships established on this battlefield would serve both nations well as Operation Enduring Freedom progressed, and carry over into the next war in Southwest Asia, in Iraq.*

In the early afternoon of December 11, some of Ali's fighters were trapped in a valley, and a large group of al Qaeda fighters was looking down on them from the ridgeline. The muhj liaison stationed at OP25-A listened carefully to the radio transmissions and described the dire situation to Jester and Dugan. He pointed over to Hilltop Moe, where some other muhj fighters were trying to relieve the trapped men. The rescue force ran up Hilltop Moe, raised their AK-47s over their heads, and sprayed a few bursts of automatic fire across the valley, toward the dug-in al Qaeda fighters. That tactic didn't work very well.

The liaison man in OP25-A then asked the Americans to put some bombs on adjoining Hilltop Larry, which would spring the muhj fighters to take Hilltop 2685. Jester had word relayed to the commander to back his men a safe distance from the anticipated impact area, and the Delta boys went to work with a couple of the Green Berets and the Afghans to match the spotted location to the map.

Not surprisingly, whenever Americans and muhj tried to interpret the same map, there was significant disagreement over the correct grid. Jester took out his compass and shot an azimuth to the center of the ridgeline in question, then using the polar plot method—distance and direction—he determined a usable set of grid coordinates, and a confirmation round marked

---

* The good relations between the United States and the United Kingdom developed since the turn of the twentieth century continue today. This is particularly true among military outfits and has proven a tremendous asset in the ongoing war on terror. See http://www .strategicstudiesinstitute.army.mil/pdffiles/PUB633.pdf.

the target. The combat controller gave his solution to a B-52 bomber which dumped twenty-five bombs on the spot. Airburst fuses exploded the weapons before they hit the ground in order to kill not only the al Qaeda fighters caught in the open but also those tucked into holes.

The muhj cheering that was overheard on the OP25-A radio couldn't be mistaken. The strike opened the way for the muhj to break the stalemate, and they charged up Hilltop 2685 in a surprising display of aggressiveness. They did not stop until they had killed every al Qaeda brother with a heartbeat on the ridgeline and had captured the last of the Three Knuckles.

Then they ruined the moment by spending the next hour looting the dead al Qaeda fighters of equipment, weapons, and ammo. With the pillaging done, the victorious and joyful muhj headed back home for the night. What a waste.

Although the muhj had once again failed to hold the captured terrain, they had by clearing the field opened another opportunity for us to inflict still more damage on the bin Laden forces. Before the al Qaeda fighters could put their heads down for some much needed sleep with the retreat of the muhj, the boys in OP25-A took control of the airspace again.

Most of the Green Berets bedded down for most of the coming night, while Jester, Dugan, and the air force controller began another twelve straight hours of guiding bombs and providing targets to the stalking warplanes. At one point, OP25-A simultaneously controlled nine aircraft, which were stacked like blocks, and called them in one at a time to attack the enemy positions, cave entrances, foot trails, and fighters still in the open.

Several times, the special intelligence interceptors at the schoolhouse heard the agonizing cries of pain and despair coming over the al Qaeda radios. The pitiful pleas were just the kind of feedback we needed, and as the bombers gave way to the AC-130 gunships and night fighters, "multiple hot spots and personnel" were reported and engaged.

After destroying three enemy vehicles, the boys saw enemy foot soldiers fleeing down a ridgeline and immediately cleared the Spectres and

F-14s to engage. It was the end of the jihad, and everything else, for those guys.

S uccess did not come without some hiccups.

A CIA owned-and-operated unmanned aerial vehicle known as the Predator entered the Tora Bora airspace and started unleashing rockets on al Qaeda targets. Without any heads-up from our friends next door, the unknown bird caught our boys as a complete surprise. They had no idea about the identity of the aircraft, which had the call sign "Wildfire" and was being driven by a computer joystick in the hands of an operator far removed from the battlefield. It was certainly welcome, but it took a while to figure out what the hell it was.

Besides the unexpected appearance of the Predator, the night was filled with a good bit of confusion, which can be expected on any fluid battlefield. Multiple aircraft entering and exiting the airspace resulted in a few bad target locations. One aircraft identified Ali's few T-55 tanks as belonging to al Qaeda, and another plane mistook the position of OP25-A as being occupied by enemy fighters.

Back at the schoolhouse, we monitored each call for fire and matched it with the colorful enemy radio intercepts. Each new bomb generated another broadcast, which in turn helped fill out the developing picture: Al Qaeda forces were withdrawing south, into secondary positions.

We identified on the map a linear terrain feature that they had to traverse and worked the grids to each end of the target line. Once the information was relayed to OP25-A, they snagged all available aircraft and relentlessly hammered the area.

Besides the CIA's armed Predator, we also received excellent support from a second one, although it carried no guns. The roving aerial camera spent eight hours helping to identify targets and providing immediate feedback after the targets were struck. This camera-carrying Predator had a direct feed to the AC-130U gunship, and was a true combat multiplier.

Few believed that the success the boys up at OP25-A had enjoyed the night before could be outdone, but on December 11 the close air support they controlled in tandem with every type of aircraft in theater—AC-130 H and U models, B-1s, B-52s, F-14s, F-15s, F-16s, F-18s, and Predators made this the mother of all sleepless nights. The boys in OP25-A were the envy of the half-dozen Green Berets who watched the light show from several miles away in OP25-B.

After handing over airspace control to their buddies across the battle-field at 0500 hours on December 12, the exhausted boys at OP25-A passed out.

Ski and his India Team, which had stayed at OP25-A the previous night, had packed their gear and headed back to the schoolhouse. Without the luxury of the donkeys, their rucksacks weighed over a hundred pounds each, since they had brought along five days' worth of food, batteries, and water. A couple of Toyota pickups met them at the original drop-off site and gave them a lift the rest of the way.

With things developing fast up in the mountains, we began cashing in some of the flexibility that we intentionally placed in the plan.

India had a day to rest and prepare for reinsertion the next day as part of another large unit, this one to be led by reconnaissance troop sergeant major Bryan. The team assumed part of his odd nickname, B-Monkey, and became MSS Monkey. It was nearly the mirror image of MSS Grinch.

Bryan took the normal complement of direct support personnel with him—combat medic Dirty, communicator Shen Dog, combat controller Spike, and a tactical signal intelligence collector. Besides the snipers of Ski's India Team, MSS Monkey included Charlie Team assaulters—team leader Catfish, as well as Stalker, Nitro, Hobbit, and Shamus. We tasked MSS Monkey to relieve the Green Berets currently in OP25-B, then press on deeper into the mountains to help seal the western Wazir Valley.

Although shorted a bit on their stay in the mountains, these Green Berets had performed superbly as they passed control of the airspace back and forth with OP25-A. They were ordered to pack up their gear, meet the relieving MSS Monkey personnel at the base of the foothills, and use the same vehicles that had brought our boys forward to return to the schoolhouse.

Outfitted with the best night vision equipment money can buy, we preferred to infiltrate at night, but Ali's men still could not be persuaded to stick around and guide us through the friendly checkpoints. Money could buy many things in Tora Bora, but could not lessen the muhj's fear of the dark. They pretty much refused to do anything after sunset other than eat, sleep, and shiver, preferably somewhere very safe, and were certainly not about to capitalize on the cover of darkness to get in among the enemy. As far as the muhj fighters were concerned, we could take our state-of-the-art NVGs and own the night all we wanted . . . just leave them out of it.

Ali and Zaman, the two rival warlords, became changed men once they saw the extraordinary effects of the bombing from the night before and heard a couple of reports that bin Laden was under duress and possibly ripe for the kill.

Ali and Zaman, locked in their own battle for status, were still trying to trump each other to secure favor with the press. Neither missed an opportunity to second-guess or complain about the other man's tactics or the other warlord's unwillingness to engage in heated battle when the recorders and cameras were running.

Returning from Jalalabad, General Ali drove right past the schoolhouse and headed directly for the front, pausing dramatically at Press Pool Ridge to update the eager reporters about his intentions to finish bin Laden that day, God willing, of course. Zaman was close on his heels.

The big lights popped on for the TV crews, and dozens of sleepy and unshaven reporters—both Western and Eastern—stuck their small tape recorders or hand mikes almost into the mouths of Ali and Zaman, who held simultaneous interviews only thirty yards apart. And, as had become customary, the media representatives listened with enormous enthusiasm and expectation as the warlords pledged that their men were on the attack.

And they were, in a crazy sort of way, with little coordination between the two forces. They moved on separate routes, and fought up ridgelines for the prize of owning Hilltop 2685.

It was a foot race with dramatic political overtones. With the effective bombing overnight, and the boys in OP25-A delivering new bomb loads during the day, the enemy had been unable to fully reoccupy its positions, and after trading small-arms and rocket fire with al Qaeda remnants, elements of both warlords reached the high peak within thirty minutes of each other.

But Zaman's people got to the top first and were quick to let Ali's men know who owned the high ground. With a quick and interesting tactic, as if this game had been played on other hilltops, they cleverly expanded their perimeter on top, not so much to protect against an al Qaeda attack as to keep Ali's men lower on the military crest, which was the less valued piece of real estate.

Understanding the importance of command presence on the battlefield, Zaman got to the hilltop and stayed there. Ali departed to return to the schoolhouse. Now Zaman had direct access to the al Qaeda fighters remaining in the area, and the subordinate commanders of the embarrassed and departed General Ali stood around dumbfounded and frustrated, unable to do anything.

The taking of Hill 2685 by the mujahideen on December 11 would prove to be a very critical point in the overall battle, for Zaman was nothing if not a sly opportunist.

Earlier in the day, on his way to the dual press conference and then the front, Ali had radioed the schoolhouse to request that we send a couple of Americans forward to direct bombs while his men attacked toward the prized hilltop. As much as we were willing to support his offensive, we had learned our lesson the hard way about sending a small team out there with the muhj because it was a safe bet that, come nightfall, they would again be left behind.

So this time we were ready with a full package, and Jim and MSS Grinch took off for the foothills. If they could link up with one of Ali's subordinate commanders, they could then push up the ridge to the contested high ground, from where they could call for precise fire on the retreating al Qaeda forces.

That was they way it was supposed to work. Few things in Tora Bora ever went as planned.

Our first attempt to infil the combat-savvy men of MSS Grinch had met exactly the problems we by now almost routinely anticipated. The narrow road to the front was one snag after another and the usual traffic jams slowed the infil down to a snail's pace. Al Qaeda would have had to be blind not to have seen Jim's convoy coming their way.

Then, our boys ran smack-dab into a mass of journalists and cameramen at one of the forward checkpoints. The muhj guides knew that under no circumstances were the American commandos to be discovered by the press, so they stopped our convoy to discuss the options.

Time seemed to stand still, and when the sun set behind the mountains and darkness overtook the area, the guides simply decided that the best plan would be for nobody to go anywhere. They had no idea where exactly Jim and the boys needed to be dropped off anyway.

Jim was fit to be tied. He wanted desperately to press on alone with MSS Grinch, to ditch the guides and just drive on through the press area, but patience had to be the better part of valor. Jim knew that if we took center stage, we would be giving the proverbial middle finger to our hosts. No matter how frustrating, we had to do this with the muhj.

My boss had made it clear that our mission was to keep General Ali moving, continue to generate momentum for his assault, and help create the conditions for his success. The guides at the front had quite another idea; they refused to continue, and that was that.

With a lot of angry muttering about having to miss still another opportunity, the powerful MSS Grinch, twenty-five Delta operators and skilled British SBS commandos, were forced to turn the convoy around and head back to the schoolhouse without even having seen the enemy. Ali had failed to coordinate his intentions with us, and now he paid the price for that mistake. That night, Zaman was king of the hill.

When George of the CIA, Adam Khan, and I went over to the general's lackluster quarters, we found a totally exhausted Ali. Wearing a clean set of snow-white pajamas, the general this time opted not to even sit up when we entered his dark room, but instead remained on his side, with his head on his pillow and a green and brown wool blanket pulled up to his shoulders. His words were slow and labored. There was little light in the room, which had a leathery, musty smell about it. He was totally whipped and discouraged.

The general said he was concerned about his fighters' stamina. They were tired, bloody, and cold, and he was not sure how long he could keep them motivated to fight. It was a veiled plea for help and exactly what we were looking for. We pounced on the chance.

"General Ali, now is the time," I said, trying to encourage him. "I know you and your men are tired, but so is al Qaeda."

The general nodded his head slowly, almost as if he was too tired to give it any more thought.

"He is right, General; bin Laden is very vulnerable right now. We can't let this opportunity to end this thing slip away," George added. "You need to order your men to support Dalton's men . . . or I will have no other choice but to bring thousands of Americans to do the job for you."

We made it as clear as we could. If he wanted to maintain the bombing, and the general certainly did, then he needed to get a handle on things and impress upon his subordinates the importance of getting us onto those damned mountains at night. The cover of darkness would keep the press off our rear ends, provide us unimpeded movement along the narrow road, and get us close enough to accurately direct bombs onto al Qaeda's positions.

We had to *be* there! It was useless providing a grid location to the muhj or pointing out where we wanted to go on a map because the muhj didn't read maps. A better technique would have been just to stand behind the schoolhouse and point to the ridgeline where we wanted to be dropped off. Even more practical would be to drive as close as we could get, then point to the correct spot and have the guides determine the best route to walk there.

After the little pep talk, Ali realized the importance of getting on with it, and issued some short commands to several aides waiting outside the doorway. As we nodded to signal our pleasure with Ali's ability to make tough calls, we couldn't help but notice the aides were visibly uneasy with the orders. The general just seemed happy to get back to sleep.

With that good news, we reset MSS Grinch's mission. They would depart at 2300 hours local, eleven o'clock, on that same night when they had already been stymied once. The convoy would now reach the drop-off point about midnight. That gave the boys a few hours to kill, so they warmed themselves with blankets and body heat, wolfed some cold MREs and powdered Gatorade, and made last-minute equipment adjustments before going out again.

All of us had arrived in Afghanistan with zero visibility as to exactly what type of fighting force the Eastern Alliance Afghan Opposition Group might be. We had assumed they possessed some fundamental sense of organization, professionalism, and skill of arms, and we expected some level of motivation to get the job done. But after encountering repeated debacles, it was clear that our new friends were anything but an organized, well-equipped, professional allied army.

It was just over two months since 9/11, and for the most important mission to date in the global war on terror, our nation was relying on a fractious bunch of AK-47-toting lawless bandits and tribal thugs who were not bound by any recognized rules of warfare or subject to any code of military justice short of random executions or firing squads. Moreover, the muhj showed little advancement from slingshot technology beyond some handheld walkie-talkies and a few aging Soviet battle tanks.

It was their turf, their fight, and for their glory, but it sure seemed that they should have been doing a lot better.

A few minutes before MSS Grinch loaded the trucks for their second attempt at reaching the mountains, Adam Khan showed up after talking to the locals and some muhj fighters. The value of this guy's ability to converse in fluent Pashto cannot be overstated. To me, he was an asset more valuable than a boatload of BLU-82s and an armory of AK-47s; he was the glue that was holding the entire scheme together.

Apparently, the CIA wasn't the only player with cash to spend. Bin Laden's minions were said to be dishing out $100 bills like candy to every local in the region. Adam Khan reported the locals said he had bought off every villager, even before we arrived, and that the recipients of his largess included some of our assumed allies.

Shortly after midnight, the radio in our corner room came alive. MSS Grinch had finally infiltrated the Tora Bora Mountains, linked up with the designated group of muhj, and was moving out. Adam Khan went with them.

They soon reached the Milawa base camp, a place that was reputed to have once been the home of Usama bin Laden, and had been attacked by bomb after bomb. On the opposite side of the ridgeline stood about a hundred muhj—Zaman's men.

13

The Surrender

This is the greatest day in the history of Afghanistan.
—AFGHAN WARLORD HAJI ZAMAN
GHAMSHAREEK, DECEMBER 12, 2001

Before the sun came up on the morning of December 12, the American and British commandos of MSS Grinch were already on the hill. They stopped momentarily in a sparsely treed area that was strewn with boulders. Just to the west and down the ridge about a hundred meters, approximately one hundred of Zaman's fighters were spread out, and their commander was sitting on a large rock with a lit joint in one hand and a folding-stock AK-47 propped beside him. Adam Khan and Jim cautiously moved down to coordinate the next move with the man.

By the way the muhj were acting, Jim realized that something big was going on. As Adam Khan talked to the commander and pieced the story together, Jim's curiosity changed to anger.

The commander said that al Qaeda had thrown in the towel! A full surrender of all al Qaeda forces was about to take place!

As Jim's fury grew, the local commander raised Zaman on his radio, and the warlord himself issued an order that the foreign commandos were not to proceed any farther into the mountains.

"Whatever it takes," Zaman said in Pashto. "Under no circumstances are the Americans allowed to attack al Qaeda. We must see the negotiations through."

The notorious warlord had left Hilltop 2685, but was directing the show from not too far away. His voice carried a cocky air of self-assurance.

Jim knew the surrender gambit was nonsense, and said so. He responded that he had his own orders and intended to see them through. Short of a gunfight, not much could stop the powerful Grinch force from advancing south into the mountains to kill as many al Qaeda fighters as possible. He told the boys to top off their Camelbaks and ruck up. Within twenty minutes after hearing Zaman insist that Americans would not be allowed to take another step toward the enemy, Jim and MSS Grinch began humping up the ridgeline.

They had covered only about fifty meters when Zaman's men appeared on the high ground and leveled their weapons—eighty AK-47s—at the commandos. Some of the fighters were only innocent-looking teenage boys who seemed uncertain, but many others were hardened warriors. The local commander yelled a warning for the Americans to halt, reiterated Zaman's orders, and vowed to follow those instructions. The commander obviously feared Zaman's wrath more than he did the twenty-five American and British commandos that morning. Only Adam Khan's calm presence prevented disaster.

He told Zaman's man that the commandos had General Ali's full support to make the attack, and scolded him: "The general will not be happy." The commander didn't really care about Ali's pleasure. He worked for Zaman.

Jim bottled his anger and weighed his options. The odds in a firefight were probably about even: one highly trained commando against every four untrained Afghans, but getting into a shootout with your supposed allies was not the most diplomatic of moves. So MSS Grinch had little choice but to hold in place and let the cease-fire situation play out a little more. An hour passed uneventfully except for the commandos stewing about being held back.

A few minutes after 6:00 A.M., Zaman arrived with another dozen of his fighters. He was an arrogant sort who played himself up in front of the

Americans whenever he had the chance and now he took full credit for arranging the surrender. He announced that he had arranged to contact the al Qaeda forces by radio in two hours, at 0800, to close the deal and provide surrender details and terms.

Jim listened intently until Zaman was done with the self-promotion.

"Okay, I hear what you are saying. Now start from the beginning," he counseled the strutting warlord. "Tell me what happened."

After the battle the previous afternoon, December 11, some of Zaman's soldiers reached the highest point of Hilltop 2685. There they found the bodies of a dozen dead al Qaeda fighters who had been left behind in their trenches. Zaman's men wasted no time in stripping them of valuable items. Any Afghan warrior worth his salt goes for the weapons and ammo first, followed by warm blankets, shoes, and foodstuffs. Afterward, a junior Zaman commander barked orders, and several muhj kicked as much dirt into the hole as they could, then rolled rocks the size of bowling balls into the pit before kneeling in prayer beside the partially filled hole.

The burial detail stood, picked up their thin prayer blankets, wrapped them around their shoulders, and stood motionless over the makeshift mass grave for a few moments before the cold got to them and they trembled. They wondered who might have the better deal, the buried martyrs who were on their way to paradise, ready to cash in on Allah's promises, or the shivering gravediggers who had to continue the fight.

With the contested hilltop finally and officially captured by the muhj, an al Qaeda lieutenant then allegedly radioed Zaman to request a cease-fire and terms for surrender, and after a little customary tribal discussion, the warlord agreed. He gave them ten minutes to surrender. Of course, nothing happens that fast.

Jim nodded, listening with a growing sense of skepticism as Zaman described how the negotiations had been going throughout the night of December 11 and the early morning of December 12.

The al Qaeda negotiator finally requested that they be turned over to the United Nations. Zaman balked, admitting he held no sway with that organization, and directed the enemy to start coming off the mountain at ten o'clock to surrender. Almost unnoticed, the talking had just let the clock slip another two hours.

The negotiator protested, telling Zaman they were worried that the Americans would kill them, and the al Qaeda fighters wanted permission to retain their weapons as they surrendered.

"Absolutely not!" Jim snorted. "No weapons. No deals."

It was possible that al Qaeda really did want to surrender, because they had been undergoing increasingly intense day-and-night bombing, and likely were low on basic supplies and morale. The signals intercepts painted a clear picture of crisis and despair. Two nights earlier, Hopper and the Admiral had crawled about among them and wreaked havoc on their frontline stronghold before OP25-A destroyed the valuable mortar position. And after last night's no-holds-barred round of bombing, al Qaeda fighters might actually have felt defeat was inevitable. It was possible, but was it likely?

But Jim was not buying the story. It sounded too clean. Too easy. Too much like a schoolyard stall tactic. Our seasoned Delta warrior raised the bullshit flag and pressed the warlord for more details.

Zaman insisted that all enemy forces would be surrendering, and although he didn't specifically mention Usama bin Laden, it was clearly implied that the big guy also would be giving up.

Jim couldn't figure out just yet who was doing the stalling. Was al Qaeda using Zaman to buy time? Or could Zaman perhaps be in cahoots with al Qaeda and delaying the fight to allow the enemy to consolidate its forces, reposition, or even escape?

Almost as a sideshow, the muhj of General Ali who had accompanied Jim and the Grinch boys were happy to come to a stop. A surrender sounded good to them. Heck, they would have been pleased to have the day's ground battle conclude before it ever got started. Then they could stroll back down with a bunch of al Qaeda prisoners who would have their arms raised high in the air and parade them around the press and local women and children like a bunch of American Indians arriving back at the teepees after a big buffalo hunt.

A centuries-old code of Afghan warrior ethics was in play. In tribal warfare, when one side is outmatched and concedes the field, the Kalashnikovs are traded for teacups and the evil adversaries become honored guests and sit cross-legged around plates of broiled sheep and fried dates, resting and fattening up until the next time. It is tradition and custom.

Jim continued to work every angle. Even should the surrender turn out to be legitimate, he demanded that Zaman agree that if any of the top twenty-two most wanted al Qaeda members listed by the U.S. State Department happened to be in the surrendering group, then Jim and the boys would take them into custody.

He demanded that Zaman pick a spot in the mountains for the surrender at which Jim could get a good look at each of the fighters' faces before the muhj whisked them away to who knows where. The place chosen was the training field directly in front of bin Laden's old rubbled home.

Then, in all seriousness, Zaman asked if Jim planned to execute the surrendering al Qaeda prisoners on sight, and if not, would he like Zaman's men to do it for him? Jim said he didn't care if they were turned over to American hands dead or alive, but the commandos would follow the established rules of engagement and not shoot prisoners.

Time dragged on, but Zaman was still exuding confidence and insisted that al Qaeda was not stalling. A time had been established on how long the surrender would take. Given the rugged terrain and the dispersal of enemy, it would take several hours for them to navigate in from the distant caves and bunkers and reach the designated surrender location. The warlord's latest promise was that by five o'clock in the afternoon, it would all be over. The two sides had been haggling since the previous day, and al Qaeda was not yet getting with the surrender program.

Jim intuitively decided that Zaman was dirty.

He told the warlord if any al Qaeda fighters refused to come out of the hills during that obviously elastic surrender time, and were seen carrying weapons by the Americans after the surrender, then he would immediately move the OP teams up and begin dropping bombs. The warlord stood silent for a few seconds after that ultimatum, then turned on his heels and left the field.

While Jim was dealing with Zaman, I dialed up Ashley on the satellite phone and filled him in. He agreed that we had to let the alleged surrender run its course until 5:00 P.M., since we really had no choice. But when that deadline expired, it was important to resume the fight immediately. The negotiation itself was a clear sign of weakness in al Qaeda. The enemy was on the run; we could feel it, and we would not take the pressure off just so the Afghans and al Qaeda could continue bargaining like they were in a marketplace.

Still more players became involved, and a new time element surfaced. News of this magnitude would never hold for long because it had too many headline possibilities for the major personalities, and too many people knew about it. The story that was passed to the media stated that a twenty-four-hour cease-fire had been agreed upon, and actually had started at eight o'clock on the morning of December 12!

We had not been told of that, and would not abide by it. It would mean that things would remain on hold overnight. A whole day and a night of granting respite to a savage enemy that was cracking under the pressure. Keep pounding them, and you hold all the cards. Instead, Zaman was frittering away that advantage. So if we played by their rules, we would have to wait around until 0800 the next morning before going to full speed again. No way.

Overhead, an irritated fighter pilot waiting to drop his load turned the bright blue sky into his personal notepad. He had been given the news, too, and wrote a message in the heavens for all to see. Turning his afterburners on and off to create contrails, he circled back and forth until he spelled out: "ON 8."

We could not have made it any clearer to everyone below that we were tired of waiting while the enemy fighters were given the priceless gift of time. By eight o'clock the next morning, our forward commandos would have established new positions and the great game would be back on with full fury.

The only time that mattered to us was Zaman's earlier pledge that it would all be done by five o'clock this afternoon. Screw tomorrow.

Six older, heavyset men with long gray beards came to the schoolhouse. All wore thick gold turbans that appeared four sizes too big and white Afghan men's dresses that draped down from their shoulders to their toes. The Shura had arrived. We crammed inside General Ali's small room to listen to the elders describe the village telegraph version of how the surrender unfolded. Word travels fast.

They confirmed that when Zaman's and Ali's forces closed in on Hilltop 2685 the previous afternoon, they were met with a surprise offer of surrender. The enemy asked only for a few minutes to collect their modest belongings, but then Zaman showed up and began directing the show.

According to the Shura, the warlord told the enemy fighters to leave their weapons and descend to the foothills, and the councilmen also confirmed that the al Qaeda fighters had asked to be turned over to the United Nations. Zaman gave them a few hours to consider their options and offered to negotiate surrender terms with the American representatives at the schoolhouse.

"Negotiate?" George, the CIA lead dog, was seething. He was in no mood to talk about any surrender with the archenemies of the United States. "America won't negotiate with terrorists who need to be killed and not pampered," he barked. "Al Qaeda is a worldwide problem. We must kill them all."

It was hard to read the Shura, but they got the point. It wasn't that hard to understand. They stared at George without responding, and then the meeting broke up.

S oon after the meeting, the signals interceptors picked up several radio calls of al Qaeda fighters still negotiating with Zaman. There was no doubt that the whole surrender gesture was a hoax. The "negotiations" were a simple stalling tactic to buy time, and the enemy wanted to drag out the discussions for as long as they could to make the battlefield safe for them to do whatever they wanted.

A few hours after the Shura departed, Zaman himself came to the schoolhouse in hopes of fulfilling his commitment to al Qaeda over terms of surrender. After listening to Jim's firm lecture that the bombing would resume, Zaman had driven somewhere to freshen up and had changed into a chocolate brown tailored suit, with shiny brown leather dress shoes and a little silver hat. Perhaps he wanted to look the part of a serious diplomat, but that image was soiled when he arrived with a couple of truckloads of ragged triggermen. Still, he strutted with pride.

George and I sat on a beautiful green, red, and gold carpet that had been spread about twenty meters north of the schoolhouse. The afternoon skies were clear and a very welcome sun warmed us. Now we would get to hear all the details of the cease-fire from Zaman himself.

As we waited for Ali to join us, Haji Zaman said to me, "This is the greatest day in the history of Afghanistan."

"Why is that?" I asked. He was not aware that we already had concluded that the surrender was a fraud.

"Because al Qaeda is no more. Bin Laden is finished!" he boasted.

General Ali arrived, clad in his standard modest clothing of browns and whites. He obviously was still aggravated that Zaman's people got to the hilltop first the day before, and now his rival warlord had used that edge to freelance surrender negotiations that Ali had not approved.

George laid the situation out clearly. The CIA deputy chief told the two leaders, in few words, that they were smoking crack if they thought a less than legitimate surrender would weaken America's resolve to kill or capture bin Laden. Nor would the Americans be leaving the Tora Bora area before that job was done.

"After this meeting, the bombs will start falling again," George pledged.

In fact, even though the Muslim armies on the battlefield were con-ducting their cease-fire, the Americans and British had never agreed to it, so some bombs were being called by the boys in OP25-A and 25-B on the higher elevations. No fighter, bomber, or gunship would return home still carrying ammunition, but without the forward observation posts, much of the target area was hidden.

Zaman said a dozen Algerians were ready to surrender immediately but feared that the American commandos would kill them on the spot. The Algerians demanded permission to retain their rifles but would come off the mountain with weapons slung across their backs.

My turn. "No weapons, or risk being shot by my men. No conditions whatsoever," I responded.

I shook my head side to side and smirked, essentially signaling that I thought Zaman was full of shit. Looking at me incredulously, he asked, "Commander Dalton, why do you not accept surrender? In every war sur-render is an option."

We were tired of his showmanship, and I answered, "Haji Zaman, you grossly underestimate our resolve here. Your al Qaeda brothers can fight or flee, hide deeper in the mountains, or they can lay down their Kalashnikovs and raise a white flag, but any conditional surrender is un-acceptable in this battle." I paused to make sure he was still following my translated words. "We attack in one hour."

After committing ourselves to resume the fight, George and I rose, deliberately turned our backs to the warlords, and walked away, an insulting and dismissive gesture that left them alone with their personal aides to ponder their next move.

The Americans had no intention of playing fair.

Bernie got on the satellite radio and arranged for some bomber support from Bagram to get on station. Throughout the fight, certain areas were designated as engagement zones, or EZs, which for all intents and purposes were free-fire areas for any bomber or aircraft willing to oblige. We intended to clear hot any available aircraft to engage at will inside those zones, with the only condition being to first make certain that none of our guys or Ali's men were in the area before hell broke loose.

There was no sign of any surrendering al Qaeda.

Jim's patience had run out and he laid the law down to Zaman's field commander, the same joint-smoking guy who had given him such a bad time earlier in the day. The surrender was a hoax, Jim declared, and pointed out that no enemy fighters had arrived. MSS Grinch were saddling up again and getting ready to head out. Jim, Hopper, and Pope planned to occupy new observation posts and get the air strikes pinpointed on better targets, expanding the battlefield. Too much valuable time had already been wasted in this surrender charade.

The senior Delta operator looked hard at the muhj commander to be sure the man took in what he had to say next: "Don't raise your weapons at us."

At exactly five o'clock in the afternoon of December 12, two teams of Delta snipers, two teams of Delta assaulters, the British commandos, and an air force combat controller shouldered their heavy rucksacks, wrapped blankets around their backs, and put one foot in front of the other, heading for the high ground beneath an umbrella of bombers and weapons at the ready. Of course, Adam Khan was along as well.

The local commander was in a panic and called Zaman again, but this time the warlord did not answer. The local guy wisely had read the determined faces of the commandos and decided not to challenge the highly trained men again. They were obviously ready for a gun battle, and possibly even hungry for one. He watched helplessly as they slowly moved out of sight.

Within two minutes after the deadline, the first warplane was cleared hot and the exploding bombs made it clear that Zaman's negotiation attempts had failed. A half-dozen other aircraft were stacked at various altitudes, waiting to hear their call signs.

Hopper led his Jackal Team up a rocky ridge along the east side, while Pope took Kilo Team off on a separate axis further west. Not too many months before, Pope and Dugan had become the first Delta operators to graduate from the grueling British 22 SAS Mountain Course, and Pope spent much of his personal time mountaineering, topping off at 18,000 feet on one excursion. But this time there would be no special climbing equipment. His expert assessment of the ugly uphill trek that lay ahead was that they were all in for a bitch of a climb.

So he made a prudent tactical decision to avoid walking like a train of ducks up the ridgeline and possibly right into the business end of an enemy machine gun. Pope split his team in half and maneuvered upward by using the bounding overwatch technique. As one team was up and moving, the second team was behind cover looking for any sign of the enemy, prepared to engage with small-arms fire. Before losing sight of each other, the teams switched roles.

Sure enough, about an hour into the climb, al Qaeda welcomed Pope's three-man team with some DShK machine-gun fire, and the heavy bullets ricocheted off the rocks, putting the commandos flat on their bellies.

"Damn, I don't like that," commented Adam Khan, who was lying close to Pope.

From somewhere up in the mountains, al Qaeda unveiled another mortar, which began lobbing rounds on Pope's forward position. The three men hugged the tan and gray quartz rocks.

The other three commandos who were in the protective overwatch position took a bead on the machine gun's location, which was a little too far for their 5.56mm weapons. One of the British commandos grabbed his radio hand mike and gave a call to an overhead fighter. Within moments, a thousand-pound JDAM took care of the DShK and gave Pope and the others some breathing room.

Both teams stayed low behind cover to prevent enemy observers from sending any more mortar rounds their way until darkness fell. When the sun vanished, total darkness cloaked the area, which created the commando comfort zone. The entire team rejoined and pressed on in search of a nice rocky outcropping from which they could overlook al Qaeda's hidden frontline defensive positions. Adam Khan had gone far enough and used the opportunity to backtrack to Jim and the assaulters of MSS Grinch.

It took another hour of moving uphill before they found a suitable perch, and not a moment to soon. Pope, the veteran climber, had developed a minor case of altitude sickness and was having a hard time staying awake. It could hit a climber at any time, and he needed to stop ascending to let the ill effects wear off. Pope dropped his eighty-seven-pound Norwegian pack, opened the top flap, and pulled out a gallon-sized Ziploc bag containing thirty small packets of GU Hardrock energy gel. It was all he needed to get him back in the fight.

The team members made themselves comfortable, put on their NVGs, and almost immediately spotted a pickup truck one ridgeline over to their west, flashing its lights on and off, signaling someone, somewhere.

An AC-130 gunship was already on station, orbiting in a tight circular pattern. Pope smiled at Lowblow and keyed the radio hand mike, his altitude sickness forgotten. He directed the Spectre's attention toward the ridgeline where the truck was sitting and blinking, and asked for the

AC-130 to "burn" the area with their onboard infrared spotlight. The gunship quickly found its prey, and Pope cleared it hot. A couple of 105mm howitzer rounds boomed out of the plane, followed by some sawing chain gun action for good measure, and the truck was ready for the junkyard.

The half-dozen men of Kilo Team had managed to slip inside al Qaeda's perimeter and were now the commandos farthest into the mountains. In doing so, they had found one heck of a location for their OP and had beautiful sightlines into al Qaeda's longtime sanctuary. Even through the green tint of their NVGs, the view was breathtaking and intimidating. Throughout the night the two Delta snipers and one British commando would work fire mission after fire mission, directing air strikes on known and suspected positions, while the other three Brits protected their teammates from any unannounced enemy appearances.

A savvy reader might notice here Pope didn't have a qualified ground force air controller with his team. A GFAC is the guy whom the military has blessed off on—certified—to talk to and control multiple aircraft at various altitudes and clear them to drop bombs on the bad guys. When MSS Grinch inserted, we only had two air force combat controllers, the Admiral and Spike, and even though one of the Brits with Pope on the Kilo Team was qualified, the vast battlefield begged for more. We requested two additional GFACs and they arrived in short order, but we had to wait for future infils to capitalize on their skills.

Pope had recognized that potential liability a very long time ago. As a Delta team leader he enjoyed great liberty as to what skills he wanted his men to learn or to sustain during their training at home. He could take them on a long-range sniper-hunting trip where the daily kills were gutted, skinned, cleaned, and roasted over an open fire. Or maybe take in a fun-packed off-road driving school where brightly colored souped-up Humvees were delicately maneuvered over boulders the size of sports cars. They could opt for some fingernail-biting level-5 technical rock climbing at some ritzy venue or even go kayaking bare-chested in the hot summer temperatures of the Texas Panhandle. Anything to make the Delta operator more valuable in an unforeseen future mission was available.

With the world of possibilities at his feet, Pope chose close air support training—fixed-wing CAS—and didn't have to leave Fort Bragg to do it. For several weeks in a row, Pope and Kilo Team latched on to the Admiral, the air force combat controller attached to the reconnaissance troop, piled into ATVs, and headed for the local bomb-impact areas to sharpen up their skills. Needless to say, Pope wasn't too popular for that, at least until they found themselves in a place called Tora Bora. The members of his team were fully versed in the finer points of terminal guidance operations. It's not rocket science, but it might as well be. Pope himself, Lowblow, Jester, and Dugan were as valuable as any air force special tactics combat controller available. They knew it, and so did we, which is why Pope was told that he could make do without a GFAC.

Being able to have eyes up on the ridgelines, deep in al Qaeda's lines, to see over and down into the next valley or across to the next ridgeline, was priceless. About a thousand meters to the east of Kilo Team, Jackal Team had found a position above the steep side of a long and twisting valley and enjoyed an awesome view for roughly a mile that pierced right through the middle of al Qaeda's defensives.

With both Jackal and Kilo teams now in positions high up on two commanding ridgelines, the tide was turning.

The snipers determined their own locations to within ten meters by using their GPSs. Next, they used laser range finders to fix the location of the target they wanted to attack. This provided distance and direction, as well as a grid location. Before the data could be packaged inside a modified fire mission—or "solution"—and radioed to the pilots upstairs, the operators had to make one final, and very critical, calculation. The multimillion-dollar aircraft above did not accept simple grid coordinates. So the data obtained with the laser rangers first had be converted to latitude and longitude coordinates, the same delicate frustration that Jester and Dugan had been dealing with for days up in OP25-A.

A handheld $150 Garmin GPS that accomplished that conversion process was one of the cheapest and most important tools on the battlefield. The aircrew punched in the coordinates and released the smart bomb, which followed its own internal GPS and impacted within a few meters of its intended location nine out of ten times.

Throughout the night, both Kilo and Jackal teams worked in tandem to control bombing runs. Enemy fighters not bright enough to maintain a low silhouette were prime targets, as were the cave entrances into which other fighters scurried. Either way, the designated targets eventually disappeared in massive orange-and-red explosions.

The cease-fire had allowed al Qaeda to reposition a Russian-made .50-caliber DShK heavy machine gun on a prominent ridgeline just south of the new observation posts, and its presence stalled the muhj. After some rudimentary coordination in Russian with the muhj commander to pinpoint the gun, Hopper and Jackal Team worked up a fire mission.

Promising to advance to the next ridgeline if the DShK was not in the way, the muhj commander backed up with his men and watched the Jackals bring in several bombers and an F-18 fighter that demolished the enemy gun emplacement with thundering explosions.

With the successful infil of MSS Grinch, things slowed significantly for the boys up at OP25-A. All of a sudden Jester and Dugan found themselves out of a job and bored. They requested permission to return to the schoolhouse to prep for reinsertion somewhere else.

Instead, we told them to stay put until we were certain Grinch was solidly positioned, and to allow the second group, MSS Monkey, time to get established. We also weren't comfortable with the unreliable radio communications as the boys moved deeper south, and Jester and Dugan provided a valuable radio-relay asset.

In addition, the muhj commander who was with them at the OP had become a great source of information about what was happening at the front with Ali's other fighters. That information would have otherwise been unavailable to us, and we used it to corroborate General Ali's situation reports during the nightly fireside chats.

After directing their final bombs of the battle for a while, the hardworking boys in OP25-A reluctantly released control of the airspace to their mates in MSS Grinch, several miles away. The JDAMs and MK-82 bombs rained down.

As had become customary, al Qaeda radio intercepts provided immediate feedback. More good news for our side. Requests for the "red truck to move wounded," frantic calls from a fighter to his commander relaying "cave too hot, can't reach others," and discussions of surrendering were all heard by Skoot and his signals interceptors at the schoolhouse.

Even with this indisputable insight about the terrible state of the enemy, the Afghan muhj were not changing their ways. We were still unable to impress upon them the importance of remaining on the battlefield and not giving up hard-earned terrain by retreating back down the mountain each evening. As per standard procedure, the muhj had marshaled about midmorning at the base of the mountains, slowly moved up the rocky trails in an uneven zigzag pattern, ripped a few dozen 7.62mm rounds each through their AK-47s, and launched a rocket or two toward al Qaeda, then promptly called it quits for the day.

The example we had set was hard to argue with, and a pleased General Ali was becoming a believer. His spirit was returning following Zaman's shady antics with the phony al Qaeda surrender and with the slaughter that our boys were pouring onto the enemy. Ali was succumbing to the pressure from George and the rest of us and would soon tell his fighters to prepare to stay in the mountains with the American commandos and take the initiative away from bin Laden.

With the boys of MSS Grinch needling through al Qaeda's weakened lines generally from the northeast, it was time to put our second group of operators—MSS Monkey—into the fight from the other side of the battlefield.

With Bryan in command, they were to link with the Green Berets at OP25-B, get a quick situation update, and then push south higher into the mountains. They would provide observation farther along the Wazir Valley, which marked the western edge of the battlefield.

The straight-line map distance from the schoolhouse to the linkup point was a mere ten kilometers, about six miles, but the uneven and brutal terrain the pickups had to follow turned it into a three-hour trip. Lieutenant Colonel Al furnished a local guide to navigate the trip, and also paid for donkeys to be waiting at the rendezvous so MSS Monkey could use the pack animals to ascend after the pickups had to stop.

Ironhead took on the job of getting Bryan and his mates safely to the linkup, then bringing the vehicles and the exfilling Green Berets back to the schoolhouse. As the squadron sergeant major, Ironhead could have gone anywhere he wanted to. He could have been with one of the two flanking OPs, or he could have jumped in with MSS Grinch or Monkey. But it wasn't his style to get in the way when the boys had work to do, and he chose to stay back at the schoolhouse, likely to keep me from doing something stupid. I took that as a compliment and was more than thankful for his adult supervision. However, as the hours turned to days and the temperature dropped, I could see the sergeant major becoming restless.

One of the junior CIA officers, Drew, desperately wanted to be involved in the action, and the young operative cautiously asked George, "Can I be in charge of the movement, so I can get my spurs?" George honored the request. Drew was to be in charge of the Afghan guides and handle the interface to get the Delta boys safely to the linkup.

Having Drew in charge on the trip did not bother Ironhead or Bryan a bit, as long as the mission got done. Besides, the two seasoned Delta operators enjoyed having him along to deal with the locals, because neither of the Afghan guides spoke or understood a word of English.

Four hours into the trip, they found themselves stopped inside a gated compound, unsure of where they were. Nasty terrain and cutback trails, when coupled with pathetically sorry directions, had led MSS Monkey to a standstill. If that was not bad enough, the two Afghan guides disappeared.

A couple of Monkey boys who spoke some elementary Russian managed to talk with some newly arrived Afghans who had picked up some rudimentary Russian while interned in a Soviet prisoner-of-war camp in the 1980s.

Bryan was a little irritated, and made his way over to Drew, "Okay, where are we?"

Looking at the screen to his handheld GPS, Drew nervously responded, "Here."

"Say again," Bryan asked, with raised eyebrows.

"Here!" Drew repeated.

One of the Russian-speaking Afghans approached, as if to help, but really to offer a deal. "One of the guides thought you needed more donkeys. If so, his uncle, the elder that lives here, can rent you some. Do you want them?"

"*No!*" Bryan snapped.

Everyone got back on the trucks to continue to the linkup point, already several hours late and with several hours to go.

They had tried without luck to reach the Green Berets at OP25-B, but once again the terrain negated the radio. Unbeknownst to any of us, those Green Berets had grown tired of waiting and decided on their own to move back to a more secure location in the mountains for the night.

So there were no Green Berets at the rendezvous point, which meant that the entire day had been wasted. There were no donkeys either. MSS Monkey had to turn the convoy around and would try again tomorrow.

14

Bomb Like There Is No Tomorrow

We are surrounded by the American commandos from above.
—AL QAEDA RADIO TRANSMISSION,
DECEMBER 14, 2001

MSS Grinch took over the lion's share of the work and continued to push deeper and higher into the mountains. The assaulters from Alpha and Bravo teams protected the rear and flanks while the Jackal and Kilo sniper teams swapped the duty of controlling the airspace and directing the persistent bombing.

Besides killing al Qaeda, we expected that the bravery of Jim and the boys would be contagious among their muhj brethren. Some of the muhj responded, albeit reluctantly and hesitantly, but most of them still went home at night.

On the morning of December 13, Jester and Dugan received the word they had been waiting for up at OP25-A. They would be able to return to the schoolhouse as soon as MSS Monkey became operational over at OP25-B on the other ridge. They were no longer calling in the warplane strikes as our people pushed deeper into the mountain stronghold, but stayed in touch with the developing action. They passed along the bad news that the weather conditions on the mountain were bad and getting worse.

The snow was creeping down from the highest peaks at an astonishing rate of about five hundred feet per day, and the wind was slicing across OP25-A in excess of fifteen miles an hour, plummeting the temperature to a painful level with the wind chill. OP25-A was totally exposed to the bad weather, literally bald of any foliage or trees for protection from the wind, and they had no sleeping bags.

It prompted the Green Berets to build a warming fire. The only tree within sight was seven hundred meters away back down the hill, and a few of the Green Berets took off with a block of C4 explosives, dropped the tree with the demo and dragged their kill back up to the OP.

Everyone gathered around to warm themselves, but kept the radios close. An AC-130 gunship circling above reported that it had spotted several fires near the established free-fire zone, and the pilot described seeing six to seven individuals near a fire. The snipers were just about to clear the AC-130 hot to engage when Dugan suddenly asked Jester, "Hey, do you think they are talking about us?"

The two of them and the Green Berets forgot all about the cold for a moment and frantically dug out their infrared strobe lights and turned them on to let the Spectre know there were friendlies around this particular fire.

Skoot and his tactical signal interceptors had been going 24/7 since they arrived four days earlier. They were an incredible asset to have on the battlefield, so we attached one of his operatives to move with MSS Grinch and another to MSS Monkey. The other two worked under Skoot's watchful eye at the schoolhouse.

Skoot was a tall, athletically lean, Bill Gates type with wire frame glasses and wavy blond hair. He had an incredible energy level and a sense of humor that helped keep everything in perspective throughout the fight. Each time a bin Laden transmission was intercepted, Skoot would jump up from the cold, hard floor, yank off his headphones and come tearing into the corner room to give us the news. His positive attitude was contagious.

Skoot worked his guys in shifts, and they either grabbed a few minutes of sleep when they could or when they were forced to go down for a few winks. It was necessary to rest the brain because of the mind-numbing nature of intercepting and interpreting al Qaeda conversations in real time, taping and replaying conversations for translation, and trying to identify al Qaeda's many radio frequencies. They kept netting information out of the air, confirming that the enemy's morale and will to fight was slipping, while their vulnerability increased.

Skoot came running into our room the morning of December 13 with new intercepts that strongly suggested al Qaeda was preparing to make a final stand. Morning enemy radio calls requesting "big and small land mines" were overheard. Another al Qaeda commander was overheard confidently stating "victory or death" before telling of plans to reposition a couple of hundred brothers. Al Qaeda fighters had no idea that they were passing critical battle damage estimates and targeting information to us each time they keyed their radio. News of each cave or tunnel that was dropped by bombs was relayed from one group to the next on the terrorist net. They weren't the voice of bin Laden, but it wouldn't be long before his lack of stomach for the fight surfaced.

General Ali was getting his second wind and stopped by our room on his way to the front on the morning of the thirteenth to express his thanks for the ruthless bombing. As I followed him out to his truck and waiting fighters, the general smiled and gave a gesture like cutting someone's throat, running his hand palm down and fingers extended across the front of his neck. He believed victory was close at hand.

Ali's cocky rival, Zaman, had left the day before, upset and embarrassed at the outcome of the surrender negotiations, and we had not heard from him since. The general did not know whether the warlord would continue the fight.

Actually, Zaman was having even more trouble at the moment.

After seeing how professional the first eight British commandos were out with our forward teams, we were tickled when four more came rolling in. But before heading to the schoolhouse, the commandos and a British intelligence operative had a meeting with Zaman in Jalalabad, during which they sternly voiced their displeasure with his antics. He obviously was not giving our closest allies their money's worth and the Brits felt it was time to adjust the warlord's attitude.

We had been pondering the idea of pairing up some of our operators with Zaman's men just to keep him honest and on track. We even considered marrying up the Green Berets with Zaman's forces, although we knew that request would be squelched back at Task Force Dagger headquarters. The entrance of the additional Brits took care of this issue nicely. They would hook up with the stumbling Zaman and keep his feet to the fire.

MSS Monkey departed for OP25-B again just before dusk on December 13 with two new Afghan guides, and neither spoke a lick of English. Having traveled part of the route once already, the navigation was much easier, but the terrain remained painfully rugged. It gets dark quickly in Tora Bora. Dusk gives way to total darkness in a blink. Within an hour and a half after leaving the schoolhouse, MSS Monkey was moving through early nighttime hours that were already pitch-black. With al Qaeda having been pushed back and their frontline mortar position destroyed, our force had the luxury of using their vehicle headlights, but the guides still managed to screw things up. They stopped in the middle of a dry streambed while the Afghans began yelling and screaming at each other about the correct route.

Air strikes were lighting up the sky just a few terrain features away, and the boys weren't sure if the guides were just frightened by the bombs or were setting them up for an ambush. Two more locals needing a lift jumped in the back of one of the pickups. One said, "Bush good!" and communicated further by making obscene screwing motions with his fingers and mumbling something about American women.

The convoy finally cleared the streambed and moved to higher ground, only to have a repeat performance by the Afghan guides. While the guides went at it again, Ironhead and Bryan unfolded their own maps to check their location.

Mysteriously, the recent hitchhiking Afghans had already disappeared, quite likely to pass the patrol's presence on to the highest bidder.

A couple of the boys sitting with Lieutenant Colonel Al decided that everything might not be going according to plan, but was pretty much as expected in this nutty land.

"Well, it's about time. Let's get them out," said one.

The other operator pointed at Lieutenant Colonel Al and asked, "He's okay, right?"

"Yeah, he's okay," the first said.

The operators reached into their assault vests and pulled out rubber clown noses, slid them into place on their faces, and honked them. One declared, "It's now an official full-up three-ring fucking circus."

They took off the noses and carefully stowed them away for use on future appropriate occasions.

One of the boys looked at Lieutenant Colonel Al and said, "Before you come back out here, I recommend you get one, too."

After a three-hour drive to the base of the mountain followed by an exhausting two-hour climb, Ski and India Team reached OP25-B just prior to nightfall on December 13. The mules, on the other hand, showed little sign of fatigue. The team was anxious to get in on the bombing and looked forward to alternating with Jackal and Kilo teams of MSS Grinch a few thousand meters away to the east.

As the team dug out their equipment, they quickly noticed the Darth

Vader thermal imager was busted. After a little delicate Delta ingenuity, detail work that would make a Swiss wristwatch artist take notice, the priceless piece of kit was back in business.

Unfortunately, the sharp advances made by MSS Grinch and the others had put MSS Monkey out of business before they even got started. Monkey would have to push farther south to get in the game.

Before they could get going again, though, we tasked them from the schoolhouse to take control of the airspace for preplanned bombing missions. MSS Monkey's combat controller, Spike, took up where MSS Grinch had left off, and for the next six hours, Monkey would not let al Qaeda rest for more than a few minutes at a time. Bryan decided to remain in place at OP25-B for the rest of the night and move south early in the morning.

At the schoolhouse early on the afternoon of December 13, Skoot and his interceptors picked up the startling call that "Father" was "moving to a new tunnel with two Yemeni brothers." And then we heard bin Laden himself break radio silence, and there was desperation in his voice. "The time is now," he said. "Arm your women and children against the infidel!"

Calling out the kids to fight wasn't going to be enough for bin Laden to retake the lead, because things were going our way.

After hours of massive and accurate bombing directed by Pope, Lowblow, and a talented Brit with Kilo Team, the Admiral with Jackal Team, and Spike with India Team, Usama bin Laden was on the radio again. Skoot threw open the flimsy door with authority, and entered our room quickly and smiling widely. His eyes were wide and wild as if he just hit a ninth-inning walk-off home run. He held the small black transistor radio up with his right hand and thrust it toward us. "Listen," he whispered softly. "It's him."

His Arabic prose sounded beautiful, soothing, and peaceful. But the words were very portentous, and I paraphrase him here. "Our prayers have not been answered. Times are dire," he said with an uncanny combination of surrender and despair. "We didn't receive support from the apostate nations who call themselves our Muslim brothers. Things might have been different."

His final words to his fighters that night revealed a tired and weary warrior, "I'm sorry for getting you involved in this battle, if you can no longer resist, you may surrender with my blessing."

Before the nightly chat with General Ali on the thirteenth, two unexpected guests arrived at the schoolhouse: One was a representative from Pakistan, the other, Zaman's brother. Both were there on behalf of the warlord and passed information that, in their opinion, bin Laden had already departed for Pakistan. Curious. Could Zaman have engineered the odd cease-fire earlier to allow bin Laden time to escape?

After the two visitors departed, George asked General Ali about the progress they had made that day. The tired but enthusiastic general said his men had uncovered a large cave stocked with weapons, ammunition, uniforms, documents, and a large carpet. The general seemed to consider the carpet the most valuable item. George accused the general of allowing his men to halt the attack to loot caves for personal gain. Ali shrugged, almost as if he felt helpless to fix the problem. Or perhaps he just didn't consider it a problem.

Ali placed blame on the journalists and the CIA. He said his men were hungry and poor, and since the media and George's people were paying such a high premium for anything coming out of the mountains, his subordinate commanders were becoming businessmen.

The tenuous relationship between the boys in MSS Monkey and their local guides worsened at sunrise of the following day. Ski and Catfish had gone forward early in the morning darkness of December 14 to scout out another forward area for MSS Monkey, and after finding a spot that provided excellent angled views into the valleys, they radioed back to tell Bryan to bring up the rest of the team. When Bryan gave the order to saddle up, their muhj escorts again hit the panic button. OP25-B was far enough removed from the real fighting now that it was relatively safe. Moving forward meant entering the dreaded no-man's land, territory owned by al Qaeda.

The escorts had been give strict orders by one of General Ali's lieutenants not to let anything happen to the Americans. Unfortunately, they took this guidance too literally. Obviously, this was bullshit and unacceptable.

After failing to convince the muhj guides to relax and let the highly trained MSS Monkey folks move out to join Charlie and India teams, Bryan grabbed the radio and dialed up the schoolhouse.

On his end, the situation had to be handled with kid gloves but at the schoolhouse, Ironhead and I could be a little more aggressive with General Ali. Unfortunately, the good general could not be found in time to overturn the decision in the field.

Bryan ordered Ski and Catfish to return to OP25-B, and MSS Monkey's combat controller, Spike, settled in where he was and resumed control of the airspace for preplanned targets for another six hours.

In the relatively finite black SOF world, assaulters and snipers are a dime a dozen. Yes, these men are trained in multiple deadly skill sets and the dark arts of counterterrorism. But if you asked what tool of the trade would be the very last thing they would leave behind, you might be surprised at the answer. You would likely hear that it is not a tool that makes one nervous when it isn't there, but rather a *capability* that is not organic to a troop of Delta operators or Navy SEALs.

Just because you are the best of the best does not mean you are the best at everything. Any Delta operator can vouch for the capabilities of the air force combat controllers, and very rarely goes on a "hit" without the men who wear the scarlet berets.

Arguably they are the best-rounded and uniquely trained operators on the planet. The initial training "pipeline" for an air force special tactics squadron combat controller costs twice as much time and sweat as does the journey to become a Navy SEAL or Delta operator. Before their training is complete someone brainwashes these guys into thinking they can climb like Spiderman, swim like Tarzan, and fly like Superman—and then they have to prove they can do so if they plan to graduate. And that is just to get to a place where they can do the job for which they are really trained, calling those deadly air strikes. The life of a combat controller is split between working with Delta and the SEALs, with a little moonlighting with the 75th Ranger Regiment now and again.

They carry the motto that would be hard to look another operator in the face and say—if it weren't true. "First There." In Tora Bora, we counted ourselves lucky to have the Admiral and Spike, and their *capability*.

Shortly after Jackal Team first started directing bombs on previously unseen al Qaeda caves and bunkers, bin Laden was picked up again on SIGINT. We plotted the location, which was only several hundred meters away from the snipers' current strikes. Unfortunately, most SIGINT hits are not real time and are often not very accurate. But we again picked up bin Laden's voice over a short-range radio the CIA had taken off a dead al Qaeda fighter.

Adam Khan and a gentleman known to us as Bilal stood in the school yard listening to the unmistakable voice of the al Qaeda leader. Bilal, himself an Arab American and former marine, was considered the CIA's foremost authority on identifying bin Laden's Arabic prose and voice. He had appeared out of the darkness one day at the schoolhouse, but in fact, unbeknownst to any of us, Bilal had been in the mountains for the past few days with General Ali's fighters. His personal assignment, and an incredibly dangerous one, had been to serve as somewhat of a liaison officer for the CIA to provide firsthand reporting of the attitude, performance, and genuine effort of Ali's men in pursuing the terrorist mastermind.

On that day, the two CIA assets and former marines listened to what would prove to be the last intercepted transmission of bin Laden to his fighters. They picked up something odd about this particular transmission. Bin Laden was giving more of a sermon than issuing orders, and it was clear to them that the primary target was on the move and intending to leave the battlefield. They also thought the transmission might have been a recorded sermon that would give the impression that bin Laden was still in the middle of the fighting when he could have been on his way out.

The Admiral noticed something odd about one of the caves on which he directed bombs that day. Typically, a bomb at the base of the cave opening or on top of a bunker resulted in the flash of a momentary fireball, a storm of hot shrapnel and debris, and then a slow and billowing thick black, gray, and brown cloud. This one particular strike ignited large secondary explosions of something hidden inside the cave. It was also answered by futile attempts to engage the U.S. aircraft high above with multiple missile launches. Something valuable had been hidden in that cave.

Within an hour or so, Murph came up on the net with an exciting report. The muhj commander with the forward Jackal OP said his forces had captured bin Laden! Murph, who was out there at the scene, was skeptical, and the communication gap on his end prevented any detailed explanation as they were without a 'terp.

Back at the schoolhouse we grabbed Ali's trusted aide Ghulbihar and brought him into our room. Murph gave his hand mike to the muhj commander and we gave ours to Ghulbihar, with instructions to ask the commander if he had captured bin Laden. After a few moments of back-and-forth discussion, Ghulbihar reported the commander had not in fact captured bin Laden but "they are very close to doing so." Being close was not at all the same as having done it.

Still, with our boys positioned in the forward OPs, this was good news. At worst it suggested bin Laden had not fled the battlefield. Interestingly, during Jackal Team's bombing missions we received another intercepted al Qaeda radio transmission which told the story very clearly. Under obvious duress, an unidentified al Qaeda commander passed a message to a fellow fighter: "We are surrounded by the American commandos from above."

The reports were sobering because they reminded us that after hundreds of thousand of taxpayer dollars in bombs alone, after weeks of bombing this same ten-mile-by-ten-mile piece of an Afghan mountain range, somehow the resilient al Qaeda leader Usama bin Laden was still alive.

As Jackal Team patiently worked its magic on the east ridgeline, the rest of MSS Grinch punched straight up the middle. Each day, with Pope, Lowblow, and four Brit commandos in the lead, the allied team linked up with the muhj forces and supported their advance by putting bomb after bomb on key terrain, suspected enemy locations, cave entrances, and al Qaeda foot soldiers.

These seemingly simple linkups were an adventure of their own as our expensive and secure radios weren't compatible with the Dollar Store versions used by the muhj. Even if they had been, it would have made little difference, since the muhj didn't speak English, nor was the word spread that they should be on the lookout for the Americans at any specific place.

In one incident in particular, a group of friendly muhj returning to the battlefield crested a hill within forty meters of Stormin's Bravo Team and MSS Grinch. The local dress of the boys perplexed and alarmed the Afghans, and an anxious fighter shouldered his RPG and leveled it at the boys. Adam Khan quickly yelled out in Pashto to stop the confrontation, but the results could have been tragic. Once the linkups were completed, the muhj could now advance some three to nine hundred meters per day, burrowing deeper and deeper into the mountains.

Much has been written about this battle being fought solely with proxy Afghan fighters supported by American bombers, the implication being that American soldiers remained safely in the background, out of harm's way. The facts are different. The muhj we were tasked with supporting flat-out refused to stay in the mountains overnight. After a day of fighting, they licked their wounds, counted their booty, slung their Kalashnikovs, and left the field.

This low tide of performance was repeated for the first three nights in the mountains. Our boys watched in amazement as the muhj left the field, each time relinquishing hard-earned terrain to al Qaeda forces. Ramadan certainly played a role, but to us Westerners, trained to keep the momentum and reinforce success, this standard tribal-warfare dick dance was annoying.

Besides leaving al Qaeda alone to rest and recuperate overnight, the muhj left behind the boys from MSS Grinch as well. We flat-out refused to leave the field. We weren't going home until the battle was decided one way or another.

Keeping their positions didn't bother the boys a bit, and besides, it was easier to hide smaller numbers.

It was not until the men of MSS Grinch proved they could survive inside al Qaeda's sanctuary after nightfall that the muhj foot soldiers started to see the benefits.

MSS Grinch continued to push up the mountains and ever forward, forcing al Qaeda to retreat. As soon as snipers Pope and Lowblow reached a commanding position offering a view of the enemy's fallback caves and bunkers, they slipped between small rock formations and began scanning the terrain through their Leopold binoculars for targets of opportunity.

While the snipers worked the high ground, the assaulters from Alpha and Bravo teams moved on the recently abandoned bunkers and caves, getting an education in the methods of al Qaeda. Outside the caves were stacks of cut firewood covered with waterproofing plastic to ward off the elements and camouflaged from the air with fir tree limbs and branches. Scattered about willy-nilly were RPG and mortar rounds and cans of ammunition. Discarded clothing and bloody bandages lay at the base of shrapnel-infested trees, and dirty wool socks dangled on broken limbs.

Inside, the caves still smoldered from warming fires, indicating a hasty retreat. Bottled water from Pakistan, abandoned modern backpacks, food, and cooking utensils sat on the dirt floors. Finally, to prevent having to venture out into the cold night air and expose themselves to the infrared camera of an overhead AC-130, discarded water bottles had been recycled nicely as urine containers.

Although the al Qaeda mortars had been relatively quiet since the night of December 10, when Dugan and Dallas worked their mojo, it was not until the afternoon of December 14 that we could confirm their word. Pope, Lowblow, and the four Brits, moving forward to create still another OP, saw firsthand the death and destruction dealt by the gunship.

The derelict 82mm mortar tube rested silently in the upturned rock and dirt. Next to the tube was an al Qaeda fighter's decomposing corpse still sitting on—and partially lying under—a dead donkey. Surrounding them was a boatload of spent mortar round containers, crates, wrappings, and the remains of a couple of the donkey rider's buddies. The entire area had been turned into mincemeat.

Like most of the team leaders in Delta, the man who led Kilo was a singular personality. I first met Pope in 1994 as a Ranger lieutenant visiting the Delta compound to rehearse for the eventually aborted invasion of Haiti. As a young assaulter in the squadron he was given the dubious task of escorting my platoon to the range and teach us the finer points of combat marksmanship so we could keep from shooting one another. During a live fire run in one of the buildings, one of my young privates made what I thought was a mental mistake in his technique.

I stepped forward, confident and feeling a sense of omniscience, and immediately brought up the infraction for everybody's benefit. Pope had watched the team's entire run through the shoot house. The problem, from his point of view, was not what the private did; it was my correction of the Ranger's action. Pope stepped forward and calmly, professionally, and very deliberately explained why what I was telling the private was not necessarily the smart thing to do and then offered an alternate solution to the group. Wow! In just a few seconds, Pope made believers out of all of us and still allowed me to retain my dignity in front of my Rangers, including the young man that I had scolded. Of course, I felt about a foot tall. That young Ranger whom I had admonished in that long-ago incident was destined to be the future Kilo Team sniper with the code name of Lowblow.

Pope is the best organized individual on the planet and a master at time management. During a normal day back at Fort Bragg, Pope could accomplish more tasks in a day than most of us could in a month and still find time to shoot and work out. His teammates would arrive in the team room on Monday morning and find that he had repacked each man's gear, shampooed the carpet, and generally cleaned the entire room. All the kit bags were retagged with not only the proper markings but with some Gucci-looking tags with fancy colors and lamination. Then he might hand out new name tags to the whole troop, embroidered with the individual's jump qualifications and matching HALO wings in two different colors. It was like he possessed some stolen alien technology to control time.

On a more serious note, Pope also knows more about commando kit and fighting gear than any manufacturer in the industry. If you needed some special item or piece of equipment, but weren't sure which one to get or who carried the top of the line, you talked to Pope. He could tell you the best product, be it a flashlight or wristwatch or cold-weather underwear, but he probably had one or two tucked away in his locker and would just give it to you, or promise to call some "people" who would get it for you at half price. It reminded me of how Richard Gere always kept a stash of new brass buckles and shiny black dress shoes in the rafters of his barracks in the movie *An Officer and a Gentleman*.

Just after sunup on December 14, Jester, Dugan, and the Green Berets closed out OP25-A for good. Before leaving, the boys had an idea to discuss with Dave, the seasoned leader of the Green Beret team. Instead of exfilling, only to be reinserted later, the Delta snipers reasoned that it might be smarter to simply ruck up and make their way on foot deeper into the mountains to take up a flanking position abreast of the advancing MSS Grinch.

As much as he might have wanted to oblige personally, Dave had orders not to get his team into a firefight, so he had no choice in the matter. To do what the Delta boys suggested would have been career suicide.

Jester and Dugan repacked their rucks with water, chow, and fresh radio batteries, confident that their stay at the schoolhouse would likely be brief before they headed out to fight again. Unfortunately, all of our trucks were tied up inserting MSS Monkey, so the boys from OP25-A would have to rely upon the donkey express; they humped halfway back to the school-house before finding some.

When they finally arrived, some were walking and some were riding. Having been so isolated, they had not yet learned how valuable their efforts had been.

After debriefing Jester and Dugan, the two snipers bagged out for a few hours inside the local stables, then volunteered to pull the radio watch that night. Bernie, Ironhead, and I were able to get the first sleep we had managed in the last several days.

On December 14, our troop received two new personnel. When I first laid eyes on them, I couldn't help but think these were the two lucki-est Delta operators in the unit. As I shook hands with them, they were all smiles. Both were in their midtwenties and recent OTC graduates. They sported excellent records and came with solid footing from growing up in the 75th Ranger Regiment and Special Forces.

Skeeter, a young Ranger from 1st Ranger Battalion, sported a shaved head and thick beard that would grow to be one of the most envied in the unit.

A year later in Afghanistan, word reached us that conventional wisdom had caught up to the unconventional ways of a special operations war zone and a rumor spread that would require us to shave our beards and cut our hair. Lieutenant Colonel Ashley remarked to Skeeter, "Don't you dare cut off that work of art." By then his beard had grown at least six inches, a length the Taliban would have been proud of, with a center streak of light gray running vertically down the middle, in between pepper-colored sides, similar to the beard of Mr. bin Laden himself.

The other operator, Bullets, just as new to us, was experienced in the craft. Already a Green Beret, his beard was a little lighter than Skeeter's, and he arrived with short-cropped hair. Hopefully, both these young men's careers inside Delta will last for decades.

After a quick in brief, Ironhead told them both they had less than an hour to configure their rucks for a minimum of several days and nights in the mountains. They stood there hanging on the squadron sergeant major's every word, not worried in the slightest about the falling temperature or going into battle.

"Only take what you need," Ironhead said. "Leave your Kevlar helmet and body armor in the hooch. You won't need a sleeping bag or a lot of snivel gear. Grab an Afghan blanket from the stables to go along with your wool muhj hat and scarf to keep you warm."

Skeeter joined MSS Grinch as an assaulter on the Bravo Team of Stormin', while Bullets went up to be an assaulter with MSS Monkey's Charlie Team. No use in having them just sit around the schoolhouse.

With the two original observation posts forced to shut down because of the advancing of Ali and Zaman's forces backed by both America and British commandos, an opportunity presented itself to increase the relentless pursuit of bin Laden.

We now had twelve Green Berets out of a job, and several of General Ali's subordinate commanders—converts to what Special Ops people could do—were begging for commandos to direct bombs along their particular axis of advance. We wanted to oblige, as this would give us better visibility and at the same time provide firm locations on each group of muhj. With the Green Berets from Cobra 25 now available, problem solved. Or so I thought.

The decision to not allow them to enter the mountains dumbfounded me and frustrated the quiet professionals from Cobra 25. The Green Berets were now out of the fight completely, and I had no option but to thank them for their efforts.

Not long after that exchange, the dreaded black Chinook arrived and whisked away the A Team commander. The eager young captain had been relieved of command. Before he left, I gave the distraught Special Forces officer the phone number to the Delta recruiter and shook his hand.

I had assumed that, by now, the Task Force Dagger risk assessment matrix would have been subordinate to killing the Most Wanted Man in the world. Apparently, it was not.

As the bombs continued to rain down on bin Laden and his henchmen, George and I settled down with the general for the nightly fireside chat.

The nightly meetings with Ali served several purposes, but probably the most important benefit to the battle was what the private conferences did for Ali's stature and reputation. He was winning the fight, and as al Qaeda was being ground into dog food in the mountains, the warlord was gaining an aura of superwarlord in the eyes of his men and the local Shura. Our regular face-to-face engagements served our needs as well, as they pressured him to do more than talk to the press and issue hollow promises. He had to match his words with deeds and make good on his deals.

Numerous topics needed attention, but tonight he led off with one that surprised me.

Ali was extremely frustrated both by his fighters' inability to locate bin Laden, and by Zaman, who reportedly was continuing discussions with the enemy. Out of the blue, he made an announcement that raised our eyebrows. The general was advertising a one million dollar reward to anyone who could take him to bin Laden. A pretty shrewd business move, but not entirely unexpected. He was expecting to receive every penny of the $25,000,000 reward that the State Department had advertised, and could afford to be generous in posting a bounty that would guarantee that big payday.

We asked the general what made him think bin Laden had not slipped out of the mountains and escaped? Ali responded confidently that he had two sources that were adamant the al Qaeda leader was still around.

George asked the general if any of his men had actually seen bin Laden yet. Ali gave us that familiar shrug to give the impression his men were doing the best they could considering the conditions.

He countered with another interesting tidbit.

One of his associates reportedly had some sort of information that bin Laden's interpreter was still in the mountains and that the interpreter's father lived nearby. The general surmised that the father would certainly leave with his son, and that was even more proof for Ali that bin Laden had not yet fled.

We read it a different way. If bin Laden was still around, we needed to press the attack and not let up the offensive, not even for a moment.

15

A Strange Kind of War

Progress always involves risk. You can't steal second base and keep your foot on first.
—FREDERICK B. WILCOX, AUTHOR

We were almost out of supplies in the mountains by December 14, and the biggest needs were batteries and water. Water was needed to maintain a man's strength for carrying heavy loads up and down the steep ridgelines and to prevent the onset of hypothermia or altitude sickness. The icy weather was about ten degrees with a steady wind, and an inch or two of snow falling each day. We could melt the snow for emergency drinking water, but the extreme temperatures sucked the life out of our radio batteries.

Coming out of the mountains while al Qaeda was bloodied, disorganized, and on the run was not an option. We didn't even discuss it. In the last seventy hours, we had pushed several thousand meters into the middle of the enemy's fabled mountain stronghold and were not about to give that territory back.

The dreadful weather also was playing havoc with some of the aircraft flying missions to blast the mountainous positions, and visibility would change by the hour. We had to replace the fire support of those planes during the bad weather with some organic all-weather assets as soon as possible. The Rangers back at Bagram owned just such weapons, and we put in several requests for some Ranger mortars. Request denied. The reasons elude me still, particularly since some of their officers told me that they were anxious to comply and get into the fight.

Resupply by helicopter was also out of the question. Besides the low visibility that was periodically choking the mountains, we had learned a lesson from the Afghan-Soviet War. The muhj knew how to patiently wait behind rock formations, inside shallow caves and dugouts, or behind thick tree formations for an attack helicopter to come darting over the ridgeline. When it appeared, they would kill it with an RPG or a shoulder-fired missile. If the muhj skills were good enough to shoot down several hundred of those fast helicopters during the Soviet jihad, it wouldn't take much to pick off a slow Special Ops Dark Horse lumbering over some high ridgeline in search of a landing zone the size of a postage stamp.

Living off the land wasn't in the cards either. We had captured dozens of caves stocked with firewood, potatoes, rice, RPGs, medical supplies, and thousands of containers of Chinese-made 7.62mm AK rifle ammunition. Almost everything but enough drinking water or batteries. But while al Qaeda had shrewdly overstocked their stores in anticipation that the Far Enemy would soon arrive to do battle, they also had protectively laced some of those caves with mines that silently awaited the first clumsy or curious attacker to enter. Picking up a tin of potatoes could be deadly.

The obvious question was how were our muhj partners resupplying themselves? The hard fact was they carried what they needed to fight on their backs as we did, but they just didn't need as much to survive. Also, they could rely on some equine help along the way. The typical muhj fighter went up the mountain with his weapon, a bag of rice the size of a baseball, three to five thirty-round magazines, a couple of RPG rockets, and a single, thin blanket to stave off the cold. The muhj rarely required water, almost as if they were perpetually hydrated, and were much more acclimated to the high altitudes than we were. And there was no use carrying food for daytime use anyway, since during the holy month of Ramadan they were forbidden to eat or drink anything from dawn to dusk.

Unfortunately for the muhj, many of them just about froze to death each night. Beneath their snow-damp blankets, they typically wore only a single layer of thin cotton clothing. The lucky ones sported some type of waist-length garment. In contrast, beneath the blankets of the Americans and Brits were layers of twenty-first-century extreme-cold-weather gear. Even that could not stave off the cold.

But the muhj could get whatever they needed hauled up to them, and were usually off the mountain by nightfall. Teenage Afghans clocked in as porters to carry what they could while tending the valuable donkeys, and a well-balanced jackass humped about 150 pounds of foodstuffs and equipment.

When MSS Grinch had moved into the mountains days earlier, we had been unable to locate or bargain for donkeys. MSS Monkey had some, but even a donkey had its limits in this place. Once Grinch entered the radically steep terrain where they were now fighting, donkeys wouldn't have helped at all.

We had another idea, and we once again went back to the Rangers. Few professional military organizations can match their physical ability and mental toughness, just the attributes required to deliver the vital supplies to MSS Grinch so the shooting could continue without letup. Two platoons of Rangers were sitting around back at Bagram, and we asked for one platoon to help. They could serve as a human logistics train from the last vehicle drop-off point in the foothills all the way up to MSS Grinch, which was located several klicks away and at an elevation several thousand meters higher. Rangers could do what helicopters and mules could not. Request denied. Again, I never learned the reasons for that refusal.

We did have one quick offer. Not surprisingly, our former commander, Gus Murdock, heard of our need for human pack animals and sent a note that he was more than willing to mule supplies up to the boys in the mountains. He doesn't know how close Ironhead and I were to taking him up on the offer, and it would not have surprised us a bit if he had stepped off the next helo landing at the schoolhouse ready to hump a pack.

In the end, we would have to do the resupply ourselves, but we had committed almost every available body to the fight, and they were already up in the mountains. Only a half-dozen Delta guys were still around, sharing a multitude of duties from handling the radios, running security, getting ready to be inserted themselves and being the only reliable quick-reaction force in the entire area.

Sergeant Major Ironhead volunteered without hesitation to lead and manage this vitally important patrol behind al Qaeda's lines. He was tired of sitting around the schoolhouse anyway, while his men were out on the high ground giving al Qaeda the business. The best-qualified Delta operator in the compound was more than willing to carry the supplies necessary to keep the fight going.

His first patrol included himself, the ever-dependable Adam Khan, and a half-dozen local Afghans who had to be paid well for the job, because most of them were still too afraid to move into the mountains and chance a fight with al Qaeda. When the group off-loaded the pickup trucks at Mortar Hill, each was loaded with water, MREs, and precious batteries. Ironhead carried his pistol and M-4 assault rifle, a few 5.56mm magazines, the clothes on his back, and that was about it. Every other ounce of energy would go to the supplies.

It took them five hours to climb the rugged four kilometers up to MSS Grinch. The boys weren't at all surprised to see that it was Ironhead who led the patrol in. Somewhere along the way, about half of the Afghan porters had fallen out, probably by design. That meant that about half of the planned resupply didn't make it, but MSS Grinch was at least now good to go for another day or two.

Ironhead knew he would have to make the trip at least one more time. Since the sergeant major had refused to bring along much in the way of personal comfort items, the boys in Grinch shared some pieces of snivel gear.

He also wanted to get a feel for the condition of the overall force and checked on the muhj scattered in the area. As they were moving higher and deeper into frigid mountains, and with the temperature steadily dropping, the muhj on the front lines were literally starving and freezing. Ironhead and Adam Khan spent the night on the icy mountain with the muhj and their fellow commandos, and the sergeant major couldn't help but wonder how they were going to be able to sustain this logistics effort a mile or so behind al Qaeda's frontline fortifications.

Back at the schoolhouse, Skoot entertained us with radio reports being whispered by several of the Afghan muhj, about a giant American whom they watched carry "much stuff" up the ridgeline, with seemingly no concern about al Qaeda. The muhj let us know, with great respect, that the hired Afghan porters who were used to such altitudes had to struggle to keep pace with Sergeant Major Ironhead.

As the sun broke over the mountains on December 15, MSS Monkey was heading to their next location. After reaching the same spot that Ski and Catfish had scoped out the previous day, Bryan pushed Ski's India Team forward even more to find a new vantage point from which they could see enemy targets that needed some attention from our bombers.

Within seconds of reaching their new observation post, Ski saw a man in black clothing only three hundred meters to his front. The al Qaeda fighter was moving cautiously and deliberately, crouching over so as to present a small silhouette and hide his presence. As Ski prepared a fire mission, the dark-clad fighter moved into a bunker made from tree trunks, rocks, and foliage. A second later, a 100mm high explosive round fired from a T-55 tank slammed a direct hit into the bunker entrance, leveling the hidden emplacement and certainly killing anyone inside. The problem was that Ski had been unaware that the big tank was nearby.

They saw numerous caves on the ridges, but all appeared abandoned. India Team did notice significant movement on two smaller hilltops and assumed they were enemy fighters, so he began working up a fire mission on them. On a sudden hunch, he grabbed a nearby muhj commander and pointed to the mysterious people. Were they al Qaeda? According to the commander, they were not. Just some of Haji Zaman's fighters scouring Hilltop 2685, looking for booty.

Ski considered the unexpected tank fire, and the way that everyone on the battlefield looked alike. There was no sure way to differentiate enemy fighters from friendly looters, even at close range, so he let the unknown men live, thinking, *Hmmm, look out for the friendlies.* The battlefield was becoming more confused as it changed.

The muhj main force finally returned to Jackal Team early in the morning on December 15, and the boys fully expected them to advance to the next ridgeline. Instead, the muhj needed babysitting.

The muhj stalled and bitched about the DShK heavy machine gun that had laid down so much fire and ignored American arguments that the weapon had been eliminated. It had not fired a shot for many hours.

No! It was still there, they insisted, and refused to advance without 100 percent confirmation that the gun, some five hundred meters away, had been destroyed. They didn't like taking risks.

The American commandos' patience had worn thin. Al Qaeda was on the run, and the continuous bombing was sapping the enemy's will to fight and forcing them to leave prepared positions. Each minute wasted, such as with this mini mutiny by the muhj, only provided much needed rest to a vulnerable and disoriented enemy. They had no choice but to prove the DShK had been taken out. Nowadays, they would send a Predator to take a look, but back in December 2001 the only way was to move forward and eyeball it yourself.

Murph and his fellow snipers Shrek and Scrawny dropped their rucks and headed out, taking along an Afghan guide. Hopper and the Admiral stayed back to cover them. If that gun was somehow still operating, then a long-range sniper shot would finish the job, the Admiral would summon an aircraft, and Murph would adjust the bombs onto the target.

So, with the muhj apparently more interested in smoking hash than dealing with al Qaeda, the Delta snipers chose to explore a different route to find the heavy gun. Three men crossing open ground was just not a smart idea, and they might as well use the chance to scout for a new path that would speed a general advance. In a training exercise over such terrain, as at Lake Tahoe or Jackson Hole, they would have been able to employ a lot of safety equipment, but this was a real-world mission where not only was such equipment unavailable, but al Qaeda might have them in their sights as they climbed.

The eastern approach took them up the face of a precariously long and ugly ridgeline. One slip on the vertical rock walls could have resulted in serious injury or even a nonbattle fatality. We couldn't afford that, since no helicopters would be sent in to evacuate an injured American although he might be barely clinging to life. The dead would just have to wait until the mission was over.

They were on their own, and pressed forward as far as they could to gain a commanding position on al Qaeda's defenses. It was an extraordinary accomplishment. Al Qaeda must have assumed the route was impassable and had decided not to waste any fighters securing it or establishing any defensive positions that might cover it. Any young soldier knows that failing to overwatch a major obstacle with at least a gun or two reduces its effectiveness from being an impregnable castle moat to being a mere speed bump for any determined foe. It was a grave tactical error.

Scrawny spotted an al Qaeda fighter about eight hundred meters away, but the enemy fighter did not see them. Instead, the man fired an RPG round in the direction of the muhj who were still lounging about on the other ridge.

For a sniper like Scrawny, such an easy target was almost too good to be true. He reached for his SR-25 rifle, ready to prone out to engage, but then realized that the sound of a shot and a dead terrorist flopping down would compromise the team. Plus, there had to be more than one up there, so instead of squeezing the trigger, he took a knee, pulled off his Nomex flight gloves, and dug his map from a cargo pocket and the Silva compass from his assault vest, placing them both gently on his thigh. He lined his leg up with the target and oriented his map to the north and quietly told Shrek, who was behind him, to ready a fire request from whatever plane was overhead so that the bigger explosions would not raise curiosity about the snipers.

Scrawny looked at the spot where the RPG gunner had appeared, looked back at his map, then checked his compass needle. He didn't have a laser range finder or laser marker with him, but he didn't need one. Scrawny estimated the target coordinates using good old-fashioned terrain association and commando know-how and passed the numbers to Shrek. Within a few minutes, the first bomb slammed into the enemy position, a direct hit that sent debris whizzing over the snipers' heads.

"Look at Scrawny!" Murph joked. "Map and compass. Ooold schooool!"

Scrawny reached down for his gloves. They were gone. He asked the other guys if they'd picked them up. No? Scrawny turned to the Afghan guide who was hiding sheepishly in the rear, with his hands hidden beneath crossed arms.

"Hey, did you take my frickin' gloves?" Scrawny growled with disgust. The young man just stared. Scrawny moved closer and asked again. The Afghan remained expressionless. Scrawny finally walked up to the young man and yanked out his hands.

"You frickin' thief, give me those damn gloves!" Scrawny demanded, and pulled each one off, finger by finger.

Within a couple of hours, they found the DShK position, plotted the location and relayed the target coordinates back to the Admiral. Soon, a pair of GBU-31 bombs zoomed in and obliterated whatever had been left of the gun emplacement.

As the debris settled, an RPG whizzed over their heads from a camouflaged firing position in a nearby cave that was cut deep into the ridgeline. A new player was in the game.

The snipers quickly sent back the new coordinates and another brace of bombs impacted center mass to crush the cave opening. Once again, before the rocks stopped falling, still another enemy fighter stepped out and launched another RPG at the snipers. More JDAMs were called. They finished the job.

With the way up having been made safe, a group of muhj fighters caught up with the snipers and pushed ahead to the twice-blown-away DShK location. By midafternoon the snipers had repositioned and for the first time were able to get a good look at several cave openings just below a ridgeline, some six hundred meters to the southwest.

A frantic muhj commander keyed his radio and began trading transmissions with another muhj. Some of the fighters excitedly reported seeing
a figure that they believed to be Usama bin Laden moving among a group
of several dozen enemy fighters. They lost sight when he disappeared into
a cave.

That was all that our snipers needed to hear. They got the word back
to the team pronto. The Admiral broke into the net and summoned all
available aircraft to check in with him and stack up while Murph plotted
the exact target location. Could this be it for bin Laden?

The bombs from the first warplane hammered in with tremendous
effect, ignited something flammable, and multiple flashes and secondary
explosions lit up the valley like an outdoor rock concert. Something beside
humans had definitely been inside that cave. More GBU-31 bombs satu-
rated the cave complex with enormous power.

The snipers hunkered behind a small rock formation to watch the
show as impact after impact shook the ground and detonated even more
secondary explosions. Fireballs rose into the air and shrapnel and debris
raced over their heads and rattled off the rocks.

For the next two hours, bombs rained on one small area of Tora
Bora.

Sundown, of course, brought the usual muhj retreat. The three snipers,
however, were unwilling either to ease up on this chance to nail bin Laden
or lessen the pain that was being inflicted on al Qaeda. They would remain on the steep ridgeline, with and without the muhj, for the next two
days.

The Delta boys were certain that they were as close to bin Laden as
any Americans had been in years, certainly since 9/11, and they were hell-
bent on ensuring that some American pilot would wake up soon and hear
that it was his bomb that killed the al Qaeda leader.

For now, the snipers didn't think about sleep. Who could? They
wrapped themselves in their thin blankets and tried not to long for all of
the cold-weather gear that had been left behind in their rucksacks, back
when they thought the mission to confirm the demise of the machine gun
would be a quick one.

They were exposed on a six-foot-wide rocky path along the high spine of the ridgeline. It was the only trail up there, but remaining on it wasn't possible. Their options were limited, and night was on them. On both sides of the path, the terrain dropped off severely, with intermittent trees and stumps protruding from the cliff walls at odd angles.

After a little discussion, they decided to take their chances as mountain goats. They sat down, slipped over the edge boots first for about ten feet, and then lodged in, as best they could, practically vertical, but within whispering distance. Having started out in daylight, they had only one pair of NVGs between them.

About an hour after squeezing into the awkward positions, they heard the unmistakable sound of weapons rattling and heavy, fast-paced footsteps approaching. The snipers froze in place and held their breaths, with thumbs on the selector switches of their rifles. Shrek slipped a grenade from his vest and held it close to his chest. As soon as the footsteps faded, Scrawny whispered, "Five or six al Qaeda. No doubt."

Scrawny had been in worse spots.

He and I were in the same Ranger Class, 10-84, and after a few years with the 2nd Ranger Battalion, he joined Delta. He stands roughly five feet, seven inches tall and has a wiry set of muscles on a fat-free frame, and many in Delta refer to him as the Punisher.

He made his rep firm as a young assaulter in 1989 during the rescue of American hostage Kurt Muse in Panama.* Scrawny toted a M-249 SAW with twelve hundred rounds of linked 5.56mm ammo onto the roof of Modelo prison. It took his mates only six minutes to breach the rooftop door, descend the stairs, secure the hostage, and return to the roof to get picked up by helicopters. During that short time, Scrawny fired a thousand rounds at Panamanian defense forces while under heavy

---

* Operation Acid Gambit was the opening mission of the invasion of Panama in 1989 by Delta to rescue American citizen Kurt Muse. Muse shares his story in his book *Six Minutes to Freedom*.

fire himself. He did not get so much as a scratch, but his number of con-firmed kills exceeded fifty.

The team of snipers hugging the cliffside like spiders discussed their next move and Murph decided their best option was to stay where they were. Within minutes, another group of the enemy passed, but this time the risk of compromise was increased, for these fighters carried several white-lens flashlights to illuminate the trail of slippery, loose, and uneven rocks. A glance over the side would have exposed the Americans.

For the next several hours, more groups of fighters used the busy trail, hustling along in both directions. Was al Qaeda reinforcing their forward lines? Were they moving into ambush positions to await the routine midday return of the muhj? Or, were they simply swapping out forces? The isolated Delta boys had no way of knowing what the footsteps in the night meant.

Any thoughts that Usama bin Laden might still have of victory and re-taining his mountainous redoubt were gone by the evening of Decem-ber 15. The top terrorist, who was apparently being chased around the battlefield by our bombs, had already apologized to his fighters for getting them into this mess. He placed blame for their failures on the apostate regimes in Saudi Arabia, Jordan, Egypt, and Pakistan, saying he expected those countries to rally around the cause and come to the rescue. He also had passed that strange permission for women and children to arm them-selves to defend the caves.

Now he was undergoing a sea change of attitude. He authorized his battered subordinate units to surrender if they so desired! That surprise guidance came as no surprise at all. In the last signals intercept we had of bin Laden the day before, on December 14, his voice indicated obvious distress, and since then our attacks had not let up.

The British commandos who went into the mountains to keep Haji

Zaman motivated radioed back that scores of al Qaeda fighters had decided to quit, opting to remain in the present world for the time being. Martyrdom would have to wait. Having lost their will to fight, they dropped their weapons and walked off the battlefield.

The image of bin Laden hiding, surviving, and contemplating surrender was confirmed by the numerous radio calls gathered by our special intelligence collectors at the schoolhouse and also being intercepted by both MSS Grinch and MSS Monkey. Al Qaeda had lost its nerve, and it appeared that their leader also was cracking.

But was he really in panic? Or was he just putting some fighters out there to surrender as a ruse to buy time and stall our attack, hoping to get breathing room to slip out the back door? Even when things are looking good, you have to consider other possibilities.

Whatever bin Laden's choice, we knew this battle would be decided shortly.

There were spies among us.

One commodity at the top of every supply wish list was a request for interpreters fluent in speaking Pashto. Adam Khan was our only trustworthy 'terp, and being unable to clone him meant that communications between the locals and the Americans continued to present problems.

In the Tora Bora Mountains, the job skills needed for these interpreters included the ability to survive in austere commando conditions—more specifically, to keep their balance, manipulate a trigger in freezing weather, and pull their own weight.

So when a suitable linguist popped up, he was put to work. A man in a passing patrol stopped for a moment near MSS Grinch and caught the eye of Adam Khan. The guy looked like a real find. Not only was he fluent in Pashto, but he also spoke and understood English at about a grade-school level. More than good enough. He was paid a handsome signing bonus.

But the new 'terp, known as "Flagg," had not been fully vetted, so Jim and the boys limited his exposure, either visually or verbally, to what they were doing. Adam Khan kept an eye on him during his probationary period and soon figured out that there was more to this guy than a smattering of English. He spoke five languages! He also was a lot less trustworthy than any of the other Afghans accompanying MSS Grinch, and Adam Khan determined he was a spy and had him detained on the spot. It was quite possible the guy was on the al Qaeda payroll. His pocket litter contained an MSNBC business card, but also handwritten notes on a few pieces of paper, including the call sign of our man Pope. The 'terp denied all allegations, but was escorted down the mountain to see General Ali.

Before Ali could figure out what to do with Flagg, the guy was caught brazenly trying to use the telephone inside the general's quarters. One of Skoot's tactical signal interceptors struck up a conversation with him and noticed that Flagg, among his other languages, spoke fairly good Arabic. This was a big enough spike to arrest him. He was interrogated, roughed up a bit, and shipped off to Kabul to be locked away in some dark, damp, and overcrowded cellblock.

But Flagg wasn't the only questionable person around. Another gentleman was constantly following and pestering Adam Khan with personal questions about where the American commandos lived in the United States, wanting to know their names, and trying to gain his trust. He had a British accent and curiously remained apart from the rank-and-file muhj as much as possible. His English was much more advanced, but the most telling discovery about the small, skinny, and dark-skinned Muslim was the way he clearly understood the sophisticated manner in which the boys used infrared lasers to guide the bombs.

To do that required some advanced training, and Adam Khan soon pegged this one as an agent of the Pakistani Intelligence Service, the ISI, who had infiltrated inside Ali's forces. He wasn't allowed anywhere near us. Afghanistan was strange.

The British intelligence officer and Haji Zaman attended the fireside chat on the night of December 15, for another important cultural turning point would arrive with the dawn. The following day, December 16, marked the end of Ramadan, and not only could the muhj start eating and drinking during the daytime, but traditionally it was supposed to be a time of rest and forgiveness of enemies.

The bulk of the meeting centered on convincing the warlords to forego that centuries-old custom and continue the attack in the mountains. Al Qaeda was on the ropes, and it was absolutely necessary to keep up the pressure. We were not in a forgiving mood.

Zaman, apparently having recovered from the false-surrender debacle, agreed, and bragged about getting an early start, saying he would have several hundred fighters ready to go at first light.

I laid my map before Zaman and asked him to point out the spot he planned to attack. That, of course, was an exercise in futility because Zaman's ability to read a map was limited. In retrospect, there really were not too many good reasons why men like Ali and Zaman needed to read a map, for this was their backyard.

As soon as Zaman left, Ali began openly to question the commitment of his nemesis. Waving his hand wildly, the general said Zaman would never be able to motivate his men to attack, at least without letting them have a regular morning meal, their first breakfast after the month of fasting. Also, Zaman would not strike until he had spent some time at Press Pool Ridge, pandering sufficiently to the media and the cameras.

Ironically, it was the presence of the press that helped ensure the customs normally attached to the end of Ramadan would be ignored this year. Both warlords understood that public perception was the key to their futures.

Nestled in a rocky outcrop with not much vegetation, Kilo Team was enjoying an unmolested view of some of al Qaeda's best positions. Not long after midnight, the crew aboard an AC-130 gunship radioed that they had spotted a dozen or so people running around on a nearby hilltop. The pilot wanted to know if these "hot spots" were friendly. Since Kilo was the forwardmost OP in the center of the battlefield, no friendlies were out there. Pope cleared the gunship "hot," and after a few minutes of hammering, the pilot relayed to the boys on the ground: "All targets neutralized."

As the Americans and Brits passed some quiet, congratulatory high fives around their OP, the distinct and comforting drone of the gunship could still be heard overhead. Then the silence gave way to a strange and ominous whistling sound that grew louder and louder, closer and closer until it stopped with a loud *Ding!* within their position. An expended piece of 40mm brass casing had spilled out of the gunship at 15,000 feet and landed in the middle of their tight perimeter, narrowly missing all six of them. They looked at each other in the darkness for a few moments, pondering what that big chunk of brass would have felt like if had crashed onto one of their heads.

Otherwise, Kilo spent another productive night by bombing al Qaeda. Like India Team, which had humped a SOFLAM up to OP25-A five days earlier, Kilo also had brought one up with them. It was a priceless piece of kit in this environment, and Pope and Lowblow knew it. They also knew once they departed the schoolhouse and moved into the mountains, the chances of being resupplied were slim to none. So both Delta snipers carried a PRC-117D radio just in case one radio shit the bed on them. They also packed two M-72 LAW rockets, five broken-down MRE rations, four gallons of water, fourteen BA-5590 radio batteries each, and assorted other items, and their personal rifles. The combined weight, and the high altitude, the bout with altitude sickness, the freezing temperatures, and small amount of food resulted in Pope dropping from 185 pounds to 152 pounds during the course of the battle.

Pope's favorite tactic was one that the Admiral had taught him a few months earlier back at Bragg. He would run in a bomber to drop a large bomb on a cave entrance or bunker. If the strike was dead on, then nothing more was required. But if it was a narrow miss, it usually resulted in shell-shocked enemy fighters dashing off in all directions to find safety. When that happened, Pope would cycle away from the bomber and call in the gunships to rake over the survivors. The technique was deadly.

Late that evening, I returned to General Ali's quarters to alert him that a resupply helicopter would be landing very soon, just outside his window. He was already tucked beneath his brown wool blanket, but sat up when I entered. Something was bothering him, and he asked in a serious tone, "Commander Dalton, why is America in such a hurry to kill bin Laden now, after he has been your enemy for so long?"

Before Ghulbihar finished translating, the general continued: "America believes they have the might to do all things, but some things are God's will."

Now I thought that was a stupid question. Al Qaeda had regularly attacked American targets abroad, but on 9/11 they hit the United States itself, hard. Osama bin Laden was behind that attack. We were at war, and where, before 9/11, we had wanted him dead or alive, now we just wanted him dead.

But rather than spell it out for Ali and get into a philosophical discussion, as I heard the *thump-thump* of the approaching MH-47 Chinook, I decided to let action speak for me. The general's room had flimsy little swing-gate windows that directly faced the helicopter landing zone, and they were open.

"General, you are about to experience American might firsthand," I said with a bit of sarcasm.

As the helicopter thundered over the building, the powerful downdraft from the rotors struck with a vengeance. Ali threw off his blanket, jumped out of bed, and, with arms outstretched in front of him, leaned against the windows like he was about to be frisked by the law to hold them shut. The powerful rotor wash and flying sand literally threatened to push the windows open as the general struggled against them. Although it was amusing to see the warlord floundering in his pajamas, I chose to allow the general to retain his dignity and walked out the door. Point proven.

16

Victory Declared . . . Bin Laden Status Unknown

If al Qaeda was still strong, they would not have left their dead brothers behind.
—GEN. HAZRET ALI, DECEMBER 17, 2001

General Ali mustered roughly fifty anxious and shivering fighters at the schoolhouse early on December 16. It was the end of Ramadan, so while they waited for their general, some ate flat bread, others drank bottled water, and some just squatted down and stared into space. Two of those three simple pleasures were not allowed during the last thirty days of daylight fasting.

My attempts to pin down the general about his exact attack position or his intended march objective had been in vain, and except for the Muslims being able to eat and drink, this was shaping up to be no different than any other day.

Before George and the general walked to the lime green SUV to head to the battle lines, I promised Ali that he would have as many bombs as he needed and that we wanted to keep the pressure on. But I also warned that the battlefield was tightening, and that we didn't want to kill any of his men by accident. "Keep my guys updated up there with your intentions," I said.

The general shook my hand, placed his right hand over his heart, shrugged his shoulders, and said, "Just keep bombing." The man smelled victory.

"I'll keep that in mind," I responded as he climbed into the passenger's seat.

The warlord Haji Zaman, recently teamed with the third British SBS team and a recently arrived air force combat controller, was now capable of directing ordnance to support his own attack.

Adam Khan accompanied the Brits to link up with Zaman's forward commander, and while moving into the foothills, he struck up a conversation with one of Zaman's fighters. The man claimed that he personally saw Usama bin Laden mounted on a white horse and escorted by twenty or so black-hooded Egyptian bodyguards on foot. Rumor had it that unyielding loyalty was not enough to land a spot on bin Laden's personal security detail. Just as important was that they had to share the same blood type as the terrorist leader.

The fighter described the atmosphere when bin Laden moved from one hiding spot to the next. A few minutes before the Sheikh's arrival, a messenger would arrive to warn the locals, and all adults were sent to their homes and told not to come out until directed to do so. The only noise heard in the streets was the sound of little children running through the narrow alleys and back streets. Once bin Laden was safe inside his transient hideout, usually only minutes after the messenger's arrival, the village resumed its normal life, as if nothing had ever happened.

Shortly after Adam Khan introduced the Brits to their new guide, they started to lumber up the hill and catch up with the commandos who were with General Ali's fighters. Zaman chose a different ridgeline to move on, because following the Ali forces would have added little value. On the political scale, it would have been a major insult to Zaman.

Just above bin Laden's destroyed home, the team of Brits, Adam Khan, and the guide encountered small-arms fire from an adjacent ridgeline occupied by some of Ali's fighters. As tracer rounds zipped overhead, the commandos made a mad dash uphill and dove into a huge bomb crater. Within a minute or so, they heard the distinct crash of rounds being fired from two T-55 tanks back near Press Pool Ridge and ducked as the shells passed overhead and exploded on the rocks farther up the ridgeline. They began to wonder what the worst of the two evils was: dying from AK-47 fire or being hit with one of those big shells from a friendly tank. The Brits figured neither choice was worth sticking around for, so everyone abandoned the crater and rushed forward to a more secure position.

Once in their place, they got to work and ordered up a B-52 strike on a suspected enemy position. After the big bomber had delivered its thundering payload and left the area, one of the Brits opened his pack and proudly produced a mini-kitchen, as if magically pulling a white rabbit from a top hat.

"It's teatime!" he announced with a sigh of relief.

A few minutes before 0900 hours, with a slight cool breeze at their backs and the sun rising to their front, both Zaman and Ali attacked, just as they had promised. It was pretty clear they intended to stay for a while, for this time, besides the standard-issue AK-47 rifles, three magazines, an RPG round or two, and a pocket of nuts, dates, or rice, the muhj fighters were carrying bedrolls! Were they actually going to stay in the mountains this time?

Some pockets of the enemy had laid down their arms and surrendered, and others were confused, having received no recent guidance from their superiors. The stubborn enemy fighters who refused to surrender either took their quest for paradise more seriously than their buddies or opted to head for the friendlier turf across the border in Pakistan.

At the schoolhouse, tactical radio intercepts overheard frantic calls begging for medicine, bandages, food, and water. Requests for guidance, or permission to retreat into the villages, or fade deeper into the mountains convinced us that the end of the battle was near. George of the CIA received a classified cable from Kabul reporting that the Pakistani military had apprehended several dozen Arab fighters just across the border.

Around the same time, a directive came from the Americans at Bagram to ask General Ali if he would accept a larger foreign presence on the battlefield—not just a few more Special Ops types, but a massive and overt buildup of American military forces.

I sprang the question on the general at the nightly chat, and his eyes showed no sign of surprise, because an operational shift on the overall battlefield was looming. He hesitated for a moment, then said he needed until the morning to decide. Ali likely would have to discuss the situation with his trusted local supporters and the Shura.

At midday on the western flank, several of the muhj fighters who were with MSS Monkey took off for a hilltop to their front, possibly irritated that they were missing out on looting the caves. Once the muhj reached the crest, they radioed back to request some Americans to come forward and drop some more bombs.

India Team arrived shortly thereafter and, sure enough, saw numerous personnel out to their front. As Spike worked up a fire mission, Kilo Team called in to stop it. In Kilo's opinion, the designated groups were friendly muhj, and not al Qaeda. The muhj commander disagreed, but was not certain. Once again, without any way to confirm friend from foe and no interpreter, the Americans were hamstrung.

The weather took a turn for the worse and blanketed the entire area with heavier snow and a strong wind that blew some of the flurries sideways while shrinking visibility to less than two hundred meters. Later that evening, Bryan radioed the schoolhouse: The muhj were coming off the mountain and heading away from the fight. Bedrolls or not, they were coming back.

We asked, "Why?"

"One-One, this is Three-Two. The commander up here is telling us that the fight is over. He says the enemy has bolted and that they are the *winners*," Bryan reported. His voice was shaky because of the hard, cold, and freezing wind, but was drenched in pessimism.

"I haven't heard that yet," I answered. "Thanks for the update. We'll keep up the bombing anyway until someone tells us different."

Numerous reports of surrendering al Qaeda forces were heard throughout December 16.

The groups numbered from twenty to twenty-five former fighters, some more, some less. Our higher headquarters now scrambled to figure out how to handle about three hundred or so prisoners. There was no large-scale holding area and the best option seemed to be moving them to Kabul by trucks.

The reports of surrender and victory had not made it to all of the enemy forces in Kilo Team's area, and Kilo itself had not received any orders to stand down. So Pope, Lowblow, and the four Brit commandos perched on the southwest side of the third highest point in the mountains continued to wreak havoc on obvious and suspected al Qaeda positions.

Throughout the battle, the hefty collection of warplanes enjoyed complete air superiority and had little to worry about, short of running into one another. On this night, Pope pushed an AC-130 ten miles to the east and into a holding pattern while he finished working with some bombers. In about five minutes, his radio crackled to life with the voice of the female pilot of the gunship, who was eager to get back into the hunt. It was strange to hear a female voice under those circumstances, and more than somewhat out of place.

Pope instructed her to stand by for clearance. After five more minutes, she keyed her radio mike again, clearly agitated at being told to stand by. Pope was finally able to clear her in, and the AC-130 immediately wheeled in for the attack, guns blazing. A determined American woman pilot was taking her turn killing the macho Muslim terrorists.

Jester and Dugan, the heroes of OP25-A, spent only a day and a half resting and refitting before getting back into the game. Joined by another four-man team of British SBS commandos, they were tasked with reinforcing the Jackal Team and helping continue the bombing.

When they reached the base of the mountain, young Afghans stood around hoping to get jobs as guides, lined up like taxicabs at a big city airport. A couple of guides were hired and led them up the trails, and after an hour of climbing, they stopped for a rest.

As they caught their breath, heavy firing by AK-47s snapped a fusillade of 7.62mm rounds overhead. The snipers and Brit commandos squirmed behind the largest rocks they could find as the gunfire stuttered on and on. But it was no attack, just a large group of muhj celebrating the end of Ramadan by wildly firing their weapons, raising the guns in the air and squeezing off 7.62mm rounds on full auto.

One of the new guides, bless his heart, yelled at the top of his lungs for them to stop. When that had no effect, he actually started throwing rocks at them, as if he could hit them from several hundred meters away. Dugan and Jester were thankful the young man did not have a weapon of his own, or they might have been in the middle of a gunfight between the rejoicing muhj and one truly unhappy guide.

Pushing uphill as fast as they could to get out of range of the happy muhj, the commandos reached Hopper and the Admiral about noon, up on the ridgeline near an old fort. A short while later, a B-52 laid a strike on a cave about eight hundred meters away, and the cave erupted with multiple secondary explosions that sent rock and debris flying everywhere. A fifty-five-gallon drum came hurtling out of the carnage like a comet and passed fifty meters over their heads. "Holy shit," yelled one of the boys. "They're throwing oil barrels at us!"

That night, just after dark, scores of muhj fighters streamed back down the ridgelines once again, no doubt hurrying to find warmth and continue celebrating the end of Ramadan. They smiled, waved, and made no secret that they felt that they had won the battle and it was time to go home.

The Jackal Team did not agree. Murph and his two snipers were still up forward and pressing the attack, although they were critically low on water. Jester, Dugan, and two of the Brits cross-loaded up to roughly eighty pounds of supplies in each of their rucksacks and waited in the snowy cold for enough light to allow them to begin their emergency resupply mission over the treacherous trails.

Meanwhile, Sergeant Major Ironhead's own resupply patrol to MSS Grinch had returned to the schoolhouse and Ironhead almost had to be forced to grab a few hours of sleep before doing an encore.

This time, we tweaked the organization of his team to eliminate having to rely on untrustworthy local Afghans such as the kind who had made off with much-needed supplies during the first climb.

The answer was to use four attached heavy breachers who had been held at the schoolhouse to provide our local security. Most were Special Forces demolition sergeants, experts in the use of explosives, oxygen, hydraulics, and making things go boom. These guys did not mind rolling up their sleeves for a tough job. They were all as heavily muscled as racehorses and were as ready to run as odds-on favorites at the Kentucky Derby.

Ironhead and the patrol used two pickup trucks to get as far as Mortar Hill, where they put the supplies on their backs, tucked their heads against the flailing show, and humped into the steep inclines, reaching MSS Grinch in just over five hours. They even brought along dry socks.

Even with such unbelievable exhibitions of endurance, our ability to maintain such a pace was unrealistic and dangerous. Had the enemy spotted any of the patrols, major drama would have unfolded, since serving as pack mules limited firepower and security during the movement. There was no easy solution, and after mulling it over with both Jim at MSS

Grinch and Bryan at MSS Monkey, we adjusted our current dispositions in the mountains.

The changes would not only help resolve the logistics problems, but also keep up the hunt for bin Laden.

Regardless of the success of laying down an umbrella of bombs, and the advances the muhj had racked up over the last four days, we could not get bottlenecked on a single hilltop. Bin Laden's location was still unknown, and we needed to be able to quickly join the fracas when the al Qaeda chief showed himself.

Moving to the new axis of advance, MSS Grinch crossed paths with a group of muhj taking some al Qaeda prisoners back to General Ali's headquarters. Upon seeing the American commandos, the muhj became nervous, clearly not wanting the boys near their prisoners. A rumor had spread after the laughable surrender deal a few days earlier that the Americans would kill all prisoners in cold blood. In a war zone, that wasn't necessarily a bad reputation to have.

The muhj tried to sneak the prisoners past, but our Alpha Team, along with the attached Special Ops Arab linguist, intercepted them. Their orders were to snap some photos, see if they recognized anyone, and take a look at how the muhj were treating the prisoners. Did they allow them to keep their weapons? Were they treating them as prisoners of war, or had the enemy simply paid off the Afghan muhj to escort an escape? Hell, the way things were going with the entire rumor, innuendo, and unanswered questions about the surrender deal, it wouldn't have surprised any of us if bin Laden and his cane were strolling along with them.

As expected, the muhj took issue with the situation, which made the picture taking and questioning in Arabic all the more entertaining. Surprisingly, at least one of the al Qaeda prisoners had a fairly good command of English and didn't mind flaunting it.

After being asked where bin Laden was located, another prisoner responded defiantly, "I could tell any Muslim brother where Sheik Usama is and they wouldn't tell you."

Every nervous muhj guard present during this exchange thought the next action would be an American commando putting a .45-caliber hard ball into the prisoner's smart-ass mouth. But we are more civilized than our terrorist adversaries, a characteristic seen as a sign of weakness by al Qaeda's ilk, and let them live. In a war zone with these people, such compassion isn't such a good reputation to have.

General Ali declared victory over the al Qaeda forces at Tora Bora. He did not mention Usama bin Laden.

The general's victory cry was at odds with the current realities of the battlefield, where the air strikes were continuing unabated. The boys called in a half-dozen "troops in the open" requests for fire from a couple of loitering B-52s. Close to forty-five bombs were dropped before noon.

By early afternoon, we decided to honor Ali's request to cease bombing to allow his fighters greater freedom of movement. The general was confident that no caves existed beyond Hilltop 3212. He said he knew this for sure because he had helped build them in the mid-1980s.

Several villages reported strangers showing up, and the muhj visited them, one by one. At this point, there was little fight and little faith left in al Qaeda's ranks.

There had been no confirmed sign of bin Laden in the last couple of days, no body to photograph, no DNA to collect. The press began reporting that the al Qaeda leader had escaped, and that led some critics to declare that the Battle of Tora Bora was a failure.

Our boss relayed the necessity that we paint a picture of victory, but without the body of our target, there were few options for convincing out-siders that the overall fight had been a success.

We could state the fact, verifiable by the press, that the al Qaeda mountain stronghold had been utterly destroyed. And we could also accu-rately point out that the enemy was on the run. The preferred choice was to fall back on the body count option of the Vietnam era.

Thus began the numbers game of meticulously soliciting figures from each subordinate commander of the rival warlords, from the CIA people who had explored particular caves and valleys, and cross-checking their tallies with our own daily notes and reports.

Regardless of the spin, General Ali's declaration of victory meant very little to us. True victory could never be claimed until there was some proof of bin Laden's demise. A bunch of dead al Qaeda types was cer-tainly a good thing, but the main mission had been to kill the mastermind and bring back proof. That didn't happen.

Jester, Dugan, and the two Brits got an early start on their resupply hike. They had about one thousand meters to cover, moving uphill and over some treacherous terrain in weather that was deteriorating every day.

Like Scrawny before him, Dugan's mountaineering expertise saved the day, and after three hard hours of climbing over slippery rocks they finally reached their teammates. It is amazing that none of them slipped over the edge and plummeted two thousand feet to the bottom of the valley.

After reaching the three snipers, the five Delta operators and two Brit commandos huddled close together in the freezing temperatures. There were seven of them, each with a thin local blanket, but there were only two sleeping bags. They took shelter from the knife-sharp wind inside an old al Qaeda trench and spent that whole horrible night rotating through security and restless sleep. None were considering getting out of there, but were just waiting for authority to start dropping bombs again. In their opinion, the lack of thunderous explosions, machine-gun chatter and radio transmissions was only a temporary condition.

The only thing breaking the eerie, ghostly silence was the keening wind.

On the other side of the battlefield, the four-man team of Brit commandos and one American combat controller that was accompanying Zaman's fighters made their way to Ski and his India Team. By now, Zaman had surrounded the second highest peak in the area, just short of 10,000 feet, and shown on our maps as Hilltop 3212.

What was left of al Qaeda fighters was in a full retreat. And without any command and control to organize and direct them, it was every man for himself. None were sticking around the mountains in hopes of a last-ditch defensive. When the weather cooperated, the desperate yet brave enemy fighters were easy targets in the daytime for our fighter jets and accurate bombers.

India Team took the opportunity to conduct some battle damage assessment of the caves and bunkers in their area. The fissures that dominated the high ground had excellent overhead cover and concealment, and were topped with blue and clear plastic to keep out the rain. The Delta boys were impressed by the work of the men who had constructed the caves, but also saluted the attention to detail of the American factory workers who built the engines of war that destroyed them.

Heaps of sheared rock, mounds of turned soil, and mangled branches and tree trunks surrounded the emplacements, severe damage that attested to the accuracy and severity of heavy bombing. A destroyed ZPU-1 antiaircraft gun, previously well camouflaged, sat open and exposed and motionless behind some tattered trees. Empty ammo cans and belts of ammunition were strewn in all directions. Bloodied bandages, discarded cans of Quaker Oatmeal and food wrappings, split firewood, abandoned RPG rounds, and old potato masher grenades gave it the look of a junkyard. A few documents written in Arabic, the only thing of value to us, were collected and passed to the CIA.

While documenting the finds with a camera, Ski struck up a conversation with a muhj fighter. The Afghan told a dramatic yarn of a helicopter swooping in fast and low to land in a small village down in the Wazir Valley. Although the muhj's memory was admittedly hazy, he told Ski the event happened about eight days earlier, and in his opinion the helicopter had belonged to Pakistan. Ski knew for sure that it had not been an American helicopter. Could it have picked up a special passenger and whisked him away? No way to prove any part of his story.

I sat down with General Ali and Adam Khan for our nightly chat and had a chance for some small talk while we waited for George to arrive with his latest CIA reports. I mentioned that since the general's earlier declaration of victory, the U.S. government had begun debating a "definition of success" for Tora Bora.

"The Voice of America is saying this battle is over, and that you won, General," I said, sipping a cup of hot tea. Obviously exhausted, but happy that the fighting was over except for some minor actions, Ali responded in a fatherly tone: "We might not have been up to the task, we might have needed more fighters, it might not have gone according to plan, or maybe this was all in God's hands."

Pausing to allow Adam Khan to translate, the general continued, "We have much work still to do. We haven't found Sheikh Usama."

"General, with all you just said, how could you claim victory?" I asked.

"To put a smile on your face. We have destroyed al Qaeda's base of the last ten years. They are confused, tired, and hurting. The sheikh has no other place as good as this," he answered with total sincerity, nodding toward the snow-sheathed peaks.

I changed the subject. "When we arrived, we were told that up to three thousand enemy fighters were in the mountains. Where did they go, and how many were killed?"

"My commanders will tell me how many died. It is difficult, though, as our culture is to care for the martyrs right away. Zaman buried many the other day. We found eighty in a valley yesterday from bombs," he explained, then paused for a few seconds. "If al Qaeda was still strong, they would not have left their dead brothers behind."

"Do you still have fifty enemy prisoners?"

"Yes. No. One had a grenade and he was shot." He pulled the knife-edge of his hand across his throat.

George entered the room with one of Ali's officers, Commander Zahir. Not a day over thirty-five, he was muscular and well groomed, had a receding dark hairline, and spoke English well. His father, Haji Qadir, had been a good friend of General Ali's before Taliban cruel justice caught up with him. The general obviously respected his longtime friend's son.

The junior warlord was a fast learner, as well as being a dependable commander for Ali. When he had discovered that the CIA provided cash, arms, and equipment based upon the number of fighters a commander had, the shrewd Zahir had claimed he had 27,000 men of his own. It was an outrageous figure.

Zahir reported capturing several dozen enemy prisoners who had refused to drop their weapons until they were certain they would be captured only by fellow Muslims because they feared the American commandos, particularly at night.

Under George's questioning, the young commander said that his men had killed about fifty al Qaeda fighters, but many others had died in the sustained bombing. He said it was hard to tell exactly how many, since so many of the bodies were headless, missing limbs, and lying in pieces here and there.

Zahir unfolded a dirty piece of paper and read twenty-two names of presumably captured al Qaeda fighters. A second CIA guy in the room, alerted to two of the names, scribbled them in his little notebook. Two others, according to Zahir, also seemed to be important because the others showed them reverence. One of them, Zahir believed, could possibly be one of bin Laden's sons.

We all woke up at that statement and George offered the assistance of the CIA in identifying the prisoners, including providing pictures of the most important al Qaeda personnel and their siblings. If the guy in question was related to bin Laden, he would be on the CIA list.

Zahir smiled and casually raised his left hand to indicate that he had it all under control, but he dodged back to the overall body count. "I will have a religious cleric ask them how many al Qaeda were in the mountains, how many were killed, and how many have fled."

"What makes you think they will respond to him?" George wanted to know.

"I have a special interrogator who will cry with them for their cause. We will wine and dine them, with high security, to get them to call for their brothers in the mountains to put their weapons down."

How could we possibly understand that thinking? These prisoners had been trying to kill us, and now were going to be pampered. "Cry with them for their cause?" Right.

Ali, Zahir, and another elder Afghan then simply closed the book on that subject and the possible identification of a young bin Laden, and dove into an intense three-way discussion about the al Qaeda loot being pulled from the caves. It was critical to divvy up the goods fairly. Somewhere in the middle of the ten-minute discussion, Ali looked up at us and apologized for the interruption, but he was adamant that this issue be solved immediately. It was custom.

By December 18, there was little left for us to do in the mountains. General Ali assured us that his men were busy searching for al Qaeda fighters who might be hiding in the valley villages. Whether or not that was true was debatable, for it seemed every muhj fighter was busy looting the caves for anything of value that might fetch a buck or two.

Journalists learned from the muhj passing by Press Pool Ridge that some Americans were still in the mountains and some set out to try and find a commando or two. Good story, better pictures.

The India and Kilo teams, along with several teams of Brits, were still in their forward positions, watching the cave-clearing escapades and awaiting orders to pack it up. They saw scores of Afghans traversing the ridgelines and valleys that had been the war zone, heading for their homes.

Realistically, we could have pulled every operator out of the mountains the night before, but we were directed to remain in place to demonstrate

American resolve. With two inches of snow on the ground and the temperature going nowhere but down, the grim snipers must have been a bizarre sight to victorious muhj. Didn't these Western commandos know the battle was done?

At midmorning, we directed Jackal team's forward OP to climb down the mountain through the latest layers of fresh snow and ice and link up with MSS Grinch. The weather made it impossible to retrace the dangerous route they had taken coming in, so Murph and Jester decided to head east and then back to the safety of the north. That would take them over territory that previously was occupied by al Qaeda and had not yet been traversed by Americans. The team shouldered their rucks and headed into the unknown.

After a thousand meters, they left the high ridge and went down into the valley heading north, stumbling across the bouldered valley floor. Two long-haired and unshaven Westerners approached from the opposite direction, one carrying a large camera. Journalists!

The boys pulled their muhj hats a little lower over their foreheads, raised their scarves over their noses and hid the guns under their blankets. As the two groups passed, one of the journalists said, "Hello, how are you all?" The boys didn't say a word and just kept walking.

Murph, the last man, couldn't resist. "How y'all doin'?" he replied, with a bit of sarcasm.

The two journalists came to a complete standstill, looks of shock on their faces. The boys continued moving away, turned another corner, hightailed it up a sloping spur, and hid behind a rock formation. The journalists were running up the valley not far behind, trying to catch the Americans and Brits and snap a few prized pictures, but unknowingly passed right underneath the Jackal Team. One moment the commandos had been right beside them, and the next moment they had vanished. The journalists continued on down the trail, and the team decided to take a break and brew up some tea on a portable butane stove. After enduring days of stress, the unexpected encounter with the journalists had brought a moment of humor.

Jim had also sent two assaulters to guide the snipers back to the base camp. The same two journalists now spotted these Delta boys and started chasing them, but the assaulters took off. In doing so, one of their sleeping bags snaked out of its carrier and was flapping behind him like a flag by the time they came into view of the snipers. It was too much. The American snipers and Brit commandos broke out in tension-melting laughter.

After sharing the pot of tea, they all descended farther into the valley and headed in the direction of the MSS Grinch base camp. For about thirty minutes, things seemed to be normal, then someone popped up from behind a large group of jagged rocks about a hundred meters away and the sun-bright lights of a camera flashed on.

The boys were startled and at first thought it was the flash of a weapon from a friendly muhj who had mistaken the approaching Americans for the enemy. They didn't want to kill the guy, so they fired a few rounds over his head to give him the message.

Instead of a muhj, it was a photographer, who immediately dove to the ground and started yelling, "Don't shoot me! Don't shoot me!"

Tora Bora was still a dangerous place, no matter what your occupation, and it could be even more dangerous if you were armed with a camera, and not a rifle.

The boys finally reached MSS Grinch just before dusk, after four hours of heavy slogging and carrying snow-soaked loads. That night, they enjoyed the luxury of a warming fire. On the nearby ridges, the muhj continued to celebrate the end of the Holy Month. All night, they chanted verses from the Quran, beat little round drums, sang songs, smoked hash, and fired their automatic weapons at the moon.

Back at the schoolhouse things were also winding down in anticipation of our return to Bagram. The show here was over.

After all of the number crunching, the final body count emerged, although it was just a guesstimate. As best we could figure, the actual number of dead al Qaeda came to 220. Another fifty-two al Qaeda fighters had been captured, most of them Arabs and about a dozen Afghan, with a few Chechen, Algerian, and Pakistani fighters mixed in. Finally, there were the one hundred or so men who were captured crossing the border by Pakistani authorities.

There is no doubt that the real number of killed and captured enemy fighters was much higher, because many of the accurate bombs impacted directly on dozens of al Qaeda positions and either sent body parts flying in all directions or just obliterated groups of fighters where they stood. Several hundred others probably managed to run from the battlefield.

No one will ever know for sure, and it is not really all that important. We had taken Tora Bora, which the Soviets had failed to do in ten years of savage fighting.

On the morning of December 19, George, General Ali, and Adam Khan jumped in the lime green SUV. The rear window had been patched with clear plastic secured in place by duct tape. A few dozen muhj climbed into a few pickup trucks.

Intelligence reports had already turned the CIA's attention from bin Laden to his deputy, Ayman al-Zawahiri, who had not been killed in an earlier bombing as first reported. Earlier that morning, a source had provided a possible location for al-Zawahiri, and the CIA was going to check it out, backed by General Hazret Ali, who was now America's favorite warlord.

I doubted I would see them again anytime soon, so as they stepped into the SUV, I approached the vehicle to say goodbye. General Ali touched his chest over his heart, shook my hand and smiled, and touched his chest again.

As I shook hands with Adam Khan, my thoughts flashed to all the important work he had done. He seemed to always be at the center of the fight, and likely had saved the lives of several Delta operators. Words cannot express how deeply we were indebted to him.

"You didn't just face a single enemy here, but battled political, regional, and personal dilemmas in a culture completely foreign to you and your men," he said.

George, never much for small talk, said, "Your guys did a great job." Before pulling away, the CIA leader leaned out the window and called, "As soon as your men get off the mountain, we have another one for you. Number Two is nearby."

And with that, our Battle of Tora Bora officially came to a close.

For several years we would cling to the hope that bin Laden's foul remains were still inside a darkened and collapsed Tora Bora cave and that the terrorist was forever an inmate in hell. It was not until October 2004 that we learned he had gotten out and was still alive.

We have to give him credit for that escape, but we also must recognize the price he paid. Bin Laden made it out, but he left behind a battered, beaten, and shell-shocked bunch of terrorists. Perhaps he also left behind some pools of his own blood, but most of all, he had to abandon buckets of self-respect.

Only two months after his spectacular and cowardly 9/11 attack on the United States, a handful of American and Brit commandos, a fleet of warplanes and an ill-trained force of Afghan muhj had ripped away his fortress and made him run for his life.

17

The Years Since

I'm just a poor slave of God. If I live or die, the war will
continue.

—USAMA BIN LADEN, VIDEOTAPE PLAYED
DECEMBER 27, 2001

A month or so after the Battle of Tora Bora, I had an opportunity to fill in the Delta command group on what happened
there. The official briefing was followed with an informal
afternoon cup of coffee and a private sit-down with Col. Jim Schwitters, the
Delta commander who was known as Flatliner for his unflappable manner.

I had known him for years, and as we spoke, I recalled a day that had
given me an unexpected glimpse of both the colonel's experience, and our
own. After a training exercise in an American desert, we were returning to
the base when the old asphalt road led us past a little-known but historically important site. Some derelict single-story buildings loomed off to our
left, and we pulled over. As the Unit chaplain and I waited at the vehicle,
Flatliner walked to an old wooden wall that had been weathered by the
fiery desert sun and was anchored by four rusted but sturdy steel support
cables. The buildings were discolored and warped from years of exposure.

Flatliner rested his hand on one of the rusty cables and rubbed it
with reverence. He spoke to us in his trademark dry manner.

"We probably went over this wall a hundred times," he said softly.
His eyes swept the area as if it were occupied by ghosts. "We had to get

over the wall of the embassy to get to the hostages." Flatliner added, looking up. "I don't remember it being this high."

It finally struck me that this was where Delta conducted its rehearsals for the planned rescue of American hostages in Iran back in 1979 and 1980. During that raid, Operation Eagle Claw, Jim Schwitters had been a young E-5 buck sergeant and was the radio operator for Delta's founder and first unit commander: Col. Charlie Beckwith.

Besides this site being the rehearsal stage for the eventually aborted rescue mission, it also was where the infant Delta Force underwent its final evaluation by the Department of the Army to validate the long, painful, and costly birthing process.

If anyone knew first-hand how a good operation can go sour, it was Flatliner. He had been there.

The Delta commander listened carefully as I described the conflicted feelings that some of us had about the outcome in Tora Bora, and I believed that I was experiencing the same bitterness felt by the original Deltas after the Eagle Claw disaster. An important job had not been completed, and it was no one's fault.

Tora Bora was yesterday, and all we could do about it was pick up and go forward to the next assignment. The war on terrorism was really only just getting under way, so there would be more battles in the future. Flatliner left the table after expressing how much he appreciated the boys' efforts and individual acts of heroism.

There is no doubt that bin Laden was in Tora Bora during the fighting. From alleged sightings to the radio intercepts to news reports from various countries, it was repeatedly confirmed that he was there. The lingering mystery was: What happened then?

In February 2002, an audiotape was released to the al-Jazeera network in which the terrorist leader himself described the fighting at Tora Bora as a "great battle." Although the tape was released at that time, it was not known when it had been made.

In May 2002, a decision was made to try and resolve the issue by sending troops back to the now-quiet battlefield and having them do some exploring. The destination was the spot where some of General Ali's fighters had reported seeing a tall individual, whom they believed to be bin Laden, enter a cave about noon on December 14, the day that his last radio transmission had been intercepted. The muhj reported the lanky figure had been accompanied by approximately fifty companions. The cave they entered had been targeted by a B-52 bomber that dumped dozens of JDAMs on the site and forever rearranged the terrain. Follow-up strikes pounded the area day and night with an extraordinary amount of ordnance.

The investigation team was preceded by several dozen Green Berets and some Navy SEALs under my command, who drove in during the early-morning darkness and mowed down trees and obstacles with explosives to create a landing zone for a couple of CH-47 helicopters. Then a combined group of the 101st Airborne Division, soldiers of the Canadian army, and a twenty-man forensic exploitation team arrived.

The Canadians and 101st paratroopers found the caves completely sealed by tons of rubble that towered several stories high. It was obvious that the few hundred pounds of explosives they had brought along with them were not going to be enough to open that rocky tomb.

The forensic team shifted its focus instead to an eerie place known by the locals as the Al Qaeda Martyr Memorial, where colorful banners fluttered lazily on graveyard sticks, a place that would later give the intel imagery analysts fits during planning for the raid to capture Gul Ahmed. An assortment of Afghan mujahideen watched them work, probably feeling ashamed and insulted as dozens of jihadist graves were exhumed.

None of the DNA recovered from the cemetery proved to be the bin Laden jackpot, and the suspect cave where the terrorist leader was believed possibly to be entombed was impenetrable. The mission was a bust, doing little more than deepen the mystery.

TV personality Geraldo Rivera had spent several days near Tora Bora during the battle and returned to the mountains for a television special in September 2002. His interview with Gen. Hazret Ali in Jalalabad was broadcast on September 8, and I tuned in.

The general looked sharp in a suit and his familiar muhj hat, no longer just a bewildered muhj commander, but someone of substance and importance in his country. Shortly after the Tora Bora battle, Afghanistan's new leader, Hamid Karzai, had promoted Hazret Ali to the rank of three-star general, and the sly fellow with only a sixth-grade education had become the most powerful warlord in eastern Afghanistan. I was biting my nails while he was on camera, but he stayed with our agreement and never even hinted that American commandos had been anywhere near the Tora Bora battlefield.

Ali remained consistent and accurate with the known facts: Usama bin Laden was seen by some of his fighters in Tora Bora and was repeatedly heard talking on the radio. Initially, the terrorist had been full of confidence and resolve, encouraging and sending instructions to his al Qaeda forces. But as the battle wore on, that confidence evaporated, and he was heard apologizing to his men and weeping for his failures.

That matched up perfectly with what I knew to be the basic reasons to show bin Laden had been there.

General Ali also used the broadcast to level blame at his archrival, Haji Zaman Ghamshareek, for orchestrating the cease-fire fiasco during the fight, and negotiating with al Qaeda fighters to buy time for bin Laden to escape. He offered no proof of the latter part of his statement.

A few years later, a newspaper in Pakistan reported an Afghan Interior Ministry spokesman who had been present at the battle as saying it was General Ali who was truly at fault, and that bin Laden paid Ali to look the other way as the terrorist fled across the border.

It was just tit-for-tat fingerpointing and got us no closer to finding out how bin Laden obtained safe passage into Pakistan.

While Ali became a three-star, his slippery rival Zaman fled the country and, at the time of this writing, remains on the run.

Several days after that interview, Rivera was back on TV from near the Afghanistan and Pakistan border. Sitting on a large boulder, the visibly exhausted television guy described having made a three-hour walk through the Tora Bora Mountains, from Afghanistan into Pakistan. He displayed a colorful tourist map on which he had marked a small black X near the border to illustrate his location. His point was that if he could do it in three hours, then bin Laden would have had plenty of time during the cease-fire to abandon the field and cross safely into Pakistan. Just a three-hour hike!

For emphasis, Rivera read off his current latitude and longitude co-ordinates. I'm not sure exactly where Rivera was, but my mates and I had a good laugh as we watched him weave this bit of show business. What he claimed was a mere three-hour trek was a stretch of his imagination, because he was there in pleasant weather; during the harsh winter campaign, that same route would have required about ten hours, if it could have been done at all. Huge peaks blocked the way, along with impassable valleys where the snow blew horizontally in a hard and wicked wind and temperatures stayed well below freezing. By the way, the only thing shooting at Geraldo during his peaceful tour was his photographer's camera.

The two events were in no way comparable. Rivera gave us nothing new.

Peter Bergen, an author and well-known terrorism expert, uncovered vital clues in doing research for his superb book, *The Osama Bin Laden I Know*. From custodial transcripts of Guantánamo Bay detainees and a few Arabic newspaper comments of al Qaeda fighters who claimed to have fought at Tora Bora, Bergen pieced together information that shored up the claim that bin Laden, two of his sons, Uthman and Mohammed, and his chief deputy, Dr. Ayman al-Zawahiri, were all in the mountains during the fight. Some even claimed that bin Laden was wounded. Bergen chillingly portrayed a man who was staring death in the face and clearly anticipating his own martyrdom.

Bergen also uncovered that in October 2002 bin Laden's personal will was published in the Saudi magazine *Al Majallah*. The al Qaeda leader had signed his on the twenty-eighth day of Ramadan 1422 Hegira, which was December 14, 2001, on our calendar. Another match.

On December 27, 2002, two days after Christmas, my troop was once again back in Afghanistan and had gathered atop a tan mud-brick and mortar building in the center of Bagram Air Field. It was the same building we had occupied when we first arrived on that cold and mysterious night the previous year.

In those days the building was a skeleton of neglect, with large bullet holes, and loose wires hanging from the roof. Since then, it had progressed from being an emergency bunkhouse, to being a movie room, to transient quarters, to the Rangers' headquarters, to becoming the Speer Medical Clinic. It was named in honor of Delta Force medic Chris Speer, who was mortally wounded in a firefight near Khost.

Bagram was now the epicenter of combat operations in Afghanistan, with dozens of large green and tan tents erected over plywood stands, indirect fire bunkers strategically placed, and a large metal hangar or two in which commanders and large battle staffs managed the war effort.

On this day, the weather was clear and cool and offered a beautiful view of those stark peaks to the north. More than a full year after the Tora Bora battle, most of the boys and air force combat controllers now wore full beards and were dressed in blue jeans, boots, and some form of light cold-weather top. They stood at attention as I pinned medals on their chests for their actions twelve months earlier—two Silver Stars and a handful of Bronze Stars for Valor.

Our little ceremony was sans fanfare. No large formations with senior officers who were nowhere near the action giving congratulations and returning hand salutes. No live news coverage, or the presence of family and friends, or tables laden with finger food and punch. Just a private session for some sterling warriors who thought the medals were more than they deserved anyway. Typical Delta.

The men who fought at Tora Bora have always believed that just having been granted the responsibility of going after bin Laden, our nation's highest priority at the time, had been reward enough. The medals might be enjoyed by the grandkids years from now, but we would gladly trade them in for confirmation that Delta had played a role in killing Usama.

For years, no positive confirmation came out to prove that bin Laden had survived. At least not on the public record, although I trusted that the intelligence community knew more than it could say.

I used to wake up daily hoping that a breaking story would scroll across the television screen, stating that forensic evidence had come to light to prove that bin Laden had died in that godforsaken place. I hoped that he had remained in his fortress to fight and defy the world and the invading infidels. After all, that's what he advertised.

During those long months, I personally believed that a wounded bin Laden had fought a good fight until a precision-guided bomb, directed by an operator on a nearby ridgeline, punched his ticket to paradise. I planned to hold on to that theory until the intelligence community could prove I was wrong.

However, it was Usama bin Laden himself who finally did that. The terrorist leader appeared on television in a taped video late in October 2004, only days before the presidential election.

I knew immediately that the tape was the real thing. His posture, the voice, his thin body, and the aged beard that seemed frosted of snow were unmistakeable. Unfortunately, the man was still alive.

But . . . How?
Another critical piece of the puzzle surfaced in January 2007. The source was Gulbuddin Hekmatyar, who had been one of the CIA's favorite sons during the Afghan war with the Soviets before changing his stripes to become one of the most wanted men in the war on terror. Alle-

giances shift rapidly over there, and Hekmatyar was now the leader of the Hezb-e-Islami militant group.

Hekmatyar bragged during an interview with Pakistan TV that his men had helped bin Laden, two of his sons, and al-Zawahiri escape from Tora Bora. He claimed that after American and Afghan troops surrounded the cave complex, his own fighters "helped them get out of the caves and led them to a safe place." Was he telling the truth or spreading the myth? Can you trust any warlord, much less one who is a dangerous terrorist?

After six years of pondering the significance of the Battle of Tora Bora, I see some things much clearer.

Perhaps the most difficult thing to watch was the painful education of the American military in the work of confronting fanatical Muslim extremists. We were naïve back in December 2001 to think that Westerners could invade a Muslim country and rely on indigenous fighters to kill their Islamic brothers with tenacity and impunity.

That idea worked like a charm when we faced the common foe, the oppressive Taliban, which had ruled Afghanistan with an iron fist while enforcing the most rigid interpretations of the Quran.

However, at Tora Bora, the mujahideen weren't fighting the Taliban, they were fighting al Qaeda and Usama bin Laden, which made the dynamics significantly different. We might as well have been asking for them to fight the Almighty Prophet Mohammed himself. What motivation did the Afghan Muslims possess for hunting down, raising their rifles, sighting in, and actually shooting an al Qaeda fighter, much less the revered leader?

I am convinced that not a single one of our muhj fighters wanted to be recognized in their mosque as the man who killed Sheikh bin Laden.

So beyond getting the Taliban off their necks, the Afghan military and tribal leaders had goals that were much different from our own. They were out to accumulate personal fortunes and political power, to clear the opium fields for business again and protect the drug distribution routes . . . not to avenge the Americans killed on 9/11.

The CIA and the British paid these warlords handsomely for their questionable loyalty, and in turn, they were expected to pay and equip the amateur fighters who filled the ranks of both the Northern and Eastern Alliances. Material blessings literally fell from the heavens for them, more than they could ever have dreamed. New weapons, ammunition, uniforms, tennis shoes, cold-weather clothing, and blankets were dropped in huge bundles from cargo planes. America was not doing this on the cheap.

The intent of the local warlords surpassed any desires of the global coalition wanting to kill bin Laden. They wanted as much military hardware as possible to stash away for future tribal conflicts. We armed them for future fights among themselves, and that day will come.

The astonishing amount of bombs that were dropped during the fight is an easy way to prove how determined our military services had become in killing terrorists. A rule was established early on that no aircraft was to fly all the way to Tora Bora and then return to its base with bombs still hung. Engagement Zones were created to be the final option on the target list, primarily places that we could not see from the OPs but likely locations of enemy fighters.

The zones were carefully established, although based on nonscientific methods. First we had to check with General Ali on the location of his fighters to make sure they were clear. Then we culled the assessments of Ali and our snipers about the current al Qaeda locations. From that came the extrapolation of where the fleeing enemy might be heading within the next twenty-four hours. The recommended coordinates were relayed to the TOC in Bagram for approval. Generally, the pilots got the coordinates before they launched, and if for some reason they were assigned a definite target before having to egress, the aircraft was free to drop its payload inside the established EZ. A controller was still handling the planes, but primarily to maintain traffic control so they were not running into each other and to ensure that there were no friendlies below them.

Hostile threats and target discrimination were not required in an EZ. Warriors or widows, orphans or machine-gunners, commanders or cooks, any ant-sized sign of movement during the day or human-sized heat source at night was fair game. A daily average of over one hundred bombs impacted inside the EZs. This harsh reality may not sit well with critics, but it speaks volumes about the willingness of American general officers to ignore political correctness and make the tough calls.

The guys in the TOC burned as much midnight oil as the guys in the mountains of Tora Bora, cycling through their own battle drill to support the fight with as many fighters, bombers, and gunships as they could wrestle away from the U.S. Central Command, which was running the war. This was PhD-level stuff and they were establishing doctrine on the fly.

Artillery experts Will, Todd, and an old Ranger buddy named Jim collaborated with intelligence chief Brian to plot the latest EZ coordinates on their digital maps. In all, over 1,200 CENTCOM targets were fat-fingered, one at a time.

Ensuring that all this great stuff could be transmitted in real time back to CENTCOM in Florida and be made useful was a small crew of communicators. Smooth talkers Tony and Happ rigged up critical UHF antennas that allowed the fires experts to update aircraft coming into Afghan airspace on the way to Tora Bora. Sean, from the IT section, hardwired the place like Microsoft headquarters and constantly manipulated the incoming data.

Once a new free fire area was complete, the team rang up the liaison officer, call sign Rasta, at the Coalition Air Operations Center. Rasta, a navy pilot stuck with staff duty, also had the dubious duty of explaining to the CAOC commanding general why every plane in the theater always seemed to be heading to Tora Bora.

An enormous amount of U.S. taxpayer money and factory worker effort was expended at Tora Bora. Over 1,100 precision-guided bombs and more than 550 dumb bombs were dropped during the assault on al Qaeda's hideout. In one single and quite busy twenty-four-hour period alone, 135 JDAMs were dropped. These totals do not include shells put through the deadly accurate 40mm chain guns and 105mm cannons of the AC-130 gunships. Those would number in the many thousands.

With such hell falling in a relatively small target area, it is easy to understand why some cold, hungry and shell-shocked al Qaeda fighters took a rain check on martyrdom and ran away. Perhaps they were thinking quietly, *"Heck, if the Sheikh himself, the Lion of Islam, is running, why shouldn't I?"*

A day after we returned from the mountains, several of us knelt around a map of the Tora Bora area and informally briefed Maj. Gen. Dell Dailey and Command Sgt. Maj. C. W. Thompson. When we were finished, Dailey stated, "This is something incredibly historical, completely out of the box for Delta, and a great tactical victory."

Today, if you Google the words "Tora Bora," in less than a second you will have at your fingertips an avalanche of documents. This number is extraordinary, but it is public-domain material and lists everything from news reports to bloggers' opinions.

Surely, the U.S. Army could do better than that because of the rigid importance placed on identifying and documenting "Lessons Learned." One might assume the Center for Army Lessons Learned would reveal a treasure trove of information about every battle conducted during Operation Enduring Freedom.

The center's mission is to collect and analyze data and disseminate the accumulated information and resulting expert opinions to commanders, staffs, and students so we don't make the same mistake twice, and can better plan for future contingencies. The words seem to make perfect sense, right? Well, for an institution that boasts on its Web site that it is the "Intellectual Center of the Army," the phrase "Tora Bora" shows up in but a single document, as of this writing. The document is entitled *National Security Strategy of the United States of America.*

Strategy was published in 2002, on the first anniversary of 9/11, and mentions Tora Bora only in context with the Battle of the Coral Sea in the early part of World War II. The navy did not lose that pivotal battle in the Pacific, but it did not win it either. Coral Sea was important because it marked the beginning of the end of the Japanese empire. Therefore, the conclusion of the center's study was that Tora Bora was significant, whether successful or not. After all, why would the editors of our *National Security Strategy* allow such a reference if it was not warranted? It was not very enlightening. In my opinion, the center didn't give it serious attention, because it was not a conventional war, but a very restricted Special Forces operation, a stiletto instead of a broadsword. Our job was to keep moving forward, and to keep the bombs falling. Although we were after the man who was the root cause of the entire conflict, the historians would save their heavy lifting for the fly jockeys and the main battle tankers.

Even so, despite the center's viewpoint, our nation has never been closer to killing or capturing bin Laden as we were at Tora Bora.

As uncomfortable as it may be to accept, we have now known for years that bin Laden was not killed or captured at Tora Bora.

So regardless of how one chooses to spin the facts, the battle must be viewed as a military failure. This harsh reality is not to imply in any way that the American and British commandos, controllers, and intelligence operatives did not perform according to billing, for they certainly did. Even so, how can any other claim of success be made? It was, without a doubt, a tremendous tactical victory. But throw in the strategic assessment, too, and the fight at Tora Bora can be classified only as being partially successful operationally.

General Ali once had promised the CIA that he would attack on November 26, 2001, but he repeatedly stalled, apparently satisfied with small daylight skirmishes in the foothills. He did not want to order his entire army of fighters to smash al Qaeda.

The mujahideen had gained a worldwide reputation as being committed, fearless, and invincible soldiers of Allah because they had defeated the Soviet Red Army in the 1980s. The problem was that the muhj commanders believed their own headlines and vastly overestimated the abilities of their shoot-and-loot troops.

During our very first meeting, General Ali had proudly stoked the embers of the muhj myth, and arrogantly reminded us that the Russians had been unable to defeat the mujahideen after a decade of fighting. He airily stated that we Americans, the latest players on the scene, likewise would be no match for the seasoned enemy defending Tora Bora.

It took only a couple of days for us to prove that reputation of fierceness was a thin cover for the muhj not doing their jobs.

When the American and British commandos became the spearhead of the assaults, led the way into the mountains, and refused to leave the field at night, Ali's men suddenly became vastly more successful. More than eight thousand meters of al Qaeda terrain was captured in less than five days, several hundred new martyrs were created, and several hundred more of the less committed al Qaeda fighters chose survival and fled the mountain redoubt that had been touted as inviolate. Usama bin Laden ran away. Even the staunchest critics might find difficulty in classifying this as anything but a success.

Only two days after insulting our capabilities, General Ali retracted his statement, and I accepted his compliment gracefully on behalf of the USA. We had made him a believer. We easily punctured the myth that al Qaeda was some kind of superforce. We didn't need ten thousand troops to rout the enemy, but maybe we did need that many to actually kill bin Laden.

Throughout the Tora Bora operations, no Delta operator killed anyone in any way other than by dropping bombs on their heads. Some of the

best snipers, explosives experts, and knife fighters in the world were forced
to curb their enthusiasm because the Afghan muhj had to be in the fore-
front, and their hearts were not in it.

It was like working in an invisible cage, and if we had been given the
ticket to engage in real war fighting, the Delta boys could have made a
huge difference.

And had Lieutenant Colonel Ashley's request been approved to push
the snipers up the mountain from the south, out of Pakistan, we probably
would have been more directly involved. It would have been an extremely
taxing climb at that altitude, but after crossing the border and then scal-
ing the high peaks down the other side, it's very likely the Delta snipers
would have gotten the drop on bin Laden.

Then there was Ashley's request to close the mountain passes and trails
by seeding them with GATOR mines. That also was rejected, but those
mines would have killed more al Qaeda fighters and possibly the man himself as they fled toward the border.

I do not recall exactly when I heard that a thousand or so U.S. Marines
had made an "amphibious assault" in landlocked Afghanistan. Their job was
to establish a forward operating base south of Kandahar in late November
2001. As far as I know, they had not been asked to participate in the Tora
Bora battle, which was a good thing, because the introduction of conventional American troops would have caused our operation to unravel.

The local Shura undoubtedly would have needed only one look at
the marines before deciding that General Ali's days as the rock-star warlord were done. I'm also convinced that many of Ali's fighters, as well as
those of his subordinate commanders such as Zaman and Haji Zahir,
would have resisted the marines' presence and possibly even have turned
their weapons on the larger American force.

Two Marine Corps general officers asked me the "what-if" question
a day of two after the Tora Bora battle. My position had nothing to do
with the capability or courage of their marines and everything to do with
the sensitivity and peculiar dynamics of the tribal mountain area and
overall battle. We had to operate in virtual invisibility to keep Ali on top
of the Afghan forces. A full introduction of combat-ready American marines
would have tilted an already dangerous alliance.

However, the marines might have made the difference if used in another way. Had they been committed to assist the Pakistan army in blocking the key passageways that threaded out of the Tora Bora mountains, or at least to keep those new allies honest about sealing the border, we almost certainly would have captured and killed more fleeing al Qaeda. And we might even have bagged bin Laden.

Leaving the back door open gave the rat a chance to run.

18

Former Unit Member

All of life is action and passion, and not to be involved in
the actions and passions of your time is to risk having not
really lived at all.

—HERODOTUS

By the end of 2002, about the time we were hunting
Mr. Gul Ahmed, an apparent reluctance to take aggressive,
pro-active action had seeped back into the overall American
military leadership. The old pre-9/11 thinking was on the rise again, and
I found the lack of urgency to be frustrating. A commander or two talked
the good game of maintaining momentum and keeping the pressure on al
Qaeda, but they were not showing the will, desire, and mental toughness
to order American troops into harm's way.

At a time when our nation expected us to be taking the greatest risks,
some officers were unable to get past worrying about the potential loss of
life among the troops. In my opinion, they should have been in a very different profession.

During a briefing about targeting a suspected al Qaeda associate, a
senior officer wondered aloud about the mission and its accompanying
risk and asked, "Is it worth getting one of your guys killed?"

The question shocked me, and I answered bluntly, "Sir, there isn't a
target out there worth getting one of the boys killed, but if the American

people can't depend on Delta to take the risk, then we might as well pack it in.

If not Delta, then who?

Certainly, a commander must weigh the stakes when making such a commitment, particularly when politics are involved. He looks at the available intelligence and debates the pros and cons during his decision-making cycle, and if the intelligence meets the threshold for action, say 80 percent or so, then the mission is likely a go.

But what happens when the intelligence is rated as only 50 percent accurate? Or if only a single source of intelligence is available and the information cannot be corroborated? Is the mission still a go?

In my opinion, postponing a decision with your fingers crossed while you hope that the intelligence might improve after another hour or another day borders on downright negligence and hypocrisy. Analytical paralysis only helps the window of opportunity close faster.

Some men may be lost because of a commander's call, and that is tragic, but war requires a steel stomach and a hardened mind. It must be understood that those who do perish are volunteers who are unafraid of paying the ultimate price in the global war on terror. They are fighting for their buddies, for their families, and for their country.

It wouldn't be until the next phase in the war on terror, the invasion of Iraq, that the enormity and pace of the war put the Special Ops forces into overdrive, and audacity found its rightful place in the psyche of many a commander.

Obviously, we did not exist in an information-free bubble. The news channels were roaring about Iraq, and the scuttlebutt inside our tents in Afghanistan was about who in Delta would be going in first. The

Afghan campaign was slipping to the back burner as resources were chan-
neled to prepare for a massive invasion of Iraq, an invasion that I was still
not sure would actually happen.

Instead of immediate redeployment to that brewing trouble spot, our
squadron was given a couple of weeks of leave back home. There would be
no yellow ribbons tied around the old oak trees, because we stayed black
even when out of the danger zone.

In Delta, when the plane lands back at home station, the post band
is not there to welcome the returning troops. There are no crowds of
family, friends, and local townspeople waving American flags and
homemade signs. There is no mustering into formation while the commander shares some emotionally charged comments over a microphone
on a podium.

Yes, this deployment is over, but the moment that the plane rolls to a
stop and the ramp is lowered, the job begins anew.

The boys load onto buses and head for the compound, where
they repack their bags for a no-notice hostage rescue anywhere in the
world.

A Delta operator may retrieve his wedding ring from his wall locker
and slide it onto his finger, but then it is immediately back to business.
They place fresh batteries in their NVGs, weapon sights, and ear protection. They clean their weapons with solvent and high-pressure air before
applying a light coat of gun oil. They charge their interteam radio batteries and load pistol and rifle magazines before replacing them in their
kit bag.

After taking a shower and winding down with a cold beer or two in
the squadron lounge, a few minutes are spent remembering their fallen
comrades, whose eyes watch over them from a wall of honor. Before
jumping in their pickup truck or on their Harley-Davidson to head home
to the families, they reach down to make a final check that their beepers
are attached to their belts.

The beepers are as meticulously maintained as a delicate heart monitor, for an operator knows if his beeper fails while inside the local movie
theater or a neighborhood bar, then he risks missing a real world call-out or
deployment to a crisis site. The worst thing you can do to a Delta operator

is leave him behind, even for just a training mission. Counterterrorists don't punch time clocks.

At home, I received a call from Bragg telling me that my troop would not be deploying to Iraq in the first wave. With this news, my frustrations with our last tour in Afghanistan led me to do some hard thinking.

The combat rules of engagement had changed significantly since the early months at Tora Bora. Gone were the days of free-fire Hellfire missile strikes on convoys of SUVs, or stalking tall men wearing white robes and black turbans. The default position had become to simply take no action. That was unacceptable to me, and the hope that my troop would get the first nod for Iraq had been about the only thing preserving our morale at the time. Now that was gone, too.

I still had about eighteen months before I hit my twenty years in the army and I had managed to live the dream as a Delta troop commander for three years and nine months. Maybe it was time for me to move on and let someone else have some fun.

It was pretty clear that the army was not going to consider me for advancement into senior leadership, for I had intentionally not punched my career ticket in the right manner. I ducked attendance at the Combined Arms and Services Staff School, but got promoted to major anyway. Then I dodged the Command and General Staff College three times, scrapping that requirement for promotion to lieutenant colonel. I enjoyed Delta too much to spend much of what little time I had left doing classroom work, and the higher you were promoted up the pyramid in a small unit, the fewer slots were available for officers. The system had caught up with me.

I decided to get out of the way and prepare for retirement by looking for an assignment close to home so that I could spend more time with my family during my last year and a half. A friend up in the U.S. Army's Personnel Command set me up with a job just forty-five minutes from my front door. My final assignment was to be an advisor to a National Guard mechanized infantry battalion. Oh, boy.

Gus Murdock warned me that the hardest part about leaving the Unit would be driving out through the front gate and seeing the compound in my rearview mirror. It was actually even more difficult than that, because I was leaving just as a real shooting war was cranking up and I felt like I was abandoning the boys in a time of need.

During thirty days of Permanent Change of Station leave, I spent many hours running country dirt roads, pounding up and down the vast rolling hills, thinking about Delta. As hard as I tried to get on with the next stage of my life, I simply couldn't.

One of our sister squadrons had been among the first units to enter Iraq, leaving from Saudi Arabia and crossing the border days before the invasion began. They drove across the desert for hundreds and hundreds of miles, pushing toward Tikrit from the west and seizing two major enemy ammunition dumps and laying waste to dozens of Iraqi fighters en route.* The much heralded air force "shock and awe" bombing campaign started the war on March 19, 2003, and the big party began without me.

I could not purge the longing for the hunt from my system.

In April 2003, the same month that Saddam Hussein's foolish statue was pulled down in Baghdad, I was well into my new job, taking a required Defensive Driving Course at Fort Stewart, Georgia, that was being taught by a kind lady instructor who had twenty-six years of experience. I wondered how she would have done behind the wheel if she was being chased by police through the dark streets in Bosnia.

I maintained a strict nondisclosure posture in regard to any former affiliation with the Unit. When someone asked the typical, "Where'd you come from?" I practiced what I was taught and responded. "Fort Bragg."

---

* Authors Michael Gordon and Bernard Trainor document well Delta Force's crossing of the Saudi border and long push into Iraq to start the war in their book *Cobra II*.

"The 82nd Airborne, huh? I used to be in that division, too," they might say, and that would be that.

As the new guy in the battalion, my presence was also required at a seemingly endless series of routine chores. There was a brigade change of command rehearsal in starch and spits for several hours on a parade field in category IV heat. Then there was combat lifesaver recertification, military driver's license testing, drownproofing, MILES 2000 certification, observer-controller certification testing, and so on.

I had forgotten how much the army thrived off of *certification* in everything. It is a cover-your-ass technique to ensure some lower-ranking officer is accountable when a soldier screws up: "Look, you signed right here that this guy was certified, so it's your fault, not mine."

I even had to take a written test on how to wear and operate the AN/PVS-5 night vision goggles. I might as well have been quizzed on eighteenth-century buggy-whip manufacturing. I had not used the PVS-5s since I was a Ranger instructor more than a decade earlier. They were technological throwbacks, for in Delta, we used the much more advanced ANVS-9 generation of night vision goggles, the same kind worn by the night-flying pilots with the daring 160th SOAR. My new battalion was not high enough on the totem pole to receive modern gear that had extraordinary clarity and depth perception.

Also, I was a fish out of water when it came to mechanized infantry. I was uncomfortable in the rolling forts called Bradley infantry fighting vehicles. Didn't know a damned thing about them. Didn't care. Had to take another class. In Tora Bora, a decent jackass that could plod a mountain trail was much more valuable than a Bradley.

To add insult to injury, I was kicked out of the Fort Stewart Field House's weight room twice in three months, once for trying to lift weights while still in my camouflage uniform, and the other time for lifting while in blue jeans, a T-shirt, and desert combat boots. That was common attire inside the Delta gym, because you were going to get sweaty later anyway, but it was taboo in the regular army.

In early May, I attended a terrain model briefing for our brigade's up-coming two weeks of annual summer training. All the lieutenant colonels and majors stood around the model while the colonels and a few starry generals sat comfortably in folding chairs, sniping at the various briefing officers about tactics and techniques, good ideas, and not so good ideas.

My personal distaste for the conventional army came rushing back at me like a big Mack truck and reminded me of just how much I despised the traditional military pomp and circumstance. I was present at that terrain model physically, but absent mentally. The rigidity, inflexibility, and rank-has-its-privileges standards were petty and abhorrent. Why did the big dogs get to sit in comfort while the guys who would really be doing the work were either not present or treated like underlings? This was leadership?

In Delta, the whole troop would have studied this problem together and then Ironhead, Grinch, B-Monkey, and the other sergeants would tell the officers whatever we needed to know.

My mind was on the war in Iraq, and I missed the action, the adrenaline rush, and the boys. I was not exactly loving my new assignment.

I had stayed in touch with the Delta loop because it would have been impossible not to do so. The boys had rotated into Iraq and things were different this time around, they told me. No sitting around the tents waiting for perfect intelligence to materialize before being given authorization to kill the enemy. As the Tom Cruise fighter-jock character said in the movie *Top Gun*, Iraq was a target-rich environment. Delta was making their own actionable intelligence and throwing down against Iraqi soldiers and Baath Party loyalists. To make the boys jealous, I could now describe how to change the oil in a Bradley.

After several months, I received a phone call from Lowblow, one of the Kilo Team snipers in Tora Bora. One of our former teammates—retired Master Sergeant William Carlson—had been killed in Afghanistan while on patrol looking for remnant Taliban and holdover al Qaeda fighters. The Chief, from the Blackfeet tribe of American Indians, had been in

Delta forever and was one of the very best when he retired and went to work for the CIA as an independent contractor. That new job came with a hefty increase in pay and a ticket back to Afghanistan.

Chief's funeral was a solemn event, but it was also incredibly uplifting for me to see so many of my former mates gathered on that sunny summer afternoon. Jim and Jester, Shrek and Murph, and a dozen others were dressed in their military Class A uniforms adorned with the Purple Hearts and various awards for valor. Several other operators were dressed in sharp custom-made suits. There were plenty of warriors there who wore the Delta trademark Oakley sunglasses, and among them were Gus Murdock and Mark Sutter.

Inside the funeral home that day, Gus asked if I would consider coming back to Delta and get into the Iraq fight. Was it even possible, given the army's stringent rules on moving soldiers around?

I knew Gus had made the inquiry not because I was anything special, nor because the Unit needed me, because they certainly didn't. As I drove along Interstate 16, chewing up the hours to reach Fort Stewart, it became clear that he was offering me a chance to deal with my personal regret at having left Delta. I had not yet paid my dues in full, and we both knew it. Keeping one hand on the steering wheel, I fat-fingered Gus's cell number into my phone with the other hand to accept his offer.

A few days after the funeral, I was on a rifle range, teaching a company of soldiers how to mount an Aimpoint sighting device to their M-16A4 rifles. These National Guard troops were preparing to go to Iraq and needed all the training they could get. My cell phone rang. The Delta adjutant was calling to say that the Department of the Army paperwork officially ordering me back to Delta was in the mail. I guess I underestimated the Unit's power. That evening I doubled my run route and doubled up on chest and biceps. I was stoked!

Not everyone was as happy. My wife, in particular, was unimpressed that I was returning to Delta and heading for Iraq. She rightly pointed out that I was a family man, too, and that my decision was totally selfish. She was right, but what could I do? But she had been through this Delta routine before, understood the magnetism, and knew that I would be back when I got back, and that the twenty service years were almost up anyway.

My brigade commander also was not a happy camper when, without explanation, he received the news that I was history with the mechanized infantry battalion. They said that I could not just up and leave, so I gave them a special telephone number, then up and left. They called the number and were curtly informed that the commander's approval had not been sought because it was unnecessary. In the midst of a real war, the petty stuff goes out the window.

Things inside the building had changed very little since I parted from Delta months earlier, and after a few days of catching up with old teammates, it seemed like I had never left.

Stormin' had prepared for my arrival by drawing my old guns from the arms room, kitting them out with all the bells and whistles, and even zeroing them on the range. It was great to see my old friend again, because we had learned the trade of small unit infantry tactics together while growing up in the 1st Ranger Battalion in Savannah, Georgia, in the early 1980s. He joined Delta just after Operation Desert Storm in 1991.

Stormin's other nickname, "the Bod," rhymes with his first name but is an inaccurate description. Typically, one associates such a nickname with rippling stomach muscles and bulging biceps, someone who is a near-perfect physical specimen. This "Bod" was different, and his nickname stuck because he looks just the opposite of a Hercules, more like a local mechanic with a small beer belly than a Delta operator.

In fact, it is that appearance that made him so valuable to Delta missions, when he easily can become a "gray man," the everyday kind of guy who fits into literally any surrounding, a chameleon who can pose as a tourist, a businessman, or a scumbag. No foreign intelligence service would look twice at the Bod when he came through their airport, and that mild appearance often made adversaries underestimate him, which in turn made it difficult for them to compromise his mission.

He has a mind that is truly a superior analytical machine, and that uncanny ability to calmly think on his feet even while enduring the most confusing and hostile situations makes him even more valuable.

Even those of us who have known and worked with him for a long time have repeatedly been surprised at how the mild physical appearance of this man veiled a tremendous athlete, who is surprisingly strong and deadly accurate with pistol and rifle. In March 2005, the Bod was leading the boys on one of hundreds of raids that were carried out during the long hunt for al Qaeda terrorists in Iraq. True to fashion, after all hell broke loose with grenades and AK-47 automatic fire, the Bod did what he always did—went to the sound of the guns. A few minutes later, the terrorists were standing before Allah at the gates of martyrdom and the Bod and several other operators were fertilizing the Iraqi soil with their own blood, wounded but alive.

The Bod took a through-and-through gunshot wound to his right butt cheek that exited out the front of his left thigh, missing his private parts by centimeters. He actually watched through his green-glowing NVGs as a second round tore into his right forearm and severed the nerve to his million-dollar pistol finger. A third bullet was a little more forgiving, as it only ripped into his tan boots and claimed his right big toe.

As usual, the Bod continued to think quickly, even while lying in an Australian field hospital bed, and remembered to reenlist for a $150,000 tax-free bonus before he was shipped home. Now that was American taxpayer money well spent, for he is still an operational member of the Unit.

I consider the Bod to be a true American hero, one of the scores who migrated to the Unit over the last quarter of a century. He has taken more of our enemy's blood than he has given of his own, and in the context of the war on terror, that probably says more about the man than anything else.

I spent less than two weeks at Bragg, redrawing the rest of my old gear, shooting, putting in some serious physical training, catching up on the intelligence picture in Iraq, and even running the obstacle course.

There was a definite sense of purpose within the Unit, which was knee-deep in another manhunt, this time for Saddam Hussein, but it was a businesslike approach by guys who acted as if they didn't have a worry in the world. Then I headed to Iraq, back in the fight and at least for the time being, no longer a *former* Delta operator.

I was lucky, and rode the Delta stallion as long as I could. When the ride was done, I officially retired in February 2005. A month earlier, my family and I stood inside the Beckwith Room, aptly named after the Unit's first commanding officer, at the Delta compound for a small and informal ceremony. I recall humbly looking around the room in awe at the warriors who had taken the time to attend.

In the room were Delta operators young and old. Standing only a few feet from me were heroes from the invasion of Grenada in 1983, Panama in 1989, some from Desert Storm, some from Somalia, and others from the Balkans. Mixed among these dedicated operators were fellow teammates in the war on terror, whose efforts and reputations in Afghanistan and Iraq meet the legacy of those who came before them.

This time, I knew I would not be coming back, but it was also a much easier parting, because it had not been so abrupt. All dues had been paid, and the personal demons were finally at rest. It was more of a passage than a retirement, for an operator represents Delta until the day he dies.

You think about it for months, even years, after you leave, and it is forever engrained in your mind. Your thought process for the rest of your life is largely affected by the way you were taught to operate, to organize, to plan, to execute, to lead, and to kill. The men with whom you served are guys you stay in close touch with for a lifetime and for whom you would do anything.

As the years pass, as the hair thins, as the knees and back go, you cling to the unrealistic idea that you still have what it takes to hang with the current operators.

Each time you pass a children's playground, you feel the urge to climb over the monkey bars instead of swing on them. You think about snaking up the swing chain and sliding over the high bar. You can't walk by a neighborhood privacy fence without thinking how fast you can get over it. You check your hands to make sure you still have the rough calluses acquired from hour upon hour of pistol shooting, climbing caving ladders, going over cinder block walls, commando crawling on or pulling yourself up the thick ropes on the obstacle courses, and routinely pumping iron. Even crazier, each time you shake another man's hand you mentally gauge the grip strength.

You compare normal human emotions with abnormal experiences. When it is really cold outside, I think, *Not as cold as Tora Bora.* When the summer temperature soars, I think, *Not as hot as Baghdad.* When I experience physical pain or mental discomfort, I think, *Not as bad as Delta selection and assessment.*

Hundreds of years ago, ordinary citizens fought for recognition of a new, free, and sovereign nation called the United States of America. They were known as the Minutemen because they had to be ready to grab their weapons and be ready within a minute's notice. Their operational battle space more than two hundred years ago was down the dirt road, across the back forty, past ole man Fiddler's pond, or a half-day hike past Broken Wagon Creek.

Today, Delta serves not as Minutemen, but rather *Momentmen,* and their battle space is the globe. The unpredictability of terrorism has them on a short leash and a full-time war footing. The operators' beepers are always on, their bags are always packed, personal wills have been signed, and notes to loved ones are taped inside their lockers with the bland instruction: "Give to my wife in the event of my death."

Today, hundreds of thousands of committed American servicemen and women face the same risks and dangers, sacrifice just the same, and pull their fair share of the load. Delta, however, remains unique and does what must be done in a manner that draws little attention. Of course, it's designed that way. It still does not officially exist.

There are no "reluctant warriors" in Delta. All are eager to enter harm's way. They aren't stupid, don't carry a death wish, and aren't necessarily

looking for any more holes in their bodies than the good Lord already provided. But these elite operators are paid more and enjoy millions of dollars more in funding than any other command. In return, they are expected to do more. It is their raison d'être, and they will not let down their mates.

As my wife, two daughters, and I pulled out of the compound shortly after the retirement ceremony, it came to me that Gus Murdock had been wrong about that last look in the rearview mirror. I had already seen that view, and now I had to look at it again.

I became a former Unit member—for the second time! It was twice as bad.

Index